Poetry
New Zealand
Yearbook

2022

Poetry
New Zealand
Yearbook
2022

Edited by Tracey Slaughter

MASSEY UNIVERSITY PRESS

Contents

NEW POEMS

Jack Ross
Marco Sonzogni / Timothy Smith
Mary Maringikura Campbell
Tayi Tibble
Ian Wedde
Ash Davida Jane
Jess Fiebig
Siobhan Harvey
Tusiata Avia / Courtney Sina Meredith
Ben Kemp / Vanessa Crofskey /
Chris Stewart
Rhys Feeney / Ria Masae /
Claudia Jardine

Editorial

Breakage

The break in a poetic line — whether that line is broken by breath or eye, by pulse, footstep or thought — always says one thing (among the myriad other signals it may send by its breakage): Pay attention. Wait — let your awareness be brushed by this pause, or jarred by this rupture. Switch your senses back on. Look, it says, we stand at the edge — stop here for a second, wake up, notice life, notice language: there are edges everywhere. Our normal routine patterns of reading risk rushing ahead like our prosaic lives, half-conscious, left-to-right, function-driven, habit-numbed, adrift on the surface, body-blind; poetic breakage tips us, abruptly, out of the illusion that it all goes on in tidy sequenced form.

It cracks the model of dealing with life via language that would have us believe that we can translate existence into safe consumable units, coherent grammatical blocks. It breaks. It breaks suddenly. There are gaps, leaps, lesions. There are flights that make you gasp in wonder; there are pleasures that press you to the crest; there are dead-ends that leave you seized in cold. Either way, pay attention. Concentrate, harder. Listen. Open your eyes.

It all breaks in an instant.

A poetic break is a 'location of interest'. What it wants, what it cracks the line for, is attention, alertness, awakening, response.

What happens at the crack then, as Leonard Cohen says, is the light gets in. The breakage fills with meaning. The breaking poet hangs that word, that trace, that tone on the gallery wall of the white and our gaze is forced to attend. The damage magnifies, whets our senses. Framed tighter, images gain translucence, call us closer to get transfixed. Our heightened witness casts light back across every line. Sound intensifies, experience deepens, presence is registered, atmosphere felt. Significance pours in, echoes proliferate, connections are illuminated.

It's a complex kind of light, because in poetry the whiteness does paradoxical work. Poet Glyn Maxwell distils poetry down to its two basic elements — 'the black (something there) and the white (nothing there)'; facets that represent 'voice upon time', human presence against mortality. The line breaks, he argues, because ultimately *we* do, the pressure of the whiteness, the silence, the terminus, the fact of our transience always washing back upon the black. Spin the poem, he suggests, so the black lines stand upright and what you have is a graph of our resistance, vertical lines that push up into the white the varying energy of our voice.

Whether that line of voice managed to blast out a long track of breath that beats or rattles, or whether it managed to offset into the white a single displaced murmur, what matters is that an animal sounded its need, a voice made a noise in the void. Someone spoke out into the white: that act might be triumphant or fragile, might be clamorous or minimal, reckless or quiet; it might be both loud and vanquished, fearless and vulnerable in a single vowel. (I'm hugely drawn to poems that can both give the middle finger and nakedly lament at the same time: it takes a special gift to deliver the punchline from triage.)

You'll find examples of all these voices within this volume, running the spectrum from stripped-back confession to exultantly costumed performative pose. Whether hot-blooded chorus or fine-boned whisper, whether strutting persona or shaken utterance, the black is the sound we send out into the soundlessness.

And it always returns to the edge.

For a second, you are made to face the white.

Look, the poem says, for whatever reason a voice could not go on here, may have struggled in this instant, taken a breath, had to blink, had to surrender, had to break off. At this place, perhaps, the sound of itself rushed into its ears, with all the pressure that floods a human voice: the heat of the solar plexus, the ache of the gut, the bloodstream's thresh, the feet in the dust, the trembling of the throat's chords. All that miraculous bodily music — whose traces the vessel of language *exists* to transmit — stood here, stilled for a moment, framed against the whiteness.

But go on, touch down again on the next line. Pay attention to the places we break, learn them: they are hard, as so many poems tell us, they are brutal, they are fatal — but for that very reason life shines stronger there. 'I came to talk you into physical splendor', writes C. D. Wright in the spectacularly broken 'Key Episodes from an Earthly Life', a poem whose 'use of space' is all 'leaning   toward / what we came for'. It's a piece composed of sensual fragments agleam amidst the whiteness, urging arousal back on the reader, demanding their full carnal range of involvement, making 'perfectly clear' the imperative to pay attention that every poem issues:

> Now it is your turn   to shake or
> provoke   or heal me   I won't say it again.

You heard the woman. Bring it all. Waste nothing. Use everything you are to open the poems in this book.

Tracey Slaughter
November 2021

Competition winners

This year's *Poetry New Zealand Yearbook* is pleased to publish the winning poems in its annual *Poetry New Zealand Yearbook* Student Poetry Competition.

'Route Back Home' by Ocean Jade (Otago Girls' High School) appears on page 133; 'South' by Caitlin Jenkins (Papatoetoe High School) on page 140; 'Gossip' by Sarah-Kate Simons (home schooled) on page 217; and 'Café Vienna' by Jade Wilson (Kaiapoi High School) on page 237.

Featured Poet

Wes Lee

You Had Fallen Asleep in the Chair

Through the closed curtain,
not terrible sounds,
I have heard those
I remember those.
And Eamon, the nurse, had just been
to check the drip:
magnesium and drugs
tipped vertical
the slow veins;
his half beard
carefully sculpted.
And he woke you
addled into consciousness
unbelieving (again) of the wall-less room
as I was so rudely awakened earlier
by my own heart
firing outside
its subterranean rhythm,
suddenly finding a way up
through ice caves
to scatter mayhem.
Earlier, I had weakly presented
my wrists as a barrier to my breasts
throughout the application of discs,
the metallic grey nipples
wired to the machine.

Frozen

The sudden burst into the living room
of two men in green uniforms.
Tanned, muscled, tattooed.
What year is it?
Can you spell *world*?
Now backwards?
Does she always have a tremor?, directed
at my husband.
And I want to drink water
and they give me a sip.
No more than a sip.
And you can live your life so quietly
and suddenly this
midnight rush down the concrete steps
the porch light turned on;
an Avondale spider, its legs frozen,
a starfish.
Was it there every night
flattened like that
unaware a harsh light could suddenly
blare it into being?

The Lasting Image

after 'Lost Highway'

The whitest white
like Franz Wright's joint in a box of cigars
or Melissa Lee-Houghton's cigarette burn on the arm
of the
'whitest smack-head in town'
what is glowing in my life
what remains
what is burned
and never leaves

a moment where the man (Robert Loggia) averts his eyes
when the woman (Patricia Arquette) is stripping,
when she is nearly down to all of it
and stands there naked
her eyes on his face, never leaving his face.

For Carbon Monoxide

after Anne Sexton

For carbon monoxide you need a garage and your mother's old fur coat.
I had a suitor in the 80s whose car filled slowly with fumes.
I was lulled to sleep as he drove me through the night.
His name was Joe.
We'd drive to parties out in the hills, hastened by the blaze of bonfires and drumming;
hair shaking; chanting; one hand waving at the moon.
As the moon becomes some glorious companion under the influence.
On the way home, the fumes, slowly leaking in the cabin of our life.
His strong arms. His eyes on the road.

Dolls' Eyes are God's Eyes

Who doesn't hate their female body?
When I was given dolls I buried them.
Given a pram, I rived out its stuffing,
tossed its foam,
mixed mud and water with a stick
then tipped it over.
I knew nothing
then, but knew
more than I will ever know.

Are they still there, buried under clay?
Glassy deep. Spiky plastic lashes
hinged (to open); the gravity of the tilt.

Unseeing/all-seeing.
One of them as large as a baby.

Archaeology of Blood

The way boys were taken, scoured and cut,
brought back in triumph
while girls hid in huts with a dark shrouded flap
and dare not cross the fire pit
or any sacred place with blood between their legs,
fearing their shadows would darken:
turn earth to ash. Bring famine, defeat.

The shame as I held my bloody gusset out.
I knew nothing, but knew there was something
wrong.

Some mothers throw parties:
crimson balloons; red velvet cake.
I was handed a nylon belt and safety pins —
a contraption long consigned
to the museum of menstruation. While other girls
pushed tubes inside and released
a spool of fluffy down,
I was stuck with outside stench
and stickiness. A constant wet reminder.

I longed for a hippie mother or a goddess
with a shield who'd strike at it.
Banish the rags and wrapping in newspaper;
reaching through kitchen waste
to hide it at the bottom of the bin.

Its excavations; its shell encrusted middens;
its lumps of blunt-edged crockery; its bones.

It's been years of heavy welling
and slick swishing, of fruitless build-up.
And the way it ended — a year of struggling
to expel something;
three days of 'emergency room' pain each month
that mimicked the pain of giving birth.
The raw throb of an organ that did not know how
to cease and desist.

A low gravel, a grave pulling,
as if my uterus longed to join the earth
and finally become
a nest of fungus.

I moved around like a
pregnant woman, trying to find
a pain-free spot (when there isn't any)
just a desperation to make it stop.
There was hysterectomy talk, and
'less invasive' — implants; of weighing
up the weeks of recovery, pitting
them against months. And testimonials
from some who bounced back
quick.
And some who took to their beds and faced the wall.

But the blood just stopped.
And I was spared the knife and the doctor's fingers
widening and watching to see if I
flinched.

Michael & George

Why did Michael make jars of coloured water
line them up on shelves in the garden shed
then later threaten to kill:
'The whole lot of you!'
Wrestled to the ground,
my grandfather's weight,
my mother, a girl watching.
And why did they put Michael away
and why did they drop off
George
one cold
winter night
outside The Salvation Army,
leave him addled in the snow.
And why, when these moments were
relived
did they laugh
and why (as children)
did we ask
for the stories again
like nursery rhymes or bedtime stories.
And Michael dips his paintbrush,
making
gradations of colour.
He could have been a concert pianist.
They put him in the army and he snapped.
George stole your pocket money to buy meths.
I like watching how angry he is,
how young he is,
I like how he holds
his head to one side
to compensate

for
the drooped eyelid.
How his body has made a frame
to shield him.
And why did no one speak
of what happened next.
The visits?
The cards received, exchanged?
The narrative has dropped
in one of the many blast holes
of *family.*

First Day

They put me in a clinic
with all men
and apologised later.

I wore dark sunglasses —
asked by a therapist to take them off.

One mannish boy drew a squirting erection on
the blackboard when the therapists left the
room
and the men laughed along

and the only one I liked was a man who had
hit his wife,
because he was ~~honest~~
trying to be honest.

Writing Poetry When I Would Rather Be Watching *The Sopranos*

after Livia Soprano
i.m. my mother

To stare again into Livia's
clouded blue eyes. Watch her scrape the last
from a jellied container.
Hear her feet *slutch* along hospital lino.
And hear my mother tell me: *Don't drag your feet*
and feel the back of her hand, sharply.
And stare again into her unfathomable eyes.
Her ancient Yorkshire toughness.
Smoking in her winceyette nightie,
unblinking. *She had your card.*
My mother, wondrous and prideful,
knew all there was to know,
knew everything before the end.
Even what death would be like.

Becoming Claire

It happened once before
while watching *House of Cards*.
The sensation of entering her body:
the military lines; steel armour
of dresses. Walking through rooms
with powerful chandeliers.
Acid greens, neutral beiges.
Savagery in silk and wool.
The mannish jaw, quiet
stealth, cold hypervigilance.
What she sees. What she knows.
Her command of a room —
sucking out all insignificance.
Her refusal to dwell. No apologies.
A metal Mona Lisa; the carriage
of a Valkyrie. To slip behind the eyes
of Medusa.

A Hole in the Wall of a Room I Lived in

A hole of mystery.
A greedy hole where no bird sings —
cut through the torso
in a surrealist painting;
hollow with no blood.
The way the surrealists
smoothed over the rubble of dreams
and made this clean
but terrible world.

To Sleep Something Off

I keep returning
to the woman I saw on New Year's Day
lying on a blanket
outside the changing sheds at Balaena Bay,
passed out under a broad straw hat.
Baring a fresh white bandage, her wrist
twisted awkwardly
around a blue electrolyte drink bottle.
Three bluebirds flying up
to her elbow.

The Nurses So Vivid and Gone Like Dreams

A post-it note with all the numbers
I carried for a week like a name
sewn inside my coat.
The hurried bag. The cold, insectoid legs
of the gurney, its steel thump. My eyes
on the back of your head.
And I thought later about ambulances,
how the patient's head is fixed the other
way, not looking through the windscreen
seeing the traffic coming toward them,
seeing nothing of the world
and this was design not accident,
so the focus was on
the body and their being in the body
and windows would be a distraction
would reveal the life outside.

Validation

Harold Pinter, I wish you were alive / then you could validate me / like
Sarah Kane / And Saatchi, you validated the girl who painted Lady Di
whispering on the phone / a speech bubble coming out of her mouth
saying / *I'm so afraid* / You brought her into the spotlight /
then she had her fake breasts cut out / She didn't need to be a stripper
anymore / The girl in the bedsit with the small child to look after / who
painted from the heart / with no art school training / Then everything
got on top of her / like Lady Di / And Germaine Greer, if only I could
find out where your house was / I could break in one night / like that girl
you helped / We could sit in your kitchen drinking red wine / and you
would listen / Like the man who sat on the Queen's bed / until the secret
service came / And Paula Abdul, I could sit in a car outside your house /
like the girl who met you on *Idol* / who took a match and gulped
that great fireball that roared through her chest / Doused herself in kerosene.

Sometimes I Forget I Was Her

I was a drunk, but it was so long ago.
I woke in other people's clothes.
My head rose up, a wobbly stalk.
Glassily, my eyes opened.
I've got by sometimes by saying
I dreamt that. There are things,
although I saw, I will never bring back.
A dark road where men got out of a car:
rain slash; gravel, like slanty scratches
on a photograph.

Sutcliffe #2

She said she had to do her own hair.
Hairdressers could not bear the dents
from the claw hammer.
Walking around in disguise. Hair and
clothes cover it all (cover most of it).
And they say wear a stab vest beneath
your clothes. Blunt the knives
in the kitchen drawers.
Never go out at night alone. Phone a friend.
Leave a note: the time you'll be home.
Be home. Stay home. Check all the airless cracks.
Check the windows. Check behind the door.
And when her mother arrived, she did not
recognise the face stretched over a football.

He has made a hole in the world.
Holes in the night sky. An anvil of his arm.

Experiments
after Dale Spender

Refusing to smile at a man risks your life. Refusing to smile
when a man smiles. Something travels up to the eyes,
something so old. Something dark begins to stalk, to hedge,
to herd, to run off a cliff.
Refusing to smile at a man opens a box never fully closed.

A woman did experiments, determined
to walk, stony-faced, refusing the eyes that tried
to elicit a glimpse. As if she were blossom and he was the sun.
Try it, see where it goes, see what disturbance.
Inside the head something primal unsheathes.

All the Furniture

I remember Helen Mirren as the queen —
sitting in bed, her hand flying up to her mouth
watching footage
of the crowds laying flowers
And I remember where I was
when death was announced
and it seemed I was the only person
living in the world
watching television
when the first report came in,
there were no lights anywhere
in the city;
the mattress on the floor
and the rooms with no furniture;
a rug scavenged from a skip laid out,
and when men followed me home
from the pub
they'd do a double-take
questioning my sanity
where's all the furniture?
And sometimes that gesture
will come back
the quick hand to the mouth
the question.

My Heart Wakes Me

I have emergency medication in the cupboard.
In a pyroglass giveaway with a snaplock lid.

Take care she would say
standing in the doorway.
Uneasily, superstitiously.
And some of the feeling links back,
jangles through history.

You have to be able to take shocks
until you can't.
The coffee is not smooth and unblown on.
There are ripples each day.
Some are like Goya's Saturn
devouring his son.

The Sunny Disguise

Desert silence. A bird's crazy tweeting. I suck a strand of my hair.
I read somewhere Mengele died that way (hair from the tips of his
moustache balled in his intestines creating a blockage).
I greet each stranger in this small seaside town: *I am I am I am*
The blast crater with its outrageous evidence. The life of the mind,
its unbooted white plains. Gut sick at the thought of filling out forms.
I was happiest when I had no home.
What will it be like when I send something out and don't expect a
reply? This shift in the workings of the world: an abdication of care.
I like finishing things. I was told I was a *gold star patient*. The mind
lists toward these things.
No one to call: your own echo chamber. This was not foreseen,
not then. I believed his words and could not understand the sudden
ghosting.
The authorities warning people to look for strangers with
distressed faces: *Passengers waiting for trains are being advised to
scan the platform for distressed or troubled faces and to stand at
least two metres away from the platform edge.*
Men pushing people under trains.
It's OK to write of loneliness, people want to read poems about
loneliness. It's OK to use the word *love* and repetitions.
I remember one friend leaning over the sink brushing her teeth.
Another friend telling me to chew properly.
I have been having a series of dreams where core things of
importance are revealed, and in the lucidity of the dream I identify
these core things and when I wake I cannot describe or hold on to them.
This violent territory of loss. Drip of limestone. Wear of mountains.
Deep time is comforting.
The orange cones are gone: yesterday's earthmover has vanished.
The road healed.
The many apocalypses past leaving a faint black seam in rock.
If I could go back in time I would follow Christ. There is no one

good enough to follow these days. Of his followers, one or two would have been pushed out, felt lonely, isolated, ignored, ashamed, not worthy. They may have taken turns on different days. *My inbox is crazy at this time of year,* I overhear a man say.

A difficult pain, a forever pain, to be outside.

If you are worried about becoming homeless, contact the housing department of your local authority to fill in a homeless application. You can use the gov.nz website to find your local council.

Why should I care about rules at the end of the world?

In the sunny disguise. In the 'Beautiful day'.

To Say It Now

I could sense your approach,
it developed a smell.
The tail of my dress
left no imprint.

And now I know it as a sense
that turns to dread,
enables the legs.

It seems this world only allows
particular things to be said.
The rest must glide behind
the eyes of a girl.

An interview with Wes Lee

The body remembers in Wes Lee's poems, pronouncing its truth in strange flashes, loading her pages with dark stills from an unconscious screen — yet simultaneously Lee articulates her lines with tense poetic control, sharpening language to scalpel point against the places the body is silenced. It is this use of acute poetic practice to chart the psyche's bloodied spaces — to tap through sheer craft to the carnal baseline of memory and its charged contortions, to front through a fierce, honed wielding of form the 'blast holes' where trauma has forged the body — that has always left me awed in reading Lee's work, accosted, exhilarated, struck.

The scenes glimpsed within a Wes Lee poem are often low-key, incidental, domestic, yet under the surreal pressure of the poet's eye the ordinary detonates and homely details seethe and seize. Dioramas of 'intimate femicide', polaroids surfaced from private violence, hair-raising radiance rendered with visceral force and unyielding precision, Wes Lee's poems set to work, with a kind of brutal magnification, on the personal core.

Tracey Slaughter: One of the qualities that has always struck me in your poetry is the way it illuminates memory as made in the body — so many of your images seem to emanate from cell and joint, skin and nerve ending. How consciously do you draw on, or delve into, the body in your writing? Or does the body simply *insist* on leaving its presence on the page?

I think of the act of writing poetry as 'going into the dream': a form of not existing; a space where a poem can arise. Then the work begins.

In the early morning, when I am reading online newspapers, my partner always knows if I have slipped into writing as a sound begins to emanate, a repetitive humming, almost a drone, which I am only partially aware of as I move in and out of this other space. Perhaps it works the same way as a mantra to block out the noise of the world, to deeply focus. And perhaps, within this process, the body is speaking, sending a message, and in this way it simply insists on leaving its presence on the page.

My poems are received, then honed and edited unsparingly (I have a strong admiration for form and craft and rhythm). Sometimes they work and sometimes they are abandoned for years as seemingly initial failures, then reread and reworked and reclaimed.

As I get older I have found that this precious thing called *your life*, which seemed real, drifts more and more into the territory of story. So-called factual truths become slippery, sometimes opening to larger truths. I enjoy this sense of slipperiness. I like to remain elusive to myself, as elusive as dreams.

Memory is a tricky beast, as I say in one of my poems: '. . . contained in a tiny part of the brain / that files things in such a sophisticated way / that no supercomputer / can mimic its function / and when you are recalling a memory / you are actually recalling the / last time you remembered it, / where it had changed shape, / and each time you remember, you experience / this changed shape and change it / a little more — / a reverberating changing particle of time'.

In my pamphlet 'Body, Remember' I try to address the persistence of past trauma to rewrite itself — to haunt. The various forms in which it manifests, plagued to relive it in flashbacks, in dreams. How, in a way, it is locked in to the body. How trauma often provokes a lifetime of making and remaking personal history (especially for the artist); continually rewritten, mythologised, a cannibalising of a life into stitched-up fictions, of events long dead. In some of the poems I address the body as a stranger, a deceiver; highlighting its worn-out protections (of the child).

The overall tone I was aiming for is provocative, questioning, with the use of multiple voices; adopting a variety of poetic personas, interrogating the body, interrogating memory. For me the central question is: What if you can't remember? What if remembering is impossible, but the compulsion remains strong and changes shape throughout a lifetime?

At the moment, because of recent emergency hospitalisations, the compartments of my bag are mentally packed with my NHI number; the names of my medications; what I might need — nightclothes, etc.— on standby, as if I am going on a trip, or am a pregnant woman with her suitcase waiting by the door. So a lot of my concern has been focused on the perilous nature of the body in a conscious way, and this is making its way into my poems. My consciousness has begun to be riveted by the body in fresh, new ways.

TS: There's a strong strand of poems in this collection that dwell on images of how female identity is formed and deformed by the social order, confronting the 'violent territory' of girls' and women's lives. How important is it to you to speak to this dimension?

In answer to this question, I will let one of my poems speak for me:

We Watch True Crime
Because we know / have known / will know. / Because the *Rohypnol* / in the glove box / is / will be / has been / could be / future cars. / A kind of future proofing / and history / all that has happened / will happen / is / happening. / Because violence / is a seam / that runs along our lives / a metro map / of blood / skin cells / broken / fingernails. / Because we know the words: / dumpsite / kill site / comfort woman / rape kit / intimate femicide. / Because we have been / will be / are / have to be / ready.

TS: Probing the myriad 'blast holes of family' is another task your poetry often undertakes — how much have these recurrent holes and lesions in domestic space shaped your poetic focus?

I gravitate towards poetry that focuses on or probes experience of disturbance in the domestic space. I admire poets who endeavour to negotiate these 'blast holes'. Survivors of generational terrorism, their work is a powerful form of debriefing, and connects deeply with others who have been scarified. For me this is a kind of public service for those who wish to avail themselves of it, but it is not for the faint-hearted. The kind of poetry I am talking about is not self-help. It won't make you feel better.

I find the most interesting contemporary poets in this vein produce work that is terrifying and provocative, such as Selima Hill. I highly recommend her latest pamphlet 'Fridge', published in 2020 by *The Rialto* magazine. And the sequence 'Sunday Afternoons at the Gravel-pits' from her 2015 collection *Jutland*, published by Bloodaxe in the UK. In her startling poems centred on childhood, Hill documents a defiled body, an owned body (not by her), and a stubborn taking back and owning of her own body.

Other poets I would mention in this context are Wayne Holloway-Smith, Dorianne Laux, Marie Howe, Alice Anderson, Sharon Olds, Martin Figura, to name but a few.

I admire poets who twist my insides, then twist a little more, because that is what I *know* they have done to themselves to bring a stunning thing onto the page. I admire and benefit from writing that costs. I like the Emily Dickinson quote: 'If I read a book and it makes my whole body so cold no fire can ever warm me, I know *that* is poetry. If I feel physically as if the top of my head were taken off, I know *that* is poetry.'[1]

In his collection *Alarum* Wayne Holloway-Smith uses the convention of redacting his lines in the form of strikethrough. He breaks up his words, as if he is hiding their content from himself, heightening the perilous cost: the task of bringing forth deep and scarifying shame.

I like to be challenged by other people's poetry. I court a full body shiver (or a sick feeling of recognition) where my sense of comfort is disrupted, such as in Fiona Benson's sequence from her collection *Vertigo & Ghost*, refiguring Zeus as a child-abusing rapist. Her powerful visions left me breathless. These poems have become part of my cells.

I read a huge amount of poetry, non-fiction and long-form journalism. Two articles that have recently influenced my poetry (and

---

1   Quoted in Martha Ackmann, 'An Encounter That Revealed a Different Side of Emily Dickinson', *The Atlantic*, 24 June 2020.

these tie in with the earlier question regarding my focus on the 'violent territory' of girls' and women's lives) are 'An Epidemic of Disbelief' by Barbara Bradley Hagerty, published in *The Atlantic*. It is a harrowing, long-form essay exposing the practice of shelving untested rape kits throughout the United States (an estimated 200,000), and, as a consequence, police departments failing to make links between rape victims to identify serial rapists.

In an article in *The New York Times*, 'The Rape Kit's Secret History', by Pagan Kennedy, Marty Goddard's extraordinary and forgotten life is reclaimed. Goddard was an activist and advocate for women, and the inventor of the rape kit (her original idea was claimed by a man). Goddard also crafted miniature dioramas as a 'hobby', depicting women and children in an idealised, safe, domestic space. The article documents Kennedy's search for what happened to Goddard, revealing how the lives of women so often sink into obscurity.

Kennedy's article inspired a recently published poem in *Landfall* 241: 'And I Suppose Poems Could Be Miniature Rooms: each time you begin with the hope of creation.' In the poem, I focus on these domestic landscapes (these miniature rooms), and align my activism with the activism of Goddard. Illuminating the rape kit: shining a light in dark corners, bringing things to attention, gathering evidence, standing as witness.

For me, focusing on these subjects is necessary and urgent work. With the decline of rape convictions, and the majority of reported cases not even going to trial,[2] lifting the visibility of these issues into public view is something I feel is crucial, both in poetry and other mediums. Sadly, the very old questions, the ancient questions are still being asked.

---

2   'Rape convictions fall to record low in England and Wales', *The Guardian*, 30 July 2020; 'Low rape conviction rate shows system is failing — Women's Refuge', *The New Zealand Herald*, 4 April 2021; 'Only 6 percent of sexual violence cases reported to police end in jail: major government study', *The New Zealand Herald*, 1 November 2019.

TS: A deep sense of dialogue with other artists also animates your poems — the imagery you witness in other writers, but also in drama, cinema and small screen, seeming to echo and evoke your own unconscious energies. How much of your work seems to arise in this way, as an 'answer' to other art forms?

I have a fine arts background, so a lot of influences naturally arise from this, echoes constantly turn up in my work. In my short stories, especially, I have often focused explicitly on the freedoms, privations and obsessions of the artistic life. I admire the outlaw nature of many artists. The disruptive force of a lot of conceptual art, installation and performance art. If I had a hero it would be David Hammons, setting out his snowballs in lines decreasing in size on a striped blanket on a New York street corner in *Bliz-aard Ball Sale*.[3]

At AUT I lectured on the photographer Cindy Sherman. I am fascinated by her ever-changing personas, her explorations through the adoption of masks. In the poem 'To Die and Die Again' I articulate this sense of the writer/artist adopting multiple perspectives and personas: '... sometimes I'm the detective, the gumshoe / locking his brown office. / His narrow eyes, the tough / set of his mouth. / And sometimes I am paint around a body / with the rain so sleety (the dumpster's handiness). / And sometimes I am a street with no lights / that only the drunk or stoned would walk down. / A searchlight from a helicopter.'

Some influences from other mediums that have recently thread their way through my poems are David Lynch's *Lost Highway*; Laia Abril's exhibition *A History of Misogyny, Chapter Two: On Rape*; Stella Vine's paintings of Lady Di; Sarah Kane's play *4.48: Psychosis*; Paula Rego's *Dog Woman* paintings; the plays of Andrea Dunbar; Steve McQueen's film on Bobby Sands, *Hunger*; Alice Maher's *Collar*; Valerie Solanas's *SCUM Manifesto*; and Carol Morley's documentary on Joyce Vincent, *Dreams of a Life*.

---

3   Elena Filipovic, *David Hammons: Bliz-aard Ball Sale*. London: Afterall Books: One Work, 2017.

I once worked as a gallery assistant for the exhibition *Tracey Emin: Fear, War and The Scream*,[4] in which Emin's Super 8 film played on a loop. Curled naked in a foetal position at the end of a jetty, Emin emits a high, terrible, long scream of anguish that convulses her body. The organisers had to shorten the time an assistant or a guard would spend in the gallery to 15-minute shifts because the sound was so distressing. And I am certain that piece of work surely had resonance for my own practice. Some visitors would hurry towards the sound, and others would turn and flee. The power it had was absolutely primal. I remember counting down the minutes until my shift would end. And I started to dread going back in there.

In another exhibition, I remember a huge photograph of an embalmed eyeball, which is forever burned into my consciousness. Working that way in a gallery allowed for moments of stillness and deep contemplation. The bodily presence of standing in those exhibitions for hours, often alone . . . the work really begins to inhabit the unconscious with its power.

Although other art forms animate my creativity, poetry is the most direct spur for my own writing, and my work is in constant dialogue with the work of other poets, echoing and evoking my own 'unconscious energies'. I am influenced and excited by so many contemporary overseas poets: Dorothea Lasky, Maggie Nelson, Mairéad Byrne, Malika Booker, Ada Limón, Tishani Doshi, Mary Ruefle, Louise Glück, Warsan Shire, Deryn Rees-Jones, Claudia Rankine, Kim Addonizio, Kate Clanchy, Natalie Scenters-Zapico, Melissa Lee-Houghton, Natalie Diaz, Catherine Smith, Vicki Feaver, Esther Morgan, and the late Adrian C. Louis. And New Zealand favourites: Hera Lindsay Bird, Elizabeth Morton, Fleur Adcock, Elizabeth Smither, Tusiata Avia, Tracey Slaughter, Hinemoana Baker, Anne Kennedy, Tim Upperton, the late Douglas Wright, the late Rachel Bush, to name but a few.

I am stuck with the compulsion to create, to strive to form the

---

4   *Tracey Emin: Fear, War and The Scream*, City Gallery Wellington, 30 May–22 August 2004.

'perfect machine', a perfect poem. To illustrate this obliquely, which is my favourite strategy, I am from a working-class family from the north of England, and when I was a child my mother entered me into a beauty pageant when we were on holiday in Blackpool. Competing for the title of Miss Rosebud, we all had ribbons tied around our wrists with our numbers printed on a disc. At some point the other children all got out of line and I proceeded to line them back up by their numbers, pulling them along the stage by their sleeves. I would not stop, and at some point I had to be taken off stage by the organisers, much to the embarrassment of my mother, who told the story with great delight over the years.

And perhaps poetry has this (seductive/obsessive) element of control, a need to re-order the world, lining it up obsessively (ruthlessly): the continuous, everyday, OCD nature of it (of writing, of art), this strange neuroses. No other child did this, just me!

And poetry allows me a life of connection, whereas, because of mental health issues, connection on other terms would be difficult. I get to have colleagues (albeit digital ones), and a feeling I am part of something, or the isolation would be unbearable. Such a body of human work to draw upon, so much I have read and seen and heard, and a fraction of it filters up, but of course forms a strong underlying base.

TS: I'm also struck by the vibrations you achieve through acute line control, 'the slow veins' of your poems 'carefully sculpted' to release a measured dosage of sound, tension and meaning. I'm interested to know if the forms of your pieces emerge instinctively and immediately, or are they slowly, methodically laboured towards?

The answer is both. From the initial burst of the poem arriving in the world, I edit unrelentingly; more often distilling a poem down to its bones, but sometimes making additions. I have spent weeks on one line! I love the process of editing. The magical feeling a poet has when the lines are right, when they are working. One of the tools I use is juxtaposition to create tension/interest/disruption/surprise. I love the resonance that forms between disparate lines. I strive toward creating an entity, a thing burnished and shaped and honed, and each time you open it, it remains the same, but can give up so much more.

And if you were to ask me what I wanted most, the answer would be: another poem.

Select bibliography

By the Lapels (Wellington: Steele Roberts Aotearoa, 2019)
Body, Remember (London: Eyewear Publishing, The Lorgnette Series, 2017)
Shooting Gallery (Wellington: Steele Roberts Aotearoa, 2016)
Cowboy Genes (United Kingdom: Grist Books, University of Huddersfield, 2014)

JOURNALS

Aesthetica Creative Writing Annual 2021, 2020, 2019, 2015, 2014, 2013, 2012; *Landfall* 242 (2021), 241 (2021), 239 (2020), 237 (2019), 233 (2017), 231 (2016), 227 (2014), 225 (2013), 223 (2012), 222 (2011), 217 (2009); *Poetry New Zealand Yearbook* (2021, 2020, 2019, 2018, 2017); *Abridged* 0:78 (2021), 0:67 (2020), 0:19 (2020), 0:59 (2020); *Banshee* 10 (2020), 8 (2019); *Best New Zealand Poems 2019* (2020); *Mayhem* 9 (2021), 8 (2020), 7 (2019); *Meniscus* volume 8/2 (2020), 8/1 (2020), 7 (2019), 5/2 (2017), 5/1 (2017), 4 (2016), 3 (2015); *Oscen* 3 (2020), 2 (2019); *Otoliths* 59 (2020), 56 (2020), 53 (2019); *NOON* 17 (2020), 15 (2019), 11 (2016), 9 (2015); *Not Very Quiet* 7 (2020), 6 (2020), 4 (2019), 2 (2018); *Poethead* (2020); *takahē* 100 (2020), 91 (2018), 58 (2006); *Another North* (2019); *Australian Poetry Journal* 9.1 (2019); *Geometry* 5 (2019); *Mimicry* 5 (2019); *Pink Cover Zine* 5 (2019), 4 (2019), 3 (2018); *Skylight 47* 11 (2019), 7 (2016); *Smithereens Literary Magazine* 3 (2019); *Strix* 7 (2019), 5 (2018), 1 (2017); *The Selkie* (2019); *Headland* 14 (2018); *Northampton Poetry Review* 2 (2018); *The Fenland Reed* 7 (2018), 5 (2017); *The Lampeter Review* 16 (2018); *The London Reader* (2018); *The Stinging Fly* 38 (2018); *Turbine | Kapohau* 18 (2018), 05 (2005); *Words for the Wild* (2018); *blackmail press* 42 (2017), 41 (2015), 37 (2014); *Demos Journal* 6 (2017), 4 (2016); *Here Comes Everyone* 6/2 (2017); *New Writing Scotland* 35 (2017); *Offset* 17 (2017); *Atlas Journal* 1 (2016); *Panning for Poems* 5 (2016); *Rabbit Poetry Journal* 19 (2016); *Shot Glass Journal* 19 (2016); *The Frogmore Papers* 88 (2016); *Zoomorphic* 7 (2016); *Cordite* 51.1 (2015); *JAAM* 33 (2015), 31 (2013), 29 (2011), 27 (2009); *The London Magazine* (2015); *Verandah Journal* 30 (2015), 28 (2013); *Westerly* 60:1 (2015), 59:1 (2014); *4th Floor Literary Journal* (2013); *Hue and Cry* 7 (2013); *Magma* 55 (2013); *Poet's Corner* (2013); *New Writing Dundee* (2012, 2009); *Poetry London* (2012); *Going Down Swinging* 32 (2011); *The Stony Thursday Book* 10 (2011); *Page Seventeen* 8 (2010); *Bravado* 17 (2009); *Cadenza* 16 (2007), 15 (2006); *The Warwick Review* (December 2007, March 2007); *Opium Magazine* (2006); *The Ugly Tree* 13 (2006), 12 (2006)

ANTHOLOGIES

Fresh Ink: A collection of voices in Aotearoa (Cloud Ink Press, 2021); *Not Very Quiet: Anthology* 2017–2021 (Recent Work Press, 2021); *Ten Poems About Clouds* (NZ Poetry Shelf, 2021); *Up Flynn Road, across Cook Strait, through the Magellanic Cloud* (Pōhutukawa Press, 2021); *Climate Matters: Climate crisis and capitalism* (Riptide Journal, 2020); *Haumi ē! Hui ē! Tāiki ē!: The NZPS Anthology 2020* (NZPS, 2020); *The Same Havoc* (The Selkie, 2020); *Heroines: An anthology of short fiction and poetry* (Neo Perennial Press, 2019); *More of Us* (Landing Press, 2019); *NOON: An anthology of short poems* (Isobar Press, 2019); *Story Cities* (Arachne Press, 2019); *The Perfect*

Weight of Blankets at Night: The NZPS anthology (NZPS, 2019); *The Sky Falls Down: An anthology of loss* (Ginninderra Press, 2019); *The University of Canberra Vice Chancellor's International Poetry Prize Anthology 2019, 2017, 2015, 2014*; *34 Short Stories: The Dan Davin Literary Award winners* (Pouakai Books, 2018); *BONSAI: Best small stories from Aotearoa New Zealand* (Canterbury University Press, 2018); *The Unnecessary Invention of Punctuation: The NZPS anthology* (NZPS, 2018); *After the Cyclone: The NZPS anthology* (NZPS, 2017); *Fresh Ink: A collection of voices in Aotearoa* (Cloud Ink Press, 2017); *I, You, He, She, It: Experiments in viewpoint* (Grist Books, 2017); *Voices from the Cave* (Revival Press, Limerick Writers' Centre, 2017); *Driftfish: A zoomorphic anthology of oceanic life* (Zoomorphic Journal, 2016); *Penguin Days: The NZPS anthology* (NZPS, 2016); *Poetry and Place Anthology* (Close-Up Books, 2016); *Remembering Oluwale* (Valley Press, 2016); *Shibboleth and other stories* (Margaret River Press, 2016); *The Best New British and Irish Poets 2016* (Eyewear Publishing, 2016); *The Elbow Room Broadsheet* (As Yet Untitled, 2016); *The Poet's Quest for God: 21st century poems of faith, doubt, and wonder* (Eyewear Publishing, 2016); *Scattered Feathers: The NZPS anthology* (NZPS, 2015); *We Society Poetry Anthology* (Printable Reality, 2015); *Hildegard: Visions & inspiration* (Wyvern Works, 2014); *Sweet As: Contemporary short stories by New Zealanders* (Sweet As Short Story Project, 2014); *Take Back Our Sky: The NZPS anthology* (NZPS, 2014); *The Sleepers Almanac* (Sleepers Publishing, 2014); *The Trouble With Flying* (Margaret River Press, 2014); *100 Tanka by 100 Poets of Australia and New Zealand* (Ginninderra Press, 2013); *Given An Ordinary Stone: The NZPS anthology* (NZPS, 2013); *Riptide Anthology* (Riptide Journal, 2013); *Bestiaro* (Wyvern Works, 2012); *Outside the Asylum: Best new fiction 2012* (Grist Books, University of Huddersfield, 2011); *The Sleepers Almanac* (Sleepers Publishing, 2011); *Flosca Anthology* (Flosca Teo, 2008); *Harlem River Blues & other stories* (Fish Publishing, 2008); *Short Fiction 2* (University of Plymouth Press, 2008); *Willesden Herald: New short stories 1* (Pretend Genius Press, 2007); *Mo(nu)ment* (Blue Print Press, 2006)

PRIZES

Poetry New Zealand Prize 2019; Grist Chapbook Prize 2014 (University of Huddersfield); Grist New Writing Prize 2011 (University of Huddersfield); The BNZ Katherine Mansfield Literary Award 2010; Rodney Writes Premier Award 2010; Ilkley Literature Festival 2010 Short Story Prize; The Dan Davin Literary Award 2009; The *Short Fiction* Prize 2008 (University of Plymouth Press); Over The Edge New Writer of the Year 2008; Whakatane Friends of the Library Short Story Competition 2008; The *Flosca* Prize 2008; The Bronwyn Tate Memorial Award 2007; *The New Writer* 2006 Prose and Poetry Prize; *Takahē* Monica Taylor Poetry Prize 2017 (Second Prize); *The London Magazine* Poetry Prize 2015 (Second Prize); Essex Poetry Festival 2011 Open Poetry Competition (Second Prize); The Kate Braverman Short Story Prize 2007, National League of American Pen Women (Second Prize); New Zealand Society of Authors National Short Story Competition 2007 (Second Prize); The Maria Edgeworth Short Story Competition 2008 (Second Prize); Writers of the Year Award 2006: London Writers' Inc. (Second Prize); Auswrite 2006 (Second Prize); New Zealand Society of Authors National Short Story Competition 2002 (Second Prize); The Bryan MacMahon

Short Story Award 2012 (Runner-up); The 2008 Fish Short Story Prize (Runner-up); New Zealand Poetry Society International Poetry Competition 2018 (Third Prize); New Zealand Poetry Society International Poetry Competition 2015 (Third Prize); The Troubadour Poetry Prize 2014 (Third Prize); Cafe Writers Open Poetry Competition 2011 (Third Prize); *Cadenza* Short Story Prize 2007 (Third Prize); The Sarah Broom Poetry Prize 2018 (Finalist); *Geometry*/Open Book National Poetry Competition 2018 (Finalist); *Takahē* Monica Taylor Poetry Prize 2019 (Highly Commended); Page & Blackmore National Short Story Award 2010 (Highly Commended); The Oxford Brookes International Poetry Competition 2015 (Special Commendation); Gregory O'Donoghue International Poetry Prize 2019 (Commended); The *Poetry London* Prize 2012 (Commended); *Magma* Editors' Prize 2012 (Commended); The Melbourne Poets Union International Poetry Prize 2011 (Commended)

ONLINE

www.weslee.co.nz

New
Poems

Prayer

Some people go on to make normal lives
untouched by thoughts of decay or waste

but this girl could feel the distance within her
the mountain firebreaks like collapsed veins
the sun angry behind the resinous pines

the religious texts on the walls seemed too thin
the warnings of afterlife and sin too lenient
and at odds with the fine boned boys

who waited naked and green on the lumpy bed.

Radio evenings stretch like dishwater
books lie that everything can be resolved
the Elder is a dry old stick propping open the Meeting House doors

his wrinkled face like a fire eater at the fair.

Out there is the vastness of the soul
with the silver planes silent and high above —
her father turns the muck in the field
as though he were digging out words

as though he were spade-cutting through bone.

At night no one speaks under a bare bulb
schoolgirls fear broken skin
her mother's lipstick and eye-shadow fill the room
like a coat on a wire-hanger on the wardrobe door

she prays to herself that the house will burn like paper
she prays all the schoolgirls will go lame like horses
she prays that love will destroy the world
that her father will go on living like a hopeless ghost.

death dealer : death doula

they are always there
familiars walking either side of me

this is not a heist but most certainly
an arresting situation

I'm the one who chatters (as usual)
while they, brother and sister

keep their silence
and a firm grip on things

they hold my future, turning it
over in their hands as if

testing a piece of fruit
for its ripeness

they smile at my jokes
still indulging me for after all

they will have the last laugh
the last word

their brief glances
confirming a job well done

as we leave the dance-hall
for the walk home

Kōtare

We stop in a carpark
to look down at the
white crests bobbing in the
Waitematā Harbour.

A halcyon bird
lands on the powerline overhead.

Nana winds up the car window and
Grandad turns the ignition.

They tell me that in Ireland,
the kingfisher is
a portent of death.

It watches us go
Tucks its black beak
into its white collar.
Its plumage is a sunset
an electric-blue omen.

Philip Armstrong

My Own Goals

Poetry happens in the flux of skill,
the lack of it, the rules, and accidents,

as on the school swim day when we were all
required to enter the events:

I could dive but couldn't do a crawl
and when I surfaced I was way behind;

wading on, I heard the starter's whistle blown
again, and by the time I reached the end

a swimmer overtook me, which meant I
placed second in the race after my own.

*

In PhysEd, during football games I played
Right Back — *left right back*, as my captain quipped

quite deftly. Soon the opposition, bored
with easy wins, chose to attempt

to ricochet the ball into the goal
off me, repeatedly. And so I scored

three times against my side in just one match.
It hurt a bit, but even then I thought

what poetry there was in it, for them.
Great days in New Zealand sport.

Ruth Arnison

Gone is gone

My night-time body refuses
to acknowledge her birth
and death.

33 years on it is still trying
to gift me my first born.

Expectant dreams are
always aborted
at daybreak.

Stu Bagby

Poem written in old age

Winter silhouetted, the ash boasts
arteries, capillaries and veins

over lived-out leaves
and my near translucent hands.

We are dying Auckland, dying.
So soon the sun (sighing)

has come and gone.
This alien tree, my stark song.

we meet at the brewery

greysteel barrels and concrete
sit on roughhewn slabs of pine
hold glass and grain to the light

a brown guitar strums heat to our cheeks
softens out chins and backs coaxes
blood to our fingers our mouths
taste of barley on our teeth

we talk of malt and fruit
the many weights of foam
those times we could sleep
without waking in darkness

behind us they lift perfumed sacks
pour hops and yeast to hungry wort
this our steam and steel
this our wheat and water

barcodes

barcodes cluster on my thighs
like constellations
each a figure any gazer might mythologise
but whose true story slips
through time
to the inconceivable

below
some things don't bear remembering
they burn too bright
blinding

other moments
more synaptic clutter

how it satisfies to see my skin part like lips

Art house

funny creaky footsteps on snow
on the soundtrack
of a Russian film

the Party man has visited
and the last fuel
gutters in the lamp

old photographs
curl at the edges
distorting faces

apple blossom becomes rain
then harder rain
then dissolves

only in mirrors
is there a future
somewhere between the long

silvery cracks
and the unreflecting blotches
where the backing has worn away

Today's sky

belongs to Tiepolo. A wisp of a man with nicotine-stained teeth
and wine-soaked breath, he lives in a white house with blue windows
and a wide view across the water. His angels of old have long since flown,
yet still he paints and scumbles, fusses beneath his frescoed dome.
Some mornings, a flock of whisper-thin sparrows hovers and on warmer days
the bumblebees visit. He says it's the blue they like which is reason enough
to keep his windows open. Even when he forgets, the bumblebees find a crack
and make their way in, stripe his house yellow and black. *They don't stay long,*
he insists, *just long enough to tap dance on my walls and sills, resting awhile
on my purple cushions and sometimes on the medieval throne in the hallway.*

the childhood means nothing

i.
the childhood means nothing; it was only an occurrence, like a star falling,
i have abandoned nostalgia; these years are lessons and yearning for what i would
have preferred soaked into them, seeped into the cracks like a sponge,
whatever spell it has is broken on me, or i am its remedy,
because, where were you?

ii.
hurt is a woman born with six masks, one for each hand;
six red mouths;
i don't know who i find when i look for you,
and this spectacle draws something rotten from the certainty
of what i am — look, i will say,
this is how i learned to cut my body into pieces.
leave my tongue and brain in jars; strangle the lightning-rod
out of my words.

iii.
why is your dying more important than mine?
the world has exploded into so many of your shades; you are everywhere
so, to me, you are nowhere; if you have given me singularity,
this lonely house, then what would be losing you? you are only one less teardrop
from a fountain; you are only one less cloud and the sky
has promised my glass, my bottle, his eye;
you are only one day of a thousand, one lonely bonfire,
one winter morning;
you are only one severed branch,
and the tree is blooming — there would be no finer amputation.

iv.
this is not my hunger, my thirst; this is the first signal
to the doorway in my mind that welcomes strangers.

v.
observe me as a passing phase, please; an illusion;
i would withdraw from your face in the black stampede of night,
the moon's stallions she sends to ferry wild women
away;
i never asked to be known so early; never asked for
the audiences, and the insult your kind projects onto the animals
you pull into your nets, although you arrive at every sea,
every lake, searching for something to cage
inside your knees;
i have had to make this animosity you sprinkle onto me
sweet as rose-petals — though you make seasons of it,
this loathing weeded onto me
so intricate that it is almost an affection of its own, almost a heart,
such vulnerability the room swells, embarrassed,
around it;
the song beneath the knife in your throat.

By lamplight

Below my roost, the street's glow
descends to wine-dark ocean.
A long tumble from summer.
Tea is served. Cold snuffles brick walls,
the faint fuzzy slipstream of wave fall
muddled in a heat pump's white noise.
Life narrows. My time is one of cares.
Parents become simpler, child-like,
children break from childhood's chrysalis.
The slow imbroglio of eggshell-dawn,
turpentine and petroleum-dawn,
when dim morning huffs impatiently
on windows smeared with brine,
to reveal an April stunner, a last gasp,
a finale show of deep heat.
Ten yards from tub-thumping breakers,
a spritz is served on ice
at the Esplanade's cafe strip.
Here the well of time
is less mesmerising, less foreboding.
A tiny knot of human-stuff
leaned up against senseless depth,
a slight interruption, barnacle fixed
to a lazy landmass lost at sea.
The fat waxy leaves of kāpuka
dapple sharp light on concrete steps.
Black-slick wave boarders dip and hunker.
Life has washed me here too,
and I won't know whether struggle
in the wash meant something or not.
I wonder now at the winnowing of life,
at lives unlived. Sometimes,

on this remote shore, they approach.
Through the veil of light, I sense
borders and voices, out of time.

Remainder

Last night, the wind sounded wounded. There is sickness

everywhere in the air but I read it most

on the internet, on email, on texts.

People in New York up late with me.

You picked three smooth round chestnuts from their wild casings

while we walked on blue pine needles, how the smell of oak reminds.

The trees trembled, the yellow sunlight of this season finds a way thru,

touches the clean forest floor. The fading lavender on my desk,

the banana passion blossom and dune wildflowers;

a perfect after-life of colour.

How can I love the sweetness of rot? I plant something in soil and

grow sad. Impossible how the morning grew from my fingertips,

blinked on as the streetlights blinked off. Days ago I drove

to a beach I love, walked thru the pōhutukawa grove

to feel alone with the salt-sky, the deafening light thru

the deep, my body parting itself, but instead, for a second,

I felt free, and I carry it in my breath for as long as I can and

for wherever I go.

Duplex

Old line and lures tangled. Twine in lariats,
fish-guts and rust, oily harbour stink

     and as the stinking harbour water sucks
     at stone steps, a bull seal claims the dock.

Slick as a side of meat, the seal docks
where salty rope and sodden nets are piled.

     Still spilling sea, he noses in the piled nets,
     coughs. His fur sheds its oily rainbows.

Greasy as offal, he's darkly rainbowed
in the sun. Turns on us a deep wet gaze —

     no knowable petition. Just a gaze.
     Then he launches, anchor-heavy, trailing

wrack from blunted flippers. His wake's a trail
of line and lures. Tangled lariats of twine.

Exile

Jets flew overhead, lashing the city with sonic booms
Glass exploded on to the street. It wasn't a war.
Sallow faced youths marched with a rattle of rifles.
Helicopters marred the night; checkpoints the day
Dogs roamed in packs & birds gathered near the sea.
Rumours of annihilation fanned the poetry of fear.

I meditated to the echo of jackboots on cobblestones,
Police raids at dawn, neighbours' cries of innocence;
Questioned whether I could return to order and civility
A paper trail and transparency, taxes.

Erick Brenstrum

Little Ice Age

Best estimate,
world's population cut by a third
by the end of the seventeenth century.

Bitter cold,
rivers froze, oceans froze,
famine, rebellion, war.

Zurbarán's painting
St Francis kneeling head bowed
hood of the cassock
hiding his face
but for the nose, the lips, the chin
catching the light
and the hands, the fingers,
hands that could make things,
harvest things, weave things, write things
hands bathed in light
clutching a skull
to his stomach
face up
eyeless sockets returning our gaze
from a century of war and famine.

Iain Britton

No Inhibitions

she scuffs at leaves
at winter's fallen scraps

she has this knack of disappearing
into the still black
still white landscape — of frozen ponds

& every minute something seeps underground — & is lost

a silhouette
glides into a statue

tree roots shrink in the cold

the boy learns quickly
          learns fast

he kisses the clay smoothness of the girl next door — winds up
her emotions — & they ride

their bikes between sunsets

they have no inhibitions
about what they do — or where they go — words
pass from his mouth to hers

she loves the orgasmic click
of mouth & breath

at night — he turns off the light

she holds his hands —

he unhinges an imaginary door

Chi

In a room with Beauden Barrett and another man I recognise as a
famous halfback, I say something like 'it's amazing to be with two of
the best rugby players on the planet'. The halfback I know slightly.
He's having a break from rugby. He's pregnant and has a nice bulge.
He's studying, an online course in poetry. I ask him where, and who
he's reading and we talk about the poets, most of whom I don't know.
A young rugby team clacks in, getting ready for a game. They stand
in lines facing the same way. One guy at the front faces back at them.
He starts chanting ee-vi-iil with a big grin on his face, very slowly.
No one takes it up, but you sense that they're preparing in a new way.
One of them says something about poetry being lame. I pipe up to
defend it, try to drop how much I love rugby, and talk about how hard
you have to work and how tough you have to be to go through 15–20
drafts of a poem. The room gets more tense, what I said interpreted
as criticism. The situation looks to get nasty. I made a mistake.

> dawn —
> your shadow
> lifting chi

Stacking

STACKING STONES DESTROYS NATURAL ECOSYSTEMS
I read in some online article far too late, piles higher than my
head, beyond even the line of trees. Oh Oh god Oh lord Oh
fuck, I wish I'd known before, never even photographed the
stacks I stacked, merely exposing soil, exacerbating erosion
AND HEATING THE COOL UNDERSIDES OF ROCKS THAT
PROVIDE SAFE HAVEN TO COUNTLESS INVERTEBRATES
leaving them diasporic and homeless and burning alive under
a sun which cannot care for her creatures the way she once did
for her existence has been so thoroughly fist-fucked by the
MANY YEARS SPENT NOT BOTHERING TO SORT THE
RECYCLING AND INSTEAD LITTERING VIA LANDFILL
simply because the registration process seemed like too much
work and you are the laziest pissy shitty-filthpot around, too
LAZY TO TURN OFF A LIGHTBULB ON YOUR WAY OUT
because you're some little lord without a care for the damage
much like your burgeoning recognition that so many items
YOU BOUGHT FOR FULL-PRICE STILL CONTAIN PALM OIL
AND ACTIVELY LED TO THE DEATH OF ANIMALS TOO
exotic for you to see outside of a zoo, too undeniably
endangered for any sense of peace, but you still criticised her
FOR BUYING VEGAN LEATHER SINCE IT IS MADE FROM
NOTHING BUT PLASTIC AND HAS A WORSE IMPACT ON
memories filtering through my skull through filmstock which
takes five hundred long unliveable years to degrade when left
WHERE BOYS FISH FOR EELS USING WHITE BREAD AND
AIR AND YOU WERE TOO SCARED TO CONFRONT THEM
the ghost of every fish and shrimp and crab and orangutan and
baby bird I ever dishomed appears to me each night swimming
in the space between my duvet and the ceiling where the guilt
always gathers in cloud formations, their bodies painted unreal
colours and expressions twisted in agony, joined by

coelacanths and tiktaaliks through shared diaspora and disappointment in me *(Although frankly, I've sat broken limbed, silent yet far from apathetic with only sharp rain for company on the hottest-coldest day on record since the last one)* and I still haven't found a way to forgive myself, when all these feelings STACK AND THEY DO STACK, THEY DO STACK, MY GOD, and it seems that all I now have left to do is to pull free the final wide flat piece from the endless fears and inactions and constant second guessing and questioning and to finally break

And let them all topple.

Jessie Burnette

hallways

hear the bump in your
    abscessed swallow
  the cold desked
  coffee cup clink
 in your
stomach
    hear the head pulse
     red brain
     echo of a
       world
           carved
     broad from
     sunburnt
eyes
          it is growing
            over blue veined
            necklines and
            mini skirt swish
              these pin up
        pale mouth
rhymes
              perhaps it will   kill you
                and you will
sink
                 into backbeat sirens
             fever
        buckle head sweat
                hang your
          file cabinet tea leaves
          and blood binned
             ink

Take me.
Take me, damn you.
Ask and I will dance your knives in
           ribbons of   hair
           scalped   fresh from
           my grandmother's
brow.

Here: I give you my liver, cut dirty in rusted nails.
Here: a slice of cerebellum; cellophane-wrapped in slurred intention.
Here: a sectioned crack of ulna, wire tripped in ivory hail.
Here: my premature placenta;

Nourish yourselves on the flesh
                  set me out for
                  the dogs.

Chris Cantillon

WW1
(12.10.1917)

I went to school with farmer children
strong thick boys, plush cliquey rough at rugby
didn't like me that much, good! — then war
we in lines, machine-gunned, folded over
me I made it, no work though at home
letalone find a bride o my shelled mind
(and lungs stuffed)., outskirts day, slow roll the
thoughts, summer gone a rain is later my
shack pelted and verandah — an ease of sorts —
and still clicking a lone cicada

a boy in the toi-toi!

You play in the toi-toi
in a mood of mud,
a right angle
against a wrong green fence.
Your *siblings* show me
skateboard knuckles,
grazed to the bone,
the intricacies of ripped skin
that *you* should —
everyone loves a scar!
but you sit there
adjacent to the complacency
of those other kids
with one of those little pink books —
a new one —
writing
downhill
in the wind
and the speed
of a deliberately injured
syntax
on the bone-white knuckles
of the moon,
an inconstant moon
that should —
but it doesn't matter anyway!
How I read you
will be the under-reed
of the toi-toi now
and the should-green of growth —
as sharp as the flick
of a carpenter's tape —

will plume the blond after-shavings
of a freshly planed two by four.
I am only sorry
for how I read you
now you are writing *me*
watching
you — a boy —
play in the toi-toi.

drought

here the dust-dry trees
sign history.
across grey paddocks

scattered green-plastic
bales, tin sheds,
misaligned wire fences,

a scrambling of mānuka —
then the yellow ubiquity of gorse,
while steadily the land fans away.

here enclosures are
boulder-riven,
spaces for deer

and cattle listless
in heat's heaviness.
it is a land once ploughed,

of ancient killings,
but the stony rivers
will not speak —

they're drought-trickles —
or ripple story.
unseen are the women

and men
who farm this land.
now a car scrap-yard,

colours like Pollock's drip-
paintings, vivid on brown.

Jenny Clay

Arrival

after midnight at Island Bay
my niece descends the concrete steps
mid-contraction
one, two, she rests on
her young Jordanian husband

I see you midday
your mother is tender with stitches
she guides your mouth to her sore nipples
sucking colostrum
your gums clamp as you tire

she says your nose and head
were squashed in delivery
the plates of your head not yet firm
I can't see the fontanelle
under a black wave of hair
you sneeze, she wraps you up

the midwife comes and unwraps you
your body red and soft
she counts your fingers and toes
wipes you clean
places you skin to skin
you lie on the no longer hard curve
of your mother's stomach
your mouth open, seeking a nipple

when I return from lunch
the nurse is about to check
the stitches of the person on the bed
but it's your father curled beside you

she tells us a man gave birth
in Wellington hospital twice
kept his 'lady bits' after the sex change

your aunt says the placenta came out whole
inside out, after you were delivered
she cut the umbilical cord

she has you curled within her arms
takes you into the corridor
to let your mother sleep

you are already changing to a pale pink
your skin adjusting to the light

In Amsterdam

You enter the upstairs refuge via a bookcase.

There is one window that looks up into the sky
haunted by a glimpse of the fingertips of a tree.

According to the guide no one is quite certain
who betrayed them all. My sister told me this.

And she didn't feel sad exactly, after, but she
wanted to sit in a café by a canal and not talk.

The Taxidermied Wife

The shop window sports the contorted body of a fox, instead of a welcome sign. A red fox who in death has been reinvented as a rocking chair. Hens remain gawked at and traded, they're the everlasting commodity. Dead hens with glass eyes showcase peridot necklaces. Hens who swapped their coops for shelf confinement.

I know.
I know they'll airbrush my face when I die. Add shadows. Cover my waxy sheen.

Domes encase a rainbow collection of butterflies in a state of quietude. The shop smells like vanilla. The heat pumped air wraps around your bones like white hot chocolate, a refuge from the lashing alpine wind. It's a place where still born kittens strut on podiums while drawing black carriages filled with the carcasses of birds. The never lived given a fantastical rebirth in black diamonds.

I know they'll dress me in the frock they like best. Pink lace.
I know they'll tame my curls until they lie flat.
I know they'll place my grandmother's pearls upon my hushed chest. Emeralds in my ears.

I stand at the interlock of repulsion and fascination. I move forward, further into the shop space. A workaday turkey's feathers adorned with vintage brooches and jewels. Jade, pink sapphires, garnets, and pearls.

I know they'll cut away the unlikeable parts of me in the eulogy. The hot-iron tempered nights.
The jealous questions. The human irrationality.
Until I fit.
Until I fit in the box of the devoted daughter/wife.

Death's a captivating mistress, worthy of an Instagram story. My friends and I stand over their corpses. And I know.

That's the person they'll bury / That's the person they'll set alight.

J. Coté

a redistribution of matter

it began in twenty fourteen
taking the time I built
to quicksand m o m e n t s
skies scraped the city like
claws and I watched
a tale of my three lovelies'
dirty youth disasters
turn dust against chili temptations
despite the rain I saw   liar, liar, r
holey wash, quick shower
these
     small
         matter (s)
hooked on the hung up
the silhouette of three rotating
dodger memories brained
puddled sorries of tuxedo vomit   the clock strikes
it's time for
a drop
         a tiny drop
ecstasy

red doves watched

ryan died yesterday
    (She picks the feijoas and regrets)
every atom of him absorb/fibrous cells
cancer tissue smells bad like high school
the pipe
the motherfucking pipe of
malleable connectivity
gets a D grade and not

the good kind
as we bonnet and die
diners of I love u gasoline
gritty litty from the girl
from Brazil
wavy curls against her mouth
columbus found us
against the corn
broken yet
alive

cigarette break . . .   take one and

Hallelujah

mull the wine for offerings
autumn equinox
a vial of tears
from liars

brown eyes   hallowed
graves placed here for lost babes
knife times and gas life
all for catastrophe
and cool cats who shit the bed
for happiness
gusty lines
leave (s) love, my hands
as I watch metal break
long tables put there for the sake of it
we all clap at disaster in
make up
alter boys . . . smirk with me?
brown haired idiots

three bands of three unfortunate (s)
lace garter dreams of another's

        I'm stuck with you

her only orgasmic cry
shed on finger curved hopes

Craig Cotter

Lilac

My boyfriend died 20 years ago.
This is a cure.

Suva to Nadi

The bus launches into the evening
backpackers and hitchhikers clump together
past the villages heading for night
lurching into the darkening west.

Each night village slides by
its single light fluorescent glowing
focus for the wakened watch dogs
who briefly object when we stop.

Village and village and village
mingle and melt behind us.
The backpackers and hitchhikers
stir in their sleep, dreaming their dreams:

tropical fruit with flown-in yoghurt,
chlorinated swimming pools.

Cut-throat

I could almost believe you were still here were it not for the hawthorn leaf chafe against the trachea, the swell of thorny prickles in the glottis, clutching at my throat like the rough hand of an assassin, the air in the windpipe clamped, the scald of breaths as the mind brawls for air, shrill and sharp. The neck of a bottle comes to mind, turning the cork to release the pressure, inside, a secret message that exhales a sweet odour. If I cut the tree I might invite misfortune. But wasn't it the hawthorn that marked the door to the underworld? This is not where I would find you — haunting an old church, more like — standing in front of St Blaise, the Armenian martyr, your head thrust backward as he blesses your throat with a crossed candelabrum, your elbow nudging me, your eyes that would say — what are you waiting for?

The burst of white hawthorn petals on my tongue.

Reading Lessons: Phase Five

Self detachment:

Oh yes, a belly yaks out in front
if I stand in the middle of
feeding myself or sit
knees bent in the bathtub,

but I hustle now — walked in
to a money trap, the kind
that sits and waits:

aloof sapphire, rubies
and a riotous Arabian gold,

      a cat, transcendent
      in the doorway. I'm earning:

Giver of all things you could screw up
and split your nose on: Paper and words,
words words — a lot of yummy words.

I can tell you what they say. They say humanity's
a condition — retching, gasping, gorgeous:

the führer, the floppy dick, the woman ripping her skirt
for feminism. Believable leviathans, sacrificed at the bugle
of world domination.

The monster — tender, green and verbal
liable to break a neck in devastating love.

A mouse, stored at the breast of a child. Intellects!
supping their relics and stiffer gin, thrusting their red cloth
at the fabulous horns. Dudes

ambling through the sandstorms of Africa
for oases. Sick baby / fat baby in the same pink cot. Choo choo —
the morality train, that some bird tossed herself in front of.

Indelicate.
And the spider whittles a word into her miracle, cos we
just   couldn't   see it.

gorgon

mine are the people of the sea
the wine-dark sea   they say
the people of boats with
blue-eyed prows
sails of silk and canvas

trace them to the stars
we will be found to be
stardust   in days after this
when the gods no longer
catasterise   Cassiopia
Andromeda   Orion   Merope

mine are the people of the octopus
mantle   beak   eight-tentacled
we are the writers of the pelagic sea
ink our histories in the coral
venomous memoirs of betrayal   stealth

trace them to the bull leapers
lithe and limber acrobats
cavorting with swallows and lilies
turn and tumble across the leathery hide
bony shoulders   bowed horns

mine are the people of the snake
viperous   double-tongued
we deal in death and
healing   wind round the staff
turn to stone with one baleful glare

let no man harm you
you will find us there
we will bare our boar-like fangs
shake our serpentine hair

Daddy, don't you know?

raised on john-cougar-mellencamp
of-course we are destined for sadness

I wish you'd taught-me more than to leave
a relationship if I were beaten (although acc-
ording to mum, that's your basis for a good
one: merely not hitting a woman)

we got drunk on rum and poverty's depression
took turns playing sad songs sung by deep-
voiced men —

'don't go out with someone who
    doesn't know who otis-redding
    is — because they won't have a
    soul' you said

would've been nice to know the threat-of
suicide makes a bad boyfriend — that getting
in the way of dreams isn't love — and for a
bent-girl: women can be cunts too, you know

it takes a women's-refuge check-list to tell me
lesbians aren't all rainbows

all the fight moves you taught-me were for
back-against wall not pinned against-mattress
guess my education left out: bad things can
start lying down

isn't it [adjective] how words can hurt so

it must have been hard being my dad when I told you about that rape
— you sat chain-smoking with open ended questions till there wasn't
a doubt when you offered retribution — and I said
I don't want you to —
'so why did you tell
  me then?'

because yesterday — you told me about your trip into town — you
said you saw Him — and told me He's a good guy — and I want you
to know: He-isn't.

Only Poetry Will Do

Inside the mouth of a soliloquy, I arrive at the
centre of my spiralling thoughts. I take off my
shoes. Odysseus is dead and maybe he was never
alive, but his ship still strives, seeks, finds the edge
of some distant horizon. After all: *that which we are,*
we are. In a carriage, Dickinson and Death, Death
and Dickinson, ride forever and, occasionally, I
join them. We sit together awhile, contemplating
the remnants of time, while Hera Lindsay Bird
dances on the edge of a simile, disrupting the bats
from their slumber. They float around the cave of my
mind, listening to Mary Oliver's wild geese honk
on about fresh mornings and the broken world. *You*
do not have to be good. You do not have to walk
on your knees, for a hundred miles, repenting. There
are too many Jeffs in Siken's psyche. None are alike
but they all have one thing in common: they don't
know what to do with their hands. Neither do I. Neither
do you. I want to sit at the bedpost in Edward Hopper's
Western Motel and have Therese Lloyd call me a
pioneering woman. *My turf, my land.* Let the horses
run rampant. Let them win the final race. Ada Limón
always does. They riot across her pages, pumping
life back into my veins and I'm just a neon star —
glowing and dying, dying, and glowing. Pull over
the car of my body, roll out the recycling bin at the end
of each day. There are *bright dead things* in the soil.
You just have to find them.

Lonely Hearts Club

The kind of love that I'm trying to find
isn't listed in the classified ads.

This forty something seeks similar to spend
those long summer nights inside the hothouse.

To slink our fingers deep into the soil
as November beetles bounce off the walls.

Someone to grow old with like compost
revitalises earth when mixed together.

To have an extra pair of hands to harvest
after eggplants have grown pregnant and round.

No need to feel lonely in your twilight
when all we can hear is each other's breath.

With someone to share as you reap what you sow
over a lifetime of myriad spring times.

Feeding station

After a time, the gathering birds of various kinds elide
their vowels completely. This morning, the tūī lied
when it sang *chloris chloris* and then *conk-la-ree* — I'd

not be surprised to see the white wattle vibe with the clack
of westerly worried flax on the cold eroding dune. There is no lack
of wind-fallen, knife-pared fruit for the waxeye's rump up apple ac-

robatics. Greenfinch, blackbird, dunnock, thrush come ravenous
through July while I feast and strain to stay fit, softly venous
in the mirror with my free weights and yogic nous —

O, sinuous memories of summer grass and berry tongue,
grazing friends toasting in the sun like even-toed ung-
ulates in bare hoof and hemp feather hair. Raise your glass to ngā

uruora, the groves of life. Usher the Symbiocene in its nascent
stages: seeds and suet set in a lemon cup for the ascent
of bird. Gardeners of the 'burbs — feed this crowning scent.

David Eggleton

fridge   magnet   poem

morning to night

shiver on

happy small refrigerator

off you r face

summer through winter

dawn to owl light

whisper this song

I freeze the harvest

from the garden

always so cold

and I make breath cloud

Amber Esau

A poem(,) of course

(flatmates, thin walls) membrane and then some.

Viscous and sad before the walls open.
The ending is continual glue, each layer hiding noise bubbles
in the plasterboard and the pink batts fuzzy and blind between them
rock

the ripples, bear the cave walls that hang conch somewhere in the
fur, lovers spin songs but get caught amongst the leaves and start
to settle in a rhythm as fast or slow as birth
making.

(the line, wet sheets) shrivelled fingers and the bath.

Soaked first then steamed, sand contours
thirst to salt before it sets to skin. Easy to scrape the underside of a
giant ripple
unused, the bottom of the tub gargles and stirs

the backwash, loose grains hidden in water
like Koko, muddy and tin, the darkest gold-panning this side of the
Pacific, like cliff banks squeezing the creek bed this is what it means
to fuck in silence.

(stovetops, spillage) the dusty and the dirt.

What's land without a little spill? The drama of the elements fished
out of Papa and chucked at the pop of a balloon dipping lower
to the ground, running out

of breath, out of belonging
the land bends down to the pressing of metal. Chicken wire fence and
shrapnel spilling tomato on the stove, spitting the hybrid wetness out
a lid less pot left for someone
else to tidy.

John Geraets

from RIVERSPELL 12

I see the green of the horse
chestnut before the buds open.
The lower side of the lopsided
pond under the bridge is fuller
than the upper side. The cake is
not the knife that cuts through
it and neither is it the cut. A
heron moves from the lower
to the upper pond. I am bits &
pieces and bits & pieces and
bits & pieces I am. I am bits
& pieces and this's the entire
story. Demogorgon: 'But a voice
/ is wanting, the deep truth is
imageless.'

from RIVERSPELL 12

Before I am in the ground
dandelions waver across
it. I picture my death. It is
colourless (Demogorgon's
prerogative). I acknowledge
those who have not known or
cared for me or only at a set
distance. Now that disappears.
My eyes are different. Things
are vaporous.

Sawdust

I'm going into a shed away from my life.
I'm taking a chainsaw even though I don't know how to use it.

Lying in the sawdust is a thick log.
I have come here to cut it.

I can deal with cuts that require band-aids.
But cuts that require compressions and screaming and *call-an-ambulance,*

they are not my thing.
The chainsaw eyes me from the corner.

Sat on the log, I stare at the spider webs in the window, waiting for movement.
I know I am not a useful human.

I'm the sort of human who likes to feel
dust landing on the hairs of my arm.

I'm the sort of human who likes to watch
dust rising in a slant of sunlight.

Michael Hall

The Boys' Changing Shed

In the keen world
of chlorine and damp
echoing
concrete, and un
pegging of
clothes — there
were
always
one or two who
liked to flick
towels, lightning
quick cracks on
legs, bare blitzkrieg bums
and once, someone's
balls — the instigator
who
crumbled thankfully
in the singularity of his pain
to the concrete laughter
of the wet floor.
And the chatter
of the girls
like a Russian summer
through
the wall.

Jordan Hamel

If you read this backwards blood becomes wine

The only difference between depression
and baptism is who gives the body,
trust me I've worn both, stiff like fixed form.
I need to keep some skin in the game,

I need to explain feeling nothing
but there's no parable for absence,
just a dead language carving itself
into the architecture of eternity.

Rule one is only communal sorrow
can fertilise the garden, but I'm a renegade
botanist built from stolen parts, the loneliest
green thumb and ribs to spare. So I collect

small miseries for every sacrament
I steal them off your plate when you're
in the bathroom, I grow them inside me,
I play them classical music, I regurgitate

bread for nutritional purposes, I fish them out
with an old rod from the shed, I weigh them
for science, I take a picture for my miserable
trophy cabinet then sell them back to you!

When I'm ready to bear fruit
it will be less . . . transubstantiation
more . . . Initial Public Offering

Can you really afford not to? I'm bullish
on all things confession and rule two is
never short the economy of sadness.

Rule three is take the seven moments
of your life that define you, let them fight
over the right to be forgotten, anoint
what remains and bury the rest.

I used to whisper last rites to myself
and pray I'd never wake up, I used to
pack my mouth with dirt to see what grew.

a *Woman's Weekly* interview with the Briscoes lady, to mark 30 years of being the Briscoes lady

Being the Briscoes lady has opened up so many doors for me. Mainly automatic doors at Briscoes stores. Although my house has a very nice door, with very nice pots on either side of it. There aren't any real plants in the pots, because Briscoes doesn't sell real plants, but they do sell fake ones, so I have those. And I don't have to remember my own name anymore, because no one uses it.

What is my real name? Um . . . Is it Mary?

I've been having an affair with one of the forklift drivers at Briscoes' Henderson store for 8 years now. The first time we had sex — on top of a wool duvet, 40% off, placed on a pallet of outdoor umbrellas — they were stunned to discover that I have a fully functioning vagina and clitoris. People assume that under the smart-yet-practical-and-never-too-expensive-looking trousers, I'm smooth and sexless as Barbie.

Is my name Barbara?

There are only 17 days in a year when Briscoes isn't having a once-in-a-lifetime, never-to-be-repeated, don't-miss-out-this-is-our-only-sale-of-the-year sale. If you're shopping at Briscoes on one of those 17 days, you're a fucking idiot.

How am I so cheerful in all the ads? How is my smile so effortless? I pop pills like you wouldn't believe.

Wait, is my name Kate?

I cry myself to sleep every night. I sleep on top of a pile of duvets, each encased in a duvet cover in one of this season's fashionable looks. With a range of pillows, to meet the differing needs of different sleeps. There isn't a pillow designed with suitable absorbency for crying yourself to sleep though.

I'm not allowed a bed, because Briscoes doesn't sell beds. I had an airbed for a while, because Briscoes does sell airbeds. But the cat kept clawing holes in it so it kept going flat. I don't own a cat. Fuck Lily from Big Save. Fuck her and all her beds.

My entire house is furnished in bar stools and outdoor dining sets. If Briscoes doesn't sell it, I'm not allowed it. I'm not allowed to be seen in other shops, including supermarkets. Or the liquor store. Briscoes has a small box of food sent to me once a week. That's all I'm allowed. One small box of food, one large box of liquor, one large box of pills, that's how I get by.

I'm told Briscoes has a luggage section. They won't let me near it. If I could get myself a matching set of suitcases, 50% off, I'd pack up my 40% off electric toaster and 60% off all towels and 30% off wine glasses, I'd pack them all up and run and run and run and run. I'd run away with the Trivago lady.

On Monday

On Monday
Mid-sentence
I stopped talking

The corners at Dr Jenny's eyes creased
As she
Uttered prompts
Related to our kōrero
To get me going again
Which is what I did

In the end
We laughed off my senior pause — a clichéd expression in this
Dementia facility
    &
On Wednesday
When I couldn't complete the sentence I'd started
And I stopped talking

Nurse Practitioner, Bridget
Made,
carry on talking gestures at me
With her hands
and gave me encouraging looks and nods
We laughed,
(as if nothing significant had just happened)
when the kōrero picked up and flowed
    &
On Thursday

I practised
    &
I practised
No-one heard the well-articulated sentence beginnings

&
No-one took notice of the abruptly muted endings

The silence

I practised, but I still couldn't complete the sentences
because I couldn't remember the beginnings
So,
I made shorter sentences
I made notes

On Friday I wondered
what I'd told myself to do on Thursday

And the skin between Dr Jenny's eyebrows creased

Karaoke tragedy

O madonna almighty it has been revealed unto me
that I am bad at karaoke a disaster diva a collapsing star
howling bad romance in the swirling lights half pop punk hottie
half abject tsunami cold sweating at the fact that raw
enthusiasm is no substitute for technical ability

& nobody in the room is familiar with the song I picked
so I am attempting a duet with myself skipping the soprano
notes for screamo shredding my throat so overcommitted
to wretched necromancy of the obscure evanescence back catalogue
O but my beautiful friends go about their duties in the dark

pouring generosity into applause & interchangeable shot glasses
they wrestle the remote to queue the backing tracks that will move us
down the hours poring through the sticky clearfile of pulp culture
O all our possible triumphs & calamities steeped in the syrupy
scam of nostalgia as I ascend for my final tortured chorus

one foot on the pleather sofa & one boot planted on the laden table
overflowing a soju cornucopia our bounty of morning laments O blue
berry O peach O grapefruit O apple sting even six pomegranate shots
to release me from the dismal pit I have sung myself into & soon
I will choke on the outro a mortified heroine O hair flips & glassware

tumbled but unbroken yes soon my friends we will press our faces
together cheeks squished sharing the microphone practically pashing
its spittly mesh O amateur starlets O party hags we won't be younger
than this again when behind the blinking lyrics the dolphins crest
into their sunsets rainbows erupting from shining blowholes
in the instant they perforate the oil slick

Thinking of Leaving

[love] like stone / like chaw
    like flint

between teeth
    sleepless nights

sift and file / sift and
    file memories

splintered shrapnel
    like roadkill

pheasant feathers
    wound tightly

round and round
    my [heart]

the reminder
    the temptation

to desert / start over
    indecision a hallmark

on the kitchen table
    calculator waiting

to run the numbers
    after another day

tying flies
    weighing anchors

doom

i am a doomed person   i weigh myself compulsively

i   wank far too often

i find no comfort in the radical freedom of my doom

    i hate my stretch marks

i dream of marrying porn stars

wholly empty and full of shit   there is something bent

i have lost all interest in prolonging my life

    i lack the will to end my life   help me

        end my   life

i have pushed the ones who love me   away

i do not desire a better world   for anyone

i want to trap others in my body

i do not believe in the soul

i want open borders

i fear for my soul   i must touch myself

i want to spill   into the universe

i pray for an end to all mankind

i smile at social gatherings   i am good   and   doomed

i pray for greater pain   i pray

i find no comfort in truth   or prayer

i wish god was real   and a fascist

              i wish i was machinery

i am a fat anorexic

i want a lover so i can end my life in front of them

i want others to feel responsible for my death

i want to traumatise my lover   to love

i want to inspire others to commit suicide there is no light   no love

        i want to dent infinity with my death

i want to brush up against tachyons   u   accelerate past lightspeed

    i see my life as a fever dream had by someone else many years
from now on a

    cloudless afternoon

        this is a cry for help   assist my suicide

i believe in a limitless human capacity for suffering

i hate ugly people

    i blame capitalism

i worry that i may be god

i watch some sick shit   sunlight   please miss

                                      me

i deserve doom

i think nothing of human connection

i am smarter than my counsellor

i hate the art i create   i hate my reflection

i would like to fuck my counsellor

i do not believe one can create something out of nothing

i miss my dog   i have come so close to death

i do not deserve better

i do not understand why others live   my partners have all moved on

i am incidental carbon

i have never failed a test

i do not understand a non temporal happiness

i laugh

i fuck

i

i

    captain

am terrified of feeling   better

a doomed person

                i cannot orgasm with the lights on

drive through

you loved driving
windows up
car built of ciggie smoke and rap
me
shotgun staring
as we trace the palms of a city that held nothing for us
just our pasts and loved ones
hostage

me and you
caught the last of that old auckland sorcery
gutter magic
made music from
blackout romance
blackeye nights no stars
just a neon jesus and some liquid judas
gusts of violence that swept the lifeless streets
an endless cycle of bad advice and lazy drugs
but man
did you make it all sound so good

on your learners in your thirties
self taught in all ways
fuck school
fuck cops
fuck uni
fuck the rich
and every other dumb motherfucker
with a fetish for authority
and yeah
sometimes we celebrated life more than we lived it

but we had a hunger in our guts and hearts
the way fire longs to burn

we'd never been overseas
saw the world through dirt streaked windscreens
exploring the city over
like telling a secret
everyone knows by heart
and when your music carried you away
we watched from afar
proud
when love and whānau brought you home
our smiles filled that airport
whole

I know you're not in heaven
full of fucking nerds
nah
you're still out there driving Todd
stereo on 10
gas on empty
when my time comes
I call shotgun

your abusive ex texts you every august from a new number

—thursday
in the soft
of my belly
i hold
grenades

you don't know
this
you text: hey, i'm
sorry

i've been
feeling low
and it's been
on my mind

how shit i was
to you
i'll leave it
alone now

but it's my birthday
soon
did you remember?

—monday
tonight's moon
is a hole
cut in the apex
of a tent

there are moths

on my window

orange pith
undersides
in the fickle light

i have a collection
of vintage pill-
boxes

i hold them all

in my two hands

—wednesday
tonight's moon
is actually
a satellite
dish

something opens
leaks into
memories

the ones where you
take advantage
of the best parts of
myself

it casts

those memories

in gold

Waiting in the Park

I was a fool to listen to him. If my Mother could see me now, coat a beggar wouldn't thank you for second hand boots, this wreck of a hat. I look a sketch, my head is thumping I'm desperate for a decent cup of strong tea. I could have married a draper, had my pick, grocer accountant maybe. If I'd been patient stuck with my job at the Convent the nuns would have found me a match. What with Uncle Michael's position, promise of a legacy. I can't speak the lingo, I have no money. He's got what he wanted out of me, what if he never comes back? It's cold It's getting dark that fella in the blue gansey over there is staring at me. The tall one with the gypsy looks is laughing gesturing with his fingers. Mother of God they think I'm a whore. I'll go to the police station, even if they put me in a cell. I wish I was back at Finn's Hotel, Nancy and me serving up dinners. I wish I'd never heard the name James Joyce. What was I thinking of, setting my cap at a penniless scribbler.

Tramadol panic dream

The after-hours doctor gave me yellow-green capsules for the pain
Located 3 to 5 centimetres to the right side of my spine

And that Friday night I dreamt so deeply it was like
That Fuseli painting with this weight on my body

And when I woke up I felt your presence, so
Sudden and dizzying like a hypnagogic jerk

That I had to scroll through months of messages
While I waited to throw up.

' . . . pushing them into so called therapy that asks "what's wrong with you?" instead of "what happened to you?"' — Chlöe Swarbrick

No one taught us to carry fire extinguishers,
so we learned to live with the flames.

Whiskey burning tracks down our throats,
trying to force some air into lungs tight with trauma.
Lighter burns etching the ache of broken childhoods
across our arms. Ash, everywhere, always.

The happy memories were smoke damaged years ago,
we had to throw them out. All that remains
is kindling and anger. They're almost the same thing now.

Our friends grew up next to the river. They don't understand
why we're always blazing, always lighting up.

Orange Flag 58

red knot
not red

hurtled into my hand
one hundred grams of miracle
riding the north wind

hiss of ice in white feathers
made in Siberia

seven years in rigorous
pursuit of summer

anchored to the Pacific
occasional stray to Australia

ancient chromosomes on wings
preceding glaciation

seeing with magnets
parsing the air
with compass needle nose

mercurial spirit
rising with the barometer

tiny eyes
giant world.

Haunted house

When the body left,
having stood in foyer to
reach for the umbrella
from the stand, turning
ever-so-slightly as if to say —
then not. It's what's been said
that lingers politely from
room-to-room. A curious
neighbour at the Sunday open
home. *They were such a quiet*
couple. Who would have thought . . .
When the neighbours left,
they left their house cat
to move in beneath the
floorboards. It gave birth to
a litter. He named each one
after what the teenagers who'd
broken in had written on the walls.
death to wife-beaters, death to pigs,
Black Sabbath forever,
Tina loves J, Psalm 19:1.
What an urge it is to name.
To let the word bubble and
fizz from the mouth. Perhaps
he was a woman once. When
each of the kittens left, checking
their coats and ties in the mirror
by the door, they turned a little —
then left.

Traveller at Lake Wakatipu

there you go, poking your head out
for that cooked breakfast smell
making its way up the stairs
crawling in to your hotel bedroom
leading you outside, via
glassed-in double doors

sunlight's crossing the road
yellowing the jetty lawn
where you're gulping freshest air
staring beyond far lake shore
to the snowy crown
of The Remarkables

down here, where tourists are meant
to stand, camera ready
for the perfect picture shot
of a windless dawn
brassy old, oily old, TS *Earnslaw*
chugging against its hawser ropes

then as it gets away, churning water
like a ploughshare turning soil
domino effect of its long tail wake
slapping metre by metre of shoreline
till its jig saw puzzle of reflections
settles back into a model postcard

Ocean Jade

*First prize (Year 12), Poetry New Zealand Yearbook Student
Poetry Competition*

Route Back Home

chalk teeth grate together, relentless, like the scraping metal in your
faulty brakes. but the erratic drone of your rotors keep me from
crawling too far into daydreams that skip to the ending sequence
where we run into a wide-shot embrace.
because sometimes every minute cramped and cornered
into the ink stained edges of my conscious is a blindspot
of complete suffocation and maybe i just need to

get some air. the haze of summer is ripe and all i could ever want
is to rest my head into its shoulder, rendered to its shallow fever
until i can find a warmth to keep safe. for now,
my head is tilted north through your slack-jawed window
with patient wind threading into my skin and

i long to stay on this road for miles until your truck is worn down
to its last huffs. because the lines between us are tattered through
to the tail-end, mimicking half-split wood,
fraying with a guilty conscience
and i can't tell if it will be our exit or our opening.
inhale or exhale?

but just in case, i honed a fine vacancy for you
hollow, but waiting, like measured   breaths.

and if a home is not what you're yearning for in the spaces
between the silence
then we could disperse together, fleeing with the monarchs.

      or we could be

perfectly unsteady like the stones lining some slender creek

or we could be

in the water already, face down in the flood like some shitty
metaphor of waterlogged impulse.
and all we can pray is that we're submerged in the shallow
(but never the depths.)

for what it's worth,
i'd scratch a split into the white lines that hoard us.
i'd grip the wheel like it was a collar and run us off-road
outside the borders
because rattling with the dry rhythm of rugged asphalt,
motion sick and wetting cracked lips
is far more gentle than the metro.

Adrienne Jansen

Our war

Above the beach a new bench is bolted
to the concrete roof of the old gun emplacement.

Was it on a day like today
in '42, weather turning southerly,
rain in the air,
that the men in khaki shorts who'd poured the walls,
who'd made the boxing for the gunner's slit,
finally levelled out this concrete slab
sealing off the black space below
for the Home Guard, crouching,
wide-eyed, machine gun primed,
scanning the sea for — what?
A U-boat surfacing, the blocky silhouette
of a Jap destroyer?

What could one machine gun do?
Blast the top off a conning tower?
Punch a hole in a metal hull?
While the U-boat, inexorably, drives forward,
deck guns swinging in a deadly arc around our bay,
picking off our small wooden houses
cowering on hillsides, while we race away —
where? Out through our backyards,
past our washing lines, past our woodsheds,
slamming out our rickety gates,
while the U-boat runs into shallower water
and soldiers swarm off, all splash and shouting
and do they reassemble in lines and march
along our main road, past the dairy,
past the post office, past the fire station
(are the men out front, making a stand?)

while we scramble up the steep clay tracks
and hide in the gorse and taupata,
holding our breath?

Splinters of rain fall on the varnish
of the newly-bolted bench.
Frenzies of small birds
scatter like gunshot.

Was it on a day like today
that the men in khaki shorts
disassembled the gun,
hefted it all onto a truck,
while we let out sighs of relief
and whipped our washing off the line
before the rain set in?

when my father dies

when my father dies
of time-drenched soul or
heart failure,
i'll pile his memories
into flatpack boxes
and pack them away in the garage.

then when my time nears,
and i'm clearing out the garage and
i'm moving into a facility and
i'm stopping all my debits,
those boxes can
guide me through the pain.

(my father was never born)
the thin wooden frames
relax their grip on
his story
(nor will he die)
his grinning face
leaning against a car
in the late seventies

& later,
when i follow my father
through that rose-wrapped gate,
or whatever,
& the same
long-term project of grief
catches my son,
he can open the box
that this poem is in

and hear
the refrain:

what did i tell you?

Bumper Cars

crisp $20 in exchange for
gold arcade coins
your
Nordic Ultra Light
Crystal Blonde friends
snatch
the tokens from
your hands
giggles
at the black strands
on your arms
Cosmo promises
pluck one by one
they'll be gone forever

Intensive Blonde Super Plus says
you definitely are part monkey

Caitlin Jenkins

*First prize (Year 13), Poetry New Zealand Yearbook Student
Poetry Competition*

South

our streets grow tread marks in the pattern of tapa cloth,
the men in blue roam them recreating
Da Vinci —
bronze skin mona lisa.
who knew your last supper would be
a $2.50 Big Ben pie and a bottle of stars —
will we ever breathe the same freedom
as our brothers north and west?
cause oceania's waves feel a little too familiar in the backseat
gps broken cause somehow it only circles round these streets —
south,
you are but a direction on auckland's map,
folded tightly into the plastic corners of
red and blue led lights,
police siren jams but not the jawsh 685 type
. . . forever branded as the bottom
the south of new zealand . . .
but it's okay,
we'll tau`olunga on their disrespect
wake them up at dawn with our cheehoos
breathe a brown colour palette back into their colourless minds
love us enough to not need it from anyone else
grow with each other
be strong with each other
block out their white noise with white noise
fill the cracks of Aotearoa's pavements
with more reasons to love south . . .
and put us back on the map . . .
unfold us out of the plastic corners of red and blue led lights

help reverse the damage of our roots
with the healing of our new generations
cause leaves still bloom even more beautiful after the fall
for when our streets grow tread marks
we'll repaint them with coconut oil and fala paongo,
when the world wants our faces to kiss the concrete
we'll still be safe in the arms of papatūānuku
cause when things go south —
we'll deal with them like south —
with the love our roots nourish us in . . .
bronze skin mona lisa,
who knew your last supper would be a feast of the colonised minds . . .
undo the bleaching of your brown colour palette
refill them with all shades of you
cause no direction will define where we're really from,
south

Survive the Future

Following his latest school dental check
my son is sent home with an orthodontist referral,

And it's one of those days when I see the futility
of sending him off for a consultation about teeth;
for expensive x-rays and discussions about
straightening braces, and an impeccable bright
white aligned smile.

And I think instead he'd be better off
if I equip him with a garden and a gun,
a pair of oars and the training to outrun
hellbent thugs and tsunamis. That'd be money
better spent. Lessons in how to beat
dreadful odds and random sods. If I
make sure he knows how things work
and how to fix them. Provision him
with reflective blankets to huddle under,
to stave off the heat and keep the cold out.

Stash sacks of seeds savings for him.
Teach him how to grow crops, so he can
feed himself and sustain any others he's with.

All so that he might survive the future.

And it makes me laugh to think
that he might need calculus,
for the tempests and troubles to come,
for the anarchy and slide of civil society
as disaster creeps and crashes indiscriminately.
Makes me laugh to think how reckless billionaires

think their gaudy rockets and publicity stunts
and bunkers will save them. When there's no
water or oxygen.

Although I can see the point of literature
and books, and how they might help
get my boy through long, lonely frightening nights.
Might help him escape from the horrors
surrounding him with flights of fancy into his mind.

Might also help remind him
how inadequate some ideas can be
when not conveyed urgently enough.
And how the words 'crisis' and 'emergency'
came to be so corrupt.

Stuff Hemingway said

Hemingway reckons all you need to write is:
Two pencils and a pencil
Sharpener
Two blue-backed notebooks
And the smell of early morning
For luck you may carry:
A horse chestnut
Or more distressing still
A rabbit's foot in your right pocket
I am writing on shitty supermarket paper
With some promotional ballpoint announcing LexisNexis!
The smell of Botany town centre has long rid of any sunshine
And is making me crave 'Hand-Cut Home-Made Fries'
But for luck I am carrying the shape of your upper lip when it
stretches
Asking me if I can write you a poem
I tuck into my right pocket your shy hands
Twisting themselves slowly in your lap
Everything you do is poetry
And I cannot stop writing it down
Pack it up Hemingway
What would you know anyway?

Hebe Kearney

night comes on

breakage / misstep
take a full bite
out the cylinder of night
with its handsome plume
all shoddy with satellite song

an open air deepbreath
wading monumental
an echo broken / the building tops
greet star-freckled sky / grinning
the simple white bones in your head
illuminate

take this night
quickly like a pill / the pull
of space cracking / ankle joints
from the stretch up
into its dark belly
gurgling acid starlight

the acrid smoke huffed
out metallic tubes / is the scent
like blood in the mouth / blood
in the inky water

/ succumb /
for when it is over
the night has come

Driving the Harvester

Engage. Lift. Turn. Follow
the edge of the last line

you harvested. Focus on
that place just beyond the reel

for what might catch in its teeth.
A couple on a blanket, say,

an abandoned bicycle.
More common was that rabbit

darting out across the stubble.
It's not captured in your drawing,

though that's me beside you;
yellow crayon for the wheat.

You're wearing the swim googles
that failed, while I drove,

to stop you rubbing your eyes.
The curved line for a smile

masks my own irritation.
And who is that figure in the cab?

Another me? Your second self?
Though the combine's facing us, child,

it couldn't mow us down.
Not until you have added for air

three or four lines trailing the machine
to show that it's moving.

Round Hill

Hill, don't shrug, well short of the sky,
a strong shout from the nearest suburb.

I see you in the middle of the day,
dented like a mattress. Trudging sullen, winter brown.

Who has folded away your sheep?
Without them you are bare,
picking at the seams of your fencelines.

It's difficult to stand out, being Round Hill.
Snow rarely descends and wind musses you often.

Down the valley of pooling frost
trucks won't let you rest, squaring and backing, their ticking lights.

Someone must drive that track I pace by eye.
Someone else must keep vigil
over your scrubby shoulders.

Hill, take heart. I have seen you careful and pale
in low sun brushed with its pollen.

i c u.

break
    a   p a
          r
            t

                on
            lake   seats
             Our spot to be
engraved
with   someone   else's   name
         in   iron   and
                wea
                 t
                  h
                    ered   p in e
              STOP

               WD
almost   became
                               Three
            not so LITTLE word
I'd   b r e a k   it   into
               The,   and throw *re*   a w a y
               The,   as in
               The pill did its job   as in
               The baby we didn't
          have close calls —
                    <——D   E   T   O   U   R

     m   o   n   o   x   i   d   e   Your
                             lungs

so   You
                                                                        can be Your
                                                                              mot
                                                                                her

                        N   O   E   X   I   T

                    cyst   g r o W S
            in place of   The bean,
                                                                        pink & bulbous
            C U T   I T   O   U   T
        flood with chloro   form ur FULL belly
                                    Cut it out,   You

                                                                                say

            on   all   IVs
                    no more,   CUT   ⌞I.T⌟   O U T

Queen's Birthday

The Queen is nearly the same age as my mum
At least she is for four months every year.
The Queen is in better nick than my mum these days.
Mum kept pace for many years but now has got decrepit.
The Queen is in amazingly rude health at 95.

The Queen's family have long-life high-powered genes
They have handbag and colourful coat genes.
My mum's family have long-life genes too
They have loud-voice have-a-cup-of-tea genes.

The Queen loves horses and little dogs
My mum likes cats. She also likes dolls that look at you like Chucky.
The Queen is a good driver
This was documented on TV.
My mum has been known to drive the wrong way
Down a one-way street and a main road roundabout.
She once drove through the glass front of a shop.
Mixed up the brake and the accelerator I expect.

The Queen likes trees and is helping to save them
My mum cut all the trees and bushes in her gardens
Down to her size and killed quite a few of them.
We gave her Randy Newman's *Short People* for a birthday present
She laughed.
I do not think anyone ever gave the Queen that particular single.

Jessica Le Bas

Let Us Go Early

from Solomon's Song of Songs, Old Testament
i.m. Dr K. Cheval

First, she gave me the miniature pomegranate bush,
the one she bought at the night market in Arorangi,
said it had not yet fruited, but was sure it would
if I looked after it. Placed it on the glass table on my deck
where it looked down Pokoinu Road and out to the reef,
to the ocean, where July to November, the whales come.
There was a large copper-bottomed pot too, she left
at my house, or maybe she just forgot to take it with her.
Now I make soup in it, with her beside me, drinking
cold beer, and laughing again about those dogs outside
the Indians' house, and the way, after dark, they chopped
chicken with machetes with a rhythm that spoke of dancing.
Today, thousands of miles south, her magnetic thermometer
clings to my fridge, set with a blip at its assembly point, to
read five degrees warmer than reality, it guarantees me
an almost tropical winter's day for the life of its batteries.
She bequeathed it to me just after her first diagnosis
that was early and optimistic. I think it was her intention
to keep the pomegranate bush, to watch it blossom
and bear fruit. It's anyone's guess where it is today.

chinese class

I always thought they named the building
after a girl/but recently it dawned on me
Brook/the stream/the babbling of grief/
what did I know of that word/except rocks/
how we flung them out of our mouths
chanting/*zài suŏ yŏu . . . wŏ zuì xĭhuān . . .*/
& out of all those years/I liked best
afternoons curdling/then scissored light/
children thrashing/incensed cries/rising
Thorndon Pool/how Wáng Iăoshī cried
consolidate!/until it sounded like a joke/
didn't matter that our Chinese faces
spoke white/all of us knew the routineness
of string/*mā má mă mà*/knotted our *xīn*
into snake bites/left our tongues parched/
dead nailed until the bell rang three.

why do we fall

1
i never knew until i watched it again
it must have been the thousandth time
but it only hit me tonight coming off
a seven day fast
my mind as clear as the water i drank for its duration
you look like the young boy bruce wayne
in batman begins 2005
with rachels hair and body
subconsciously i hunted for you
in the streets all those years
there you are with your dark eyes
seated before the stage play with the spinning bats
afraid all the time worried that youve done wrong
you havent
you didnt

2
there have been times when i loved you more
and times when i loved you the most
twice when you had smoked way too much
and like the scarecrow says
the mind can only take so much
in the passenger seat in our car
as i drove us back to my room
you sounded like you wouldve as a little girl
maybe thats who you are deep down
and who i know you as is only who youve become
i put your coat around you
then my body
ill take off my mask if you will
i thought

before we fell asleep like
children

3
when does eptesicus play
you think you played it over and over
because you liked the sound of it
but its when it plays in the film
whats happening on screen
what are they saying doing
the music is just a stand in to remind you of it
thats why you listened to it over and over
over all the other tracks
google when does eptesicus play in the film
no answer
why has none else asked this question
it doesnt matter
i remember now
its at the end when they kiss
and she forgives him

finders keepers

Better

Today I learned about the flowers in your body,
the ones I wanted to pull out at the roots
but modern medicine can only stunt their growth
Forgive me for thinking they do not
have the right to take refuge
in a haven like yours

I wrap my coat around me against the autumn chill
but its warmth fails to reach my heart
the way your presence does
Hope rolls from the corner of my eyes
like mermaid beads, if only to splatter
onto my scarf, your couch,
and saturate everything in their path
It is as if I am five again, pigtails trembling
and asking the same question
I am too afraid to voice
but know the answer to

Are you better now?

Frances Libeau

new blood

the old asylum is
    up for sale again.
    looking for new
blood.
    long before it was
    a horror house where
        people pay to be
        frighted
        shot at
        lost   we
        drive right by
in the back of the   red Holden wagon
    the one too old to be cool. power
lines track the corner in angling
webs; i wonder at their
suspension. opposite the Kingseat
takeaway   halfway thru the S
bend on McRobbie road, it's hard
to stop   so
we never do   ..... just jibe
the long butt of the car & lolly
doze between my siblings.

it's hard to stop & see it
standing the corner since
before the second war a place
of sanitation ..... cleansing ..... confine-
meant   [held apart.... *sacer*]
under the secure care of a
King   raising the nation by
eugenics dubbed 'mothercraft'. the

first patients
built the very
    building
    they were to   *i used to work in insurance*
    wander .... like
    digging your own
    grave. it's hard to.   make your own bed
                & see shackles. bite down.

    everyone's smiling   on the blue packet
    a trade in futures   void of memory. i swallow
    spit & backseat
    stomach at the bend. don't
    stop & see the nurses' quarters
    stellate the grass   they themselves
            locked in   form.   see the paranormal
            geeks photograph the shadow of the Grey
                 Nurse
                 lost his own soul
                 on that corner.

                         now i am paid to scare people
the Spookers' 'weak freak'   clause
states   *don't be chicken*
               you won't get   your money back. so
               don't stop >>> there is a coffin
               for sale on Trade Me:
        got it from spookers but
        was mix up in communication so
        actually got a real full size coffin.
        which I turned into my coffee table.
        would fit maximum a 6ft male

dream   of a bed floating
in ocean or is it sky
in welcome, crying Fly
(or Drown) in me
don't stop >>> splice old
barking memories   mean
to my face with prosthetic lick   *i used to be scared of clowns*
don't stop >>> give me a minute
to   bloody up
these beheaded plastic
            babies ....
to   splinter this seat
        of heaven. don't stop

            at the carpark   it's worth the queue
            come out &   pay to be scared. it's not
            real just CornEvil. performed
            madness looks the same as real
            madness. don't stop   to
            imagine not
        leaving.   don't stop >>>run thru
        this maze of image   wheat
            chafing each wet cheek   *now i am one*
                warren of troubling
                doors walked from
                their hinges

                into private
                collections
                hedging
                daylight
are we scared of the place or
the people? of becoming the. of
        already being

the. of how many
coats   away   we are. how
much fake blood it
would take
to slip into
something
a little
more .... too much. not
much at all >>>don't
        stop   stockpiling
        crass   latex faces by
        day>>>   don't
        stop   gauding
        night's corners w/
        rubber weapons &
        sfx   vomit
        in the backseat of
        the wagon. don't stop
        here.   sick for it

                the fear

This poem features quotes from the film *Spookers*, directed by Florian Habicht
(Madman Production Company, 2017) [on DVD].

'*got it from Spookers . . . would fit maximum a 6ft male*', from a November 2019 TradeMe
auction for a full-sized coffin purchased online from Spookers webstore, apparently by
accident. The listing closed and did not sell.

'in welcome, crying Fly / (or Drown) in me', from Janet Frame, 'The End', *NZ Listener
Archive*, 27 August 2004, www.noted.co.nz/archive/archive-listener-nz-2004/three-
poems-by-janet-frame

Not a Poem about Peonies

So slow and imperceptible that from under here,
it's almost comfortable
the first buds are budding and I can see their lime green sheaths
like runway lights at twilight with rain misting my eyes a little

There's a picture of a man lying face down,
a strip of astroturf half covering him
but this doesn't feel quite like that — he's visible
and easily stepped around
I'm pretty sure no one can see me down here

The green shoots are shooting off, tutus and sequins
and 2 dollar shop lippy
this feels inevitable, somehow
This loamy peat, or peaty loam is insulated to fuck
and I was wrong, it is perfectly lovely down here

there's probably a few of us now, who've made this our home
we don't mingle, but there's comfort in knowing they're here
tucked away in dark corners

Everybody loves a peony
shockingly soapy and seductive, and built to last
as long as they last. I could never bring myself
to include a peony in a poem
(but I used to think that about loam too, so there you go).
Change happens, and you spend most of your life repelling it
or craving it. A bit like that time I got really skinny. Let me tell you,
strange things happen in the world of the thin.

And those gardens full of flowers, owning every sensory pleasure
unashamedly beautiful. I want to reach out and pick one, or two,
or ten. I want to imprison them in my home, and look at them
till they die and return to the earth
where they will feed off me and the others
just as I did.

Inconsolable

First we had to dance around the name for meeting then was the one
for being called on telephones the third was the name for murmuring
as dusk turned the white hotel towels a tender grey and a few
obedient sparrows began their desultory calls he said how do I know
you're not an ugly girl in your own culture and I laughed but how do I
know we were laughing at the same part of that?

> I am holding you now like a bird snapped by the cat of me
> soothe your wings down, make things worse in your chest
> let us refuse to know that the cause is not also the solution.

That catch in his voice when he said her hair was black as a raven
there are no ravens here I no longer believe he ever gave his name
and when you came you were the mirror of those inconsolable
afternoons your eyes became my eyes when you started dancing I
could hardly look at anyone amongst them the ethnocentric night
unfurling its disastrous hooks how do you know I'm not an ugly
girl? and all the while the gentlemen asking you to turn and turn.

from The Commonplace Book

Someone has put hydrangeas on the table
and replaced the island which is like
a dog that, having turned its half-circle
on the waves, has crossed its paws and fallen asleep.
A gull writes a lazy 'S' across a cloud.
The sea is 'out there', equable and pale.
The girls are still asleep, sleeping late
in a bedroom wincing from the night-wind
in its nails. I am wholly given over
to the slanted shadows of someone else's house,
when, for no reason I can think of, there's
my father stepping from a train, a kitbag
hoicked across his arm. How strange he looks
in uniform as he walks down Station Road
past the scrumping orchard to where unbowing
high street limes are neither confetti
nor flags, with no-one rushing out to greet him,
kiss him, his Burma-tan and milk-brow, so
war-changed even the dogs don't recognise him
as he slips inside the shadow of the yard
and opens the kitchen door to his mother
drying her hands and saying, as if it were
any weekday morning, 'There you are . . .'

from Animal Etymologies

Hybrid
from PIE ud 'out' and gwerə 'heavy', to hybrida 'mongrel', specifically
'offspring of a tame sow and a wild boar' or witch spouting snakes or
merman with feathers; related to hubris 'wanton violence, outrage',
όταν π.χ. κάποιος υπερεκτιμώντας τις ικανότητες και τη δύναμή
του, συμπεριφερόταν με βίαιο, αλαζονικό και προσβλητικό
τρόπο, or 'presumption towards the gods' often in relation to acting
against the laws of the city and heaven which places limits on, for
example, running SUVs, gutting plastics; that is, being in a state of
ὕβρις and therefore fires, floods, all the tools, all the foils against
any trait not wilding the straights: monologue, monotype (vs. horse
and bird, dog and eel, eagle and lion and goat, deer and microbe
and elephant and pig) και ανάλογες λαζονικές συμπεριφορές; or
really, you could think of it this way: more than half your body isn't
human

Extinction
from PIE steig, to stinguere 'to wipe out', or stizein 'to prick', for
example to tattoo through the upper layers drawing blood and
receiving risk like being run over like a fox η Μεσογειακή φώκια
(Monachus monachus); but not forgetting bears and wolves, birds
and skinks, ants and bees and termites and worms, η δραματική
μείωση του πληθυσμού της Μεσογείου Θάλασσας; and although
pertaining originally to fires, lights, and the wiping out of a material
thing, eventually also of debt, phrasing, a species; a family tree; an
order; or in the case of εξαφανιση from PIE eghs, ek, ex 'out', and
bhā 'to shine', you might think of being the possum in the headlights,
being your own ανεπανόρθωτο τέλος ενός οργανισμού roadkill
against logic or instinct, in spite of, you know, how dumb it is to slice
off your nose to spite your face

Stomach

from PIE geus 'to taste', or magh 'to have power'; also 'machine, machina, deus ex machina'; eventually stomachus for 'throat, gullet', also 'taste, liking, distaste, dislike', 'θυμός, άγχος, θλίψη, έντονη χαρά' or 'pride or indignation'; also seat of one's psyche, pulse, insight, the spot to insert the mummy's heart, to inside the warm, to belly the desire, or appetite οπου η ίδια η σκέψη του φαγητού μπορεί να απελευθερώσει υγρά στο στομάχι προτού κἄν φτάσει η τροφή, bigger than will be possible to sate; literally 'opening' from stoma, the 'mouth' or maw, your whet maw, your wanting maw, your mawing maw, your maw or muzzle or labrador scull despite δυσφορία στο στομάχι η αιτία ή το προϊόν άγχους ή κατάθλιψης the acid reflux sugar crash and no, you won't get another shot, you're Castor not Pollux

Haunted

You drove a powder blue Mercedes to the shops
just because you could. Strapped on your bullet proof makeup,
gripped your handbag tight, heavy with bricks.

Just in case.

There was always the running, the hiding from the thing
that you would not name. But we were ready, you and I.
We were battle ready, prepared. Our own army.
At the shopping centre you ran your hands over everything
you could not afford to take home. Hissed at sales assistants
when they said *hello*.

In antique jewellery shops you'd stand at the window
and count all of the ruby rings, the emerald rings,
the dark blue sapphires with their outdated settings
and picture the hands they came from, limp and cold.
Twisted topaz and gold around your finger, catching facets
with your eyes, walking cleanly through the doorway without alarm.

Your cigarettes in packets of fifty. Your cigarettes
at the side of your mouth. Your cigarettes piled
like broken bodies in the ashtray at the end of the day.
I could smell you before I saw you. The same wood-rough skin,
mint burning at the solstice bonfire.

Arms swinging, treading water, your ring scratched the surface of my eye.
Told me I shouldn't have been so close. I saw you. I really *saw* you
with the fine film broken. Your bathers still soaked with seawater.
Nails varnished, frosted pink. Imprints of you on the park bench,
the leather seat of the Mercedes, the tartan picnic blanket.
Knew your skin was cold from the ocean, though I never dared to reach.

You learned how to use the computer at the local library.
Sent me an email with my name misspelled, signed *kind regards.*
A geriatric pregnancy reversed. Me from you, then you as the child.
And still your breath follows me. I visited you at the nursing home.
Mint slices and tea. I visited you in the hospital.
Fishermen's Friend and apple juice. I visited you
at Springvale Cemetery. Inhaled the air amongst roses,
pruned within an inch of their life.

Kept your knees together, your hands together,
your lips tightly sealed.
Kept applauding the apparition of me at the top of the stairs.
Pretended I was not falling. Your daughter doesn't shriek at shadows.
I don't need to make a sound to tell you. Fists raised. I am not afraid.
I am not afraid of air. You are not solid anymore.
Hollow, floating pieces. A container of nothing.

The crematorium for close family only. Just me in the front row.
Metallic thread curtains. Smoke above pressed metal roofs.
Family assorted biscuits and instant coffee in my mouth afterwards.
I wished you gone, disappeared. Imagined your body over cliffs,
bobbing in the ocean, a landing for seabirds.
Your topaz deep under roses. None of us here are angels.

I keep you in my handbag.

Just in case.

Good to have a ghost on my side.
Prefer to be the one doing the haunting.
Instead of being one of the haunted.

Fish of New Zealand

Do you remember?
The day the fuel light came on
somewhere between Awakino and Urenui?
Coasting down Mount Messenger,
barely touching the brakes,
praying we made
a Caltex.

I was once
with a girl on Otago Peninsula,
somewhere near the albatross preservation.
We ate cheese rolls at Huffington Point
and made out on the beach
at Portobello.

Our names
carved a heart,
dug into the salt-white cliffs.
An apparition of her face in the glow of a bonfire,
burns slow on a somewhere black sand beach.
Ocean grass tangles with fishing wire.
Sea foam and driftwood
bivouacs.

We took
the Picton Ferry home,
watching dolphins surf the wake.
I held her hair as she vomited in a brown paper bag.
Probably the cheese rolls from earlier.
Probably.

We drank
Speight's at a hotel bar
in Ōmakau, singing old songs about leaky boats.
The waitress complimented you on your 'Fish of New Zealand' t-shirt.
It's like the Fish 'n' Chip shop poster, right?
That night I went back to your room
in search of gold.

Have you ever seen
the breaking waves off the Cape?
Where the Tasman Sea and the Pacific Ocean meet?
The ancient pōhutukawa, where spirits drift
up the coast, to climb down its roots
into the sea?

We stayed
on the Pouakais's,
trudging through Taranaki petrichor.
We swam in the ice-cold waters of Dawson's falls.
You took off your 'Fish of New Zealand' t-shirt
and put the mountain
to shame.

I
want to dance
along your pink and white terraces,
run my hands along your limestone arch.
I want your eyes to light up like the cave's starry ceiling,
and for you to put your mouth on mine as if it were a brown sick bag,
and you had just eaten a plate
of your mother's
cheese rolls.

Jack McConnell

Empty Vessel, Empty Words

A charge builds in the cloud
a pouched house strange marsupial
I must be to lack conviction

what makes you look torn is just
seeing yourself beside what you present

the impression of a knotted boundary
given by just a few barbs
deviations over directness

but what is striking is bricks bordering houses
in rows loaves of bread particular robes
all saying the same kind of thing

the enterprise of establishment is
eventually an enterprise of removal
requiring diligent hands

wheel of water at your feet
when the sun starts out
grinding down your spine

a reminder that this is not simultaneous
clouds predict a shift to rough seas
while boats slide out

your reflection is not
broken up by turbulence
it is made of just the same stuff

somehow your dispersion is
a forward motion

scavengers look for scraps
of you in vertebral grass

peeked at safely through
a fog which eliminates details

specks of dark green
and faint sun cast
their tint to threads

the pouring out of a jug
all this time
never this side of you.

Lucy Miles

Ghosts

Do not go to Santorini,
The dead talk too easily there,
You think you know islands,
But you don't,
There's something wrong with this one.
Crete's been good to you,
But stop listening to cherry trees,
And drinking too much raki,
Why not take your advice from bells and pigeons?
Be kind to the dead,
Be kind to the dead,
Be kind to the dead,
They're closer than you think.
What songs do the soldiers sing,
On still afternoons in the Imbros?
(They're still there, I know, I know,
But everybody knows.)
Don't go to Santorini,
There's nowhere to hide on Santorini,
You're young, you think that's okay,
But it's not,
You don't know that yet but you will.

The Beach

Last summer we found a beach
Stretching five miles into oblivion
Out from the sandhills into the sea
And it was nobody's beach but ours

Ours and the sea's five miles of meandering
Dragging the depths disgorging its finds

A Japanese float a jewel of the sea
Singing in sea colours it shall never go home

And over beyond the blown and the bloated
The stinking porpoise rotting sand into sand

Last summer we found a body
Lying three miles up the bay
Three days before a man
A fisherman we're told
They took a truck up to get him

Anuja Mitra

by any other name

a news site runs an article:
'at his local Starbucks
Sanjeev goes by Steve'

and I consider the ways
in which we shrink ourselves

how the uncertain pause
after someone reads my name
is the space between my name

and me
owning it

how it drops
from my mouth
like a jumbled admission

marking me
an import from elsewhere

no blank slate luxury
no ambiguity
to my 'ethnic'

how it must be a privilege
to have a name that behaves

on the resumé
sits still without declaring
its *difference*

how many of us go on
correcting the mishearings

rejecting the nicknames
in some small rebellion
against self-deletion

but in line for your morning coffee
when you must be heard

among the uncaring crowd
it is easy
to be Steve

Connections

Grain of rice
sticks to crutch
attacking sushi in my car
post wine-gin cure
after night of vomiting
beetroot hummus.

Then back to school
for English class
to discuss connections between texts
with 17-year-old boys . . .
Today
all texts are apophanous.

Red Nightgown

after Anne Ferran

In the photogram, a burst of light in darkness, the red nightgown glows like burning coals. Flames instead of legs, breasts rounded in an orange glow above carbonised seams and encircled with a line of glittering embers. The nightgown, settling against the skin of the photographic paper seems to billow, incandescent with light like heat rising from the absent body. I went naked to bed in our first months together until winter in our draughty Thorndon flat. Made a joke about the comfort of my childish flannelette, its faded roses, tattered ribbons. The slippery red silk in that thin flat box, your gift meant to restore your hands to my breasts, made me feel possessed, not luminous. The dye that stained my hands the first time I washed it, like blood, not flames.

Josiah Morgan

By Degrees

'I can't really remember earlier in the dream now, there was more backstory but I forget. We were having some drinks, kinda tipsy, having a good time at like a party or out somewhere. We started wandering up a ramp, like a car size curved ramp that goes up to a 2nd level car park. As we were wandering up it, you were a little ahead, and jumped up on the ledge bit. It had a wide-ish raised edge, with a small barrier on inner, and you jumped up on the raised bit and were just jumping/ skipping up the ramp. But then you missed and I just saw you fall, it was super realistically quick. I ran to the edge and looked over and you were sort of laying uncomfortable looking on the ground, 1–2 stories down. I watched for a split second, then found a rough but manageable way down. On the way I was trying to call 111 but I only had a can of coke on me and somehow I'd managed to dial it, the numbers floating in white on top, but it looked like a driver of a stopped car nearby was calling for an ambulance, I assumed. When I got to you you'd crawled up a bit and propped yourself against a wall and were clearly in a bit of shock. I was trying to calm you a bit, but also trying to assess you, and from what I could see you'd definitely broken one leg real bad, unsure about the other. It was all very stressful and I wasn't sure that someone had called an ambulance, though I could feel there were at least a few people around. But just watching you was so hard, like you were some mix of small injured bird, confused and in shock, and trying to slink away from the pain and the people. It was like you knew I was there to help you, but you were so afraid you kept trying to stand or move your legs underneath you and I just wanted you to stop moving. After a little of this I woke up and just felt generally a bit ill. Had to focus to clear my mind after that. I didn't even want to cuddle you because I'd just feel your bones and it'd be so fresh in my mind. (Matthew Lang, 2021).

I am a man of triangles.
Pointy edges that struggle to cohere, shatter

upon contact. Millions of shards scatter
the floor, reflect back, paralyse. Tangled

up somehow in the thing looking down
at my pieces. (The outside world,
soft, external, keeping me curled
up inside itself, edges turned round.)

Tangled down to the thing I'm looking up
at, I attempt to cohere upon contact, so
that I uncurl softly, I catalyse.
Angular, is the man I am.

Elizabeth Morton

Stalker

What if I am a tree falling in a forest and nobody hears

What I would give to heal   the dull thud   of a kitchen light,

to touch the   filament, gently and wet.   I stand at night-time
hedges

   building worlds in other people's yards. A technician of lives

that pass gently   as mosquitoes, taking little parts of my   kith

and holding them in lukewarm bellies. Spreading love

   like the third-world disease it is.   I want you to know I take

batteries and batteries. My torch   forces itself into a future

cryptic and dark like these poems. Your dogs bleat — two
brontosauruses,

big and dumb, and   I have inherited them.

   I   have inherited the bicycles in the carport,

   your television shows,

the way you leave your teabag on the saucer.   When I deliver

your newspaper, I want you to   look for me —

in the connections columns   or in the deaths. The kitchen light

is a lonely thing.   I hope somebody is looking in   from the hedge from the biblical crosshairs or   from behind a tree in a forest

where the trunks are ringbarked   or someplace else. Listen.

What if my brain is in a vat, and I don't know

Cogito ergo   something. I am a brain in the chlorinated pool, sun webbing

the surfaces.   I am   meat cannibalising   other meat.

Do you know I loved you once — loved you by your numberplate, by the cul de sac

that ends with your   front door. Hell,

   I remember walking past you in the supermarket. Your mouth-hollow,

your shellac-fingertips, your gym gear worn with   premeditated indifference.

Did you see me? I was   there. A warm organ steeping in a summer full of curtains.

   You were there. That was the summer the sinkhole sank the carpark.

   People with parcels of ham-hocks and squash,   clucking like poultry.

I watched   them watch. I was glad for complicity, the   snugness of proximity. The cockles of my cortices were bathwater-warm.

I was a blue hill in the background of a scene about   happiness.

I like to think my inputs and outputs register on the machine. Grid paper

that charts sentiment, up and up.   What am I,

but a bain-marie of leftovers. Love is something to swill a little, to expectorate

into a spittoon.   What am I, but the tannins that catch in your throat.

Whatever.   You were there. I see you.

Trolley problems

Would I save Syria or my dog?   My sister or the trade towers?

  Flight 370 or my dignity?   If the train is heading for Mengele, tied to the tracks,

would I re-route it?   If six children are on one course   and you are on the other

  how will I know if you love me as much as I love you?

Thought experiments make villains of us all. I'll never be on a desert island with just one

1980s anthem. I'll never have to choose between my parents and my country — just between

Advanced Whitening or Maxi White or Enamel Pro or Ultra Cavity
Protection.

   Death is a loser   who watches *Judge Judy* and reheats sweet and sour
chicken.

Death drinks Redbull and does Sudoku,   and I can see something of

myself there — unsolicited house-calls and standing by night-time
hedges,

looking in.   You see, I want to die in the daisy constellations of your
front yard,

like the mawkish   romantic I am. I want to ride my   BMX

past the swing-set to your porch, and I want you to ring the police

and peg me down with your two kind hands.   That is what   love is.

   I would re-route the nexus of causality and time,   for you.

I would send trains smashing through a Rube Goldberg machine, one
domino

falling another, because that's what love is   too. Hell, I want to hold

the kitchen light by the filament,   gently and wet,

   to conduct heat and have it pass through me. And hope somebody

will pay witness,   maybe.

Janet Newman

Ducks

I heard a clack like wire slipping
against a batten. A drake and duck,
she, tan and speckled as hay,
he, brown as butcher's paper,

slide across the pond, smooth
as bumper cars, become motionless
as posts, as the windless gorse.

I wait for movement, stir,
splash. Nothing gives.

If I could wait as quiet, as calm
for the dangerous world to pass,
settle in instead of always pushing out.

I look away,
and looking back
the ducks are gone, not flown,
I would have seen them lift,
but settled further in, become
the dappled pond, the bank,
the rushes' thrown, mottled shadows.

News from nowhere

When the vigorous night bleeds with abundant plums
we speak the language of clematis, blossoming opals
your body takes shapes of my hands, the earth
is blue like an orange, with a necklace of wings the black
flag of the sky is sown with stars of muka flax woven
we are all African in the dancing water of the curved shore,
breathing mountains, and the wondrous fruits of the earth

- (like/with/as) pomegranates on fire
- nectarine breasts dressed with silk
- mathematical nights of avocado
- flavours of long distance phone calls
- voices un-quarantined in mahogany jungle chants
- a dance of liquid hieroglyphics
- scents of hair in oceanic starfish
- silvery bonito fibril flash
- submarine explosions of kisses
- crescendos of dark weeping
- pūriri trees cloaked in black lightning
- hyperactive frontal systems
- shattered mirrors of our selves
- dissolving

The Debt Collector

She's got a lot of souvenir teaspoons, all different. Some have names, some don't; some are memorable, some not. Like the Queenstown one where she ran a marathon, or the Murchison one where she tramped in the rain, or the tarnished one obscured underneath. I wonder which one of us is plunged into hot black tea, sweetened with a little honey, which one of us is munted prying the paint tin open, which one of us digs with dirty knees making indents for seeds to be planted. Which one of us is hidden away, aching with lies.

Te Moana-nui-a-Kiwa

As usual and might be expected
in the southern hemisphere, it's
almost spring, the godwits have

flown beyond Waikumete where
no bird sings, well, not today but
where you can make a choice

of what you prefer, earth or urn,
while east of the ranges everything
moves along the sea front

as far as the rock paintings
of Lascaux (the Magdalenien era,
circa 15,300 BCE), is carried

windborne, by the sea to where
in Tuscany people speak French
which here is a foreign language

as might be expected
because it's European, unrelated
to the languages of the Pacific

to the language of Aotearoa
the voice of the tangata whenua
te reo, te reo, reo . . .

I know that the trees are speaking
although I can't understand them
don't understand their language

haven't learnt enough of it
to tell them what I want to say
and if I can't speak to them

I need to learn more of it because
I don't know enough about Tainui
Tākitimu, Tokomaru, Te Arawa

te whetu o te tau, the venerated star
of the year, Te Moana-nui-a-Kiwa
that brought all of us here . . .

Departure

When someone leaves, your bed lacks their vintage smell —
tasting notes are now singularly yours.
When someone leaves, you make hospital corners —
sweep hands across the sheets with
unnecessary deliberation.

When someone leaves, cleaning is the indoor sport that
makes you sweat.
The Dyson skims the seas of carpet
and with skin chapped
your kitchen sink shines back at you.

Haughty lilies in a tall vase nod their approval.

But what the fuck would they know?

When someone leaves, the radio blares as you clear out the fridge —
on the door a magnetic couple
uneven heights
wearing wetsuits with masks
and snorkels that dangle like a flapper's headpiece.

When someone leaves weekends are days to dive under —
breath held you grapple coral sharpness
till you emerge on Monday morning
pleasantly numb and gasping for air,
however stale.

On Wednesday you open the wardrobe
its cavernous innards gape —
devoid of the corduroy jacket
but not its woodsy smell

Hangers chime as you step inside
serenade your slide to the floor
to forage for fluff,
anchor buttons, harpoon pins
tarnished coins.
Eyes closed to
tacky household treasures

you breathe in

in

in

till, with a wail from crimson depths
fury spews from stagnant guts.
It ricochets, spatters flimsy walls
and lashes pristine carpets —
foaming, lonely

detritus.

`inangaro

That day you left me entombed in bed sheets
I waited for an hour, then a day, then a week, then a month

I'm having a child you told me as we sat in a car in South Auckland
I didn't know what to say so I watched while
you cultivated her, your seed taking root
becoming a canoe to drift you far away

When Raro called your grandmother
she told you to marry me
you'd both laughed that `utu pānu, a floating berry
had wanted to crochet bright coloured rectangles
a parangikete to uncover me
like the tide pulling out

So I'd waited on the bed naked
as my skin grew into bark, my legs taking root, my arms wings
ready for flight

Until somewhere in Titirangi: E tumurangi matangi kāre ra i ua
a storm cloud that gives no rain could
drop my narration over the forest for you to hear

Amoré

In a dream
a poet was outside
a night club, beat,
bouncing ideas.

He stamped
them, words & phrases,
on people's hands, entering,
knowing they would wear off

with the moon, the night . . .
He hoped they would all
'come together' as one
forming an imperfect lyric.

It wouldn't make sense
of course, another *amoré* . . .
His poem could be like perfume
or a sensual touch.

Mark Prisco

dystopia

when we meet
i squeeze thru the crack of u.

i eat nothing.

i fuckin fainted in the toilet
hit my head on the wooden ledge
of the bathtub;

saw no star but
darkness &

if it happens again i go to a doctor.
see what they say.
what they give me.

i'm nowhere.
that's the fear,
the fear i'm
deadend. i declare,

for something to say, to be
— to snap
yr fingers to. thru w
shit job w
no job, i'm
gone

drift across &
cloud
winters
Bitter Cold It Was

boy. from milan we sail north
to zurich & when we get there it's —

i mist something because
when we left in the morning
it was nineteen

eightynine & there *was*
no fucking euro & the Belgium cops
hauled me off the bus & said
in demotic French:

                    you, Sir,
are a fucking criminal.

will the howling winds never cease?

Shakespeare Outta Apia

sitting with your knees pointing out
a metal table holding the last of your paper
noise had become butter because
you were writing

your pe`a glowed dark under fluorescents
your pen flicked like cigarette ash
you burnt the sea into your words and
then said to me, *could you post this?*

home is an island in the South Pacific
a fermented memory in the waves
and though you wrote elegantly in English
none of your family could read it

before one of us died, I asked why
you didn't write in Samoan, but the schools
only gave you Shakespeare you said
and you can't talanoa from prison

Mary Raleigh

The dump

You in your shabbiest gardening finery
blue towelling hat, mustard aertex
smelling of lawn clippings and carwash brush industry

chirpy
purposeful
so damn happy to turf
old junk

Palmy's dump was little Ngauruhoes forming
a mountain range of pong
seagull covered (didn't they miss the sea?)
an open air environmental horror
in 1983

that man
who emerged from nowhere
bent down for our record player speakers
        and was off,
picking his grasshopper legs through the dross
before Dad even turned back to see
I was impressed
by his efficiency

Erin Ramsay

The Veiled Years

A pomegranate seed, the bright
scar — let it be pushed into my mouth, moving

downtown — a cartographidigital
touching, the notified tongue nearing

swirled Sunday, a plastic womb to
feed the hollow cat-a-comb

through every cave-damp reflection
of communiqués too closed to call

love
to satiate the Admiral of the Underworld.

I expect I will do my duty
to Admiral, to Charon's regent and

unsteady platform — to Fullers' heady sleep,
and dawn's tannoy Kia Ora.

47

The doctor said
it's just a cyst Mary
but there is another lump
under your nipple

The surgeon said
we took the left breast
the lymph glands too

The nurses said
you may feel a little nausea
after each treatment

Dad stopped the Austin
so you could vomit in the gutter
on the way home

Your curly hair fell out
in clumps
your belly swelled

The wit at work said
when's it due?
you cried when you told me
I wanted to kill him

You said
who's this?
didn't know your own child

The hospice said
it's the morphine
your bones crumbling

My father said
I'm so proud of the way you coped
the frightened child inside me
wept

The neighbour said
I worried about you
saw you cross the road without looking
walked around in a daze

The principal said
don't say anything but be kind
her mother's dead

The priest said
these things happen
for a reason

My bones say
fuck you God
I want my mother

(when)_2(g(a)e(ther).exe

the world has gone   old tv and
the sinuses have a cord snaking around!
in a voice made of slip   ping
generate   the energy required   i
to take all the land +   return it
in one   mass email
bcc: all my friend(s)
cc: all my enem(y)(ies)
the great leather of   this movement
revolves   around   viole t
warms the cockles of   my weird
cyber   space   heart
shit-posting in   the lasers of my brain
i dance around   on the bed
and call u a line   in a poem
that i would   never forget
what a wreckage   this meeting is!
we are a punched coin   unspent

Vaughan Rapatahana

sixteen years

[*whatia pototia te tihi o Taranaki* — Māori — the peak of Taranaki is broken off]

kua tekau mā ono ngā tau

sixteen years have trundled by,
like a wounded locomotive.
had my bouts of breakdowns, break ups,
break throughs.
& came off the rails   then
                              and there.
your death still pervades,
my side-track maunder,
this erratic journey
through the tunnels of life,
across those ramshackle aqueducts
between stable station
& depots of disrepair.

misplaced my ticket stub decades ago,
never made first class.
guess I never will.

kua tekau mā ono ngā tau

sixteen years have trudged past.
& I'm still at that crossing.
those infernal bells never cease
                              their strident trill.
while the barriers taunt me
in fissiparous semaphore
                              that never fades.

your death is my own   l I f e l o n g   transit.

when I finally alight,
I pray you're waiting,
                at the terminus

Veronica interrupted

fifteen terracotta soldiers
twenty silver teaspoons
one hundred books (mostly fiction)
pills on the rimu side table
(Methotrexate for arthritis
Tamoxifen for the cancer)
a photo of her great niece
the cushion where the cat sat
a half-done cross word puzzle
a post it note 'Call Mavis!'
brochures for cruises
her mother's Crown Lynn tea set
Warehouse slippers with bunny ears
stale shortbread in the tartan tin

She was old. It was her time.

All of this is rubbish, and it all goes in the bin.

permanent wave

In my mother's old hairdressing manual, authored by S. G. Flitman M.I.T. (master hairdresser and executive of the Fellowship of Hair Artists of Great Britain) I find a woman set and plasticised in a photograph above a paragraph about her husband's achievements. The model for the man who invented the permanent wave, *the girl who later became his wife*, her hair in three large plaits tied close to her scalp, moistened with a 'secret mixture' (likely cow's urine and water), and wound about solid brass curlers that protrude from her head like horns. Karl Ludwig Nessler, curl-obsessed polymath, is preparing to heat the plait-covered rods with his self-constructed, electrically heated tongs in yet another attempt to fix the curl in her natural hair. Eventually he will perfect this ten hour process and make his fortune in America under the name Charles Nestle, but not before he burns her hair off at least three times. In this moment, his restless experimentation is counterbalanced by her stillness, her ability to bear boredom, pain, humiliation, danger. Will she cry as her hair fries and smokes, as blisters form on her scalp? Is she an enthusiastic supporter or bullied martyr? S. G. Flitman does not record. If she has her period, a stomach upset or UTI, those peculiarly female complaints well known to young lady apprentices and their clients alike, what matters that to a master hairdresser? He notes Karl Ludwig was born at Todtnau in the Black Forest in 1872, wore thick, tinted spectacles as a child and dabbled in dentistry. We do not learn her name. Yet here she is, dodging past S. G. Flitman, his passive voice and insistent male pronouns, to wave at us down the years. Waving and burning. Katharina Laible from Langenau.

Little Jack Kerouac

Ambulatin' thru the arteries of Hancock Park —
I gotta tip my cap to the sky.
I mean,
damn, that's a fine blue —
blue as a cathedral window!
This 'burb is full of satisfied faces
humongous houses
bodacious cars
immaculate lawns —
no shortage of legal tender!
& good times 24/7:
volleyball at the pool party
bitchin' tunes
ice-cold brews
the luxuriant smell of *Mary Jane* . . .
We made it, man!
Hey — this is what we were born to do, dude!
& then along comes little Jack Kerouac —
uninvited, saying that thing nobody wants to hear:

Don't you people know that you're all going to die?

Bowie at Slane

It was 1987
driving around Ireland
in my beat-up Ford
with a friend

Mike Dean
and every five minutes
a bit of a song
would come on the radio

part of a contest for tickets
to Bowie's live concert
at Slane
and Mike'd shout out

'Diamond Dogs'
'Ashes to Ashes'
since it turned out he knew
not only the words

to *everything*
the Thin White Duke
had done
but all the riffs

he tried at one point
to explain
the greatness of the man
I think *à propos* of the song

'We built this City'
by Starship
no we didn't
he'd shout

we didn't *build this city*
on rock'n'roll
no bullshit
that's what it came down to

no lies
(or not such obvious ones)
in Bowie's songs
which makes me feel sad

to read the ridiculous crap
in the guise of tributes
in the news this morning
for someone who was something

out of the box
not just another
interchangeable name
It's a dirty job   he said

but someone had to do it

Dadon Rowell

Runaway Song
for S.

I went to London to find you
filled my chest with sunflowers & wore patent leather shoes you'd have
loved

you weren't in the café or behind iron railings at Green Park
I looked for your sweet head & red wool cloche at the train station
tried to find your quicksilver laugh in the gaps between paving stones
prayed I would find you before
                    the plaque
a small apartment up too many stairs   cat claws in net curtains
                                        fractures in my eyes kept growing
                                        till I couldn't see what was left

later they showed me your green typewriter
paler than the avocado bathroom of my childhood, brighter than your
kitchen walls
where I grew up, houses weren't crushed together till you just had
streetlights for stars

why did you die in London, darling?
it rains too much   water gets in your head   after a few days your hair
fattens with mould

you could've come to Aotearoa
we'd sit in pink sand & thread totorere on seagrass
your name would be shortened to something more Tairua   less
Oxford
there'd be poems dedicated   to me   though we'd both agree I should
be nameless
epitaphs to a mystery woman who had breasts like rose petals & sliced
her thumbs peeling kūmara

darling, we'd live so many lives
        crack our eyeteeth in champagne corks & men's spines
raise garden beds, smother them in tulips   fill our
cheeks with the twang of tūī our hands with oh-so soft beestings
you would turn 31

we'd drink cheap Sav
& swing salt-kissed legs off the wharf
taste the October night & know we had made it into spring

of such is the kingdom of heaven
(fragments of childhood #13)

his sound goes
like an axe
thin   precise
hacking with
each cough   one
of those sounds
you feel it
flinchingly
one of those
sounds that keeps
you awake
with echoes
long after he
coughs himself
out of the
cradle and
they lock the
coffin closed

Borderline

cobbled stone of roman history
                fourteen times she repeats
behind the lion knocker
      roars echo
             ash turns to broken bone
and forgotten memories
      left alone in the stair well
...
      green salt air insults cavities
     a better alterative
to limp flesh
    or
  small graves
      the moon sobs for her lover
glass shards for tears
         pink ribbon from the banister
last moments of green pill pops
        tally charts and white wall rooms
JUMP!

   i cannot stay
     he is coming home soon

Our Drunken Uncle Wind

Our drunken uncle wind
staggers through tī kōuka
and tussles harakeke's hair
as we huddle under blankets,
a couple of ducks hiding in raupō.

His laughter rattles ribcages,
cheeky fat bugger
always grinning.
Dad says his upturned moon
smirk holds water.
There'll be no rain this week.

Our drunken uncle wind,
hear his beer pop and hiss
as he drinks piss, dances
with plastic chairs on the porch
at 3am.

Our drunken uncle wind
dies calmly at dawn.
The korimako chimes in his silence.
We lean obtusely into his absence.

Ila Selwyn

lost and found

I am lost since Peter has gone
look for myself in a dance class
but he isn't there to hold me

search for him in the zig-zag track
feel him out there just out of reach
my heart so full it leaks down my face

go home, on my monitor, come across Peter
on Frank's farm, smiling with his arm around me
only six months before he disappears

later check my emails, find myself for a few moments
beside him, both of us grinning broadly on a bridge
London Hospital in the background

throw myself into life, join an art class, discover a bit of me
in the 3-dimensional picture I create from foliage,
shells and ties which knot us together at the ribs

told to bring found objects for another creation
in his workshop downstairs find a rough piece of wood
a small plastic kewpie doll standing in a hole

hand to mouth as though thinking, what should I do?
what is happening now? where do I go? a gesture
repeated in several pictures of Peter on my laptop

cover the wood with plaster bandages, play around with clay
form a prow and stern, gesso the wood, then paint the boat
Peter stands on his craft, looking lost, gazing into the future

uncertain where he is going but confident
if he continues sailing and searching
this pair of agnostics will find each other

Kerrin P. Sharpe

the scaffolding of wings

my mother never cared
for Icarus and kept away
from feathers and wind sailor
boys   boys who held moonlight
like water and swam
in hammocks slung between
high rises   boys on cell phones
far from conversations
on the street *not listening*
not listening   boys flying poems
page by spinning page
too close to the sky

she lay on the pavement
squinting at clouds
and never made out
my father roosting
in cranes and carillons
even her dress   pressed
with paintings of the domes
of Budapest   made
her giddy sun downing
giddy   this way
                    and that

Sarah-Kate Simons

First prize (Year 12), Poetry New Zealand Yearbook Student Poetry Competition

Gossip

the flowers are telling tales in the street —
next door, she's packing her bags since a striped
carnation is a striped carnation and so's a yellow rose. her
husband stands holding every other pure pink
carnation, watching as she goes, and wondering if
he should have picked her hyacinth instead. Across
the road, the little boy's picked every peony in the patch
to take to the hospital for his mommy to hold. his father
doesn't know there's an asphodel among his bouquet of daisies and
soon he'll be taking his darling chrysanthemums instead. the
widow across the way has planted tulips in the window
box this year, rumour has it she's in love again. when
I step outside, there's a posy on my doorstep and a card
with your name. turns out you've mixed the roses because
you've never been in love and don't know how it feels
but you know there's something special about me you've
never encountered before. everyone says the best reply is
anemone or apple blossom, to keep my distance and
let you find your feet. yet if inside I am nothing but roses
and forget-me-nots and honeysuckle at the thought of you,
shouldn't you not have to eavesdrop on flowers
to be the first to know?

Striped carnation — no
Yellow rose — infidelity
Pink carnation — love and apology
Hyacinth — begging for forgiveness
Peony — healing
Daisy — good cheer
Asphodel — death is coming
Chrysanthemums — death

Tulips — love
Mixed roses — I think I like you, but I don't know
Apple blossom — anticipation
Anemone — hope
Roses — love
Forget-me-nots — love
Honeysuckle — love

Never mind her manners

My hand is a digger, scooping up gravy and peas
in a yard of tattoos and high vis vests.

If her eyes were daggers drawn, her spoon
had the thinnest edge of a hunting knife.

I sit in her chair, my arm trussed up
like the roast turkey she insisted we have.

My mother was a goddess with
a thousand arms, earth-etched hands.

Her mouth slew men with a single word —
kept priests and bishops at bay — declared

war, stabbed cloth with needles to make
banners invading the male sanctuary.

I sit in her chair, closest to the kitchen,
as my father and son hull the strawberries,

sprinkle over caster sugar and spoon out
dollops of cream.

What to Do with the Last Dante

showers at night
    whatever the weather
        loving that Florentine
            lather sliding on skin
        a luxury of serpents
    or a silk cascade
foaming endless
    on his body's shore
        new cake lies fresh
            racked and chiselled
        words bear witness
    to its lineage smells
like pomegranates
    and her mockery
        but he knows there
            is thyme somewhere
        the sin of cinnamon
    sown in the morsel
remnant clenched
    awaiting its corruption
        an assimilation old
            moulded into new
        some echo of clay
    immutable this soft
amalgamation

Untitled

a magician never reveals their
tricks to the joker is what you
told me that sunday night last
september as you had sloppily
crashed into a river and made
both of our cold bones shiver.
we both knew this was not a
typical drive down the road
because you had broken the
moral code and would soon
be towed while i lay with still
bones and frantic phone calls
on a stretcher in the back of
an ambulance with hands
holding my body together
as you asked the police to
give you a moment so you
could have a breather and
a cigarette or two because
you knew you were through.
they asked if you wanted to
leave me alone and head
down to the police station
and you just shrugged like
this was not your creation
because your court costs
were more expensive than
the knowledge of my pain
and i wished i had caught
that last sunday night train
instead of drinking with you
in the rain and making fog

against the window pane.
i was told not to move as
i waited for the helicopter
and you were pushed up
against the side of a cop
car and cuffed with angry
resistant will and the tears
spilled down hard and fast
from your pretty little face
because for once i would
not save your damned ass
and get you out of this gory
mess that had turned your
sunday best into a disgrace
and made my bones buckle
and cry out for some rest
for they had been pressed
and strained under the now
drowned window pane with
blood creating a vivid stain.
your head ducked down as
you were pushed into the
back of the police car and
you glanced up to see my
motionless mangled body
watching you from afar.
how's that for a date night?
you laughed as the tube
down my throat made me
cough and the police officer
gave you a stern look before
slamming the door on your

smirking face so hard that
the car shook like my body
did with hollow echoing sobs
that made my eyes run like the
river that had made both of us
shiver as you had claimed that
the joker would always deliver
even if the magician would not
reveal their spells for the joker
had his own secret way to hell.

Michael Steven

Dropped Pin: Addington, Christchurch

for Jordan Hamel

*

My one honest job while living in Christchurch
was working night shift at the PDL factory,
on the outskirts of Addington.
We sat like monkeys in a windowless room
for nine hours straight: collared with earth strap
bonds to metal workbenches,
soldering weevil-shaped resistors
and capacitors to printed circuit boards.
The three of us sat at the same bench.
Rona came in each night from Hornby,
her breath gassy with bad port.
Dave with his spade beard,
snarling, 'Whoever masters the weather
is the master of our emotions.'
I was grateful for any gig I could get.
The three of us sitting together —
our sponges and soldering irons,
our thimbles of flux and conspiracy theories.

*

We killed time with the same bad jokes,
the same sad Classic Hits playlist.
I scribbled secret lines of unspeakable
poetry inside notebooks, eager
for the buzzer to sound the shift's ending,
for the gelid air to freshen my lungs
when I stepped into the night.
Five decades earlier my paternal grandfather
moved his young family north

to flee his tranquiliser addiction
and the blood-beat of Wesleyan hymns.
The only sermons I needed to hear
came through my headphones,
crossing the avenues and districts
of sirens and empty churches
of the dark city, back to my bedsitter
and hungry poem in my typewriter
waiting patiently to be fed another line.

Melinda Szymanik

Ancestry

Studies show that children who have grandparents in their lives are
happier

I did an ancestry test —
I am mostly Eastern European
and a few per cent poetry.
My mother
said her mother was a bit poetry too
but I never met my mother's mother.
I did not meet my father's mother either
I heard she was kind and loving
with big eyes.
It might have been her.
My grandfathers were a hard man, and a drinking womaniser
respectively.
I only met the hard man
and I don't think it was him.
Because poetry
is not what you carve away
but the things that are missing.

D. A. Taylor

After Amsterdam
for T.

you know   i thought about you in
amsterdam   after the rain   in
the morning   my shirt smelled of
the canals and the smoke of the open
streets   of an energetic
but mechanical stagefuck
between a husband and wife
working a darker 9–5   i ate
stroopwafel

and made sure I got a photo
by iam   these are the obligations

i felt

that morning without you   as if i
were musty with the closed drawers
where we keep the forgotten

    as if we would
run out of time before i could find the day

to take you across

the bridge to the rijksmuseum   maybe on
an overcast like today where
students pay 17 euro to
climb the stairs past the
candelabras   the cameos as small
as the buttons on your winter coat   the

slowdim rooms with ships sleeping
behind the glass   enough to sail for
helen in miniature   and on to the third

floor where vincent refuses to meet their
eyes

and after a quick photo   like me
they are gone   see
they have the wheat in his beard
the stroke of blue in his throat and black in his head
   what they need
and a bored young
attendant looks on from behind the rope
to remind us

they are here for the giants   so
no one stops to witness
toorop's unguarded and misty seas or the
butterflies still on a peach
leaf for van neems   or van
os' meadows   whom one critic faulted for
not rendering nature more beautiful
but he was honest   and   i hope
you would love him for it

Richard Taylor

Change

In desire's last locks
last looked dark desire.
Eye-green from black
shudders in lust the fiend of fire.

Chained by chains she burns
yet all is as milk
and white life returns
that all creatures lap —

The lamb, the lion, and the head:
dark coils the curls of flame
whose roar engenders red —
and spins in mad confuse.

For none knows why the word.
None knows why wrong;
or why rises the imperilled bird
whose golden beak

sings a sweet song
that all pulsate
and re-unite with that great gong
that sings all night

to the lonely boys who madly dance
that light of life
enter them at last:
Lovely they come, to prance.

country cousins

we didn't know
we were country kids
our cousins from the big
smoke in timaru sought

to put us in our place
with their city airs and graces
temuka after all was a town
so small that mum knew

before we arrived home
on our bikes if we didn't
stop to give way before
crossing king street and

neighbours felt free to
join in our parenting with
harsh words and even the odd
wallop or three — there was

nothing anonymous about
growing up in temuka
but we went to town on
friday nights like they did and

our shoe shop — king's shoes
(no relation to the street)
was every bit as good as theirs
we had banks a post office a phone exchange

a collection of pubs and a flash brick library
our swimming holes were deeper
wetter and more mysterious and we
could pick walnuts and blackberries for free

how dare they feel more important
as if their tūrangawaewae could hold
a candle to ours as if gungy
old timaru could ever compete

with the glories of temuka
hell even our pottery was famous
made at the insulators just around the corner
no such thing as timaru pottery is there?

'Our Ancestors Are Watching'

We are settlers on an aching land.
In a tongue like ours we hear it whisper the histories of its people.
Their whenua still stolen, no apology offered,
but Māori hongi us, light the path towards a penitent Prime Minister
and offer the stage for our tapa & our Panthers & our Princess.

All our ancestors are watching.

Police dogs bark through the loudspeaker,
babies cry in tune with untied shoes slamming silent streets.
This is the soundscape of sorry.
Our people ran & ran & ran.
Today we stop running, if only for an afternoon.

Everyone we love is here.
They gather the light with their fans and spread it through the room.
The light apologises for the dawn.
Our ancestors stream it through the screen
& it flows on to the streets where they once were harassed.

We roll up the paper apologies and tie the scroll tight with coconut
leaves,
place them into our vaka
and keep paddling.

John Tuke

The Kiss

It was like the time
I kissed my friend
From down the street,
When the fluttering light
Down the side of the house
Kept the other kids away.
When I say
She was bright and red,
I mean a girl's frame
With two bars sloping gently down.
And under the curiosity
Of plum trees
In my grandfather's garden,
Where the lawns rolled on
Into the Pacific, the Indian
And even the Atlantic,
We wobbled along,
Me, my bike, my Grandpa,
Keep pedalling!
The hard rubber tyres
Squashing the dark fruit,
The crimson blood
Spilling into the earth.
Then suddenly flight, orbit,
With grand da Vinci arcs
Drawn across the green,
Just the beginning
Of the longest kiss.

I've always preferred counterfeit to the original

Hot tea is a perfect
Thirst quencher
Almost as good
As the pristine pool
We broke into the other day
And where we splashed in
Before you cut my hair

I was once told
I shouldn't wear gold
For it is bad bad luck
But I couldn't let go of your earring

Rasping buzzing of cicadas
Droplet on an eyebrow
And a funny taste of chlorine on your lips

The boiling water in the kettle
Whistles the end of summer
While middle class couples
Are looking for a last bargain
On two bucks happiness
But I love
My new haircut

The Ceremony of Another World

The ceremony of another world,
what would its music be like?
Sometimes I can hear the first notes
in the back garden
behind the chirping of sparrows.

The sunflowers have lowered their heads
spilling their black seeds.
I could collect them in a tambourine
and watch them vibrate.

Maracas filled with emeralds
fail to produce a green sound.

The ceremony of another world,
where are all the costumes stored?
Long ago we spent an afternoon
transforming ourselves
into fish and amphibians.
Derek decorated the head of his frog mask
with pink hair curlers.
It was a suburban frog
living in an opaque pond
among the eggbeaters and the mops,
the frying pans and the ironing boards.

A train departs, never to return
whenever you speak
an unconvincing word.

The ceremony of another world,
how long will the rehearsal last?

I've spent a lifetime
practising my entrance
pacing backwards and forwards
and now the light is fading.

By the side of the house,
near the washing line
crickets have begun their chorus.

Janet Wainscott

Scorpius

The Western Desert, sand on the pages
of his diary. He wrote of magnificent
sunsets, cakes from home, scorpions
in their beds, tankers of fuel aflame at night
glowing red, billowing black into black.

As a child he knew the birds by their songs
the trees by their rain-soaked leaves, could
name the boats on the bay and the stars
in the silent sky — the Southern Cross,
Orion, Scorpius.

At the centre of Scorpius, Antares,
a dying red giant, the fifteenth brightest
star. Fifteenth. As impressive
as a curtain-raiser or a dress rehearsal,
as a minor front in a major war in a foreign desert.

More threats than you can wave a stick at.
On his nights off, he wandered the desert
with a staff, looking for scorpions.
One spring morning, he noted the songs
of five different birds he could not name.

Scorpius is in no position
to scoff at such futility, with Antares
at its heart, fast on its way to becoming
a supernova, fuel spent, a brilliant blaze
collapsing into a black hole.

Jade Wilson

First prize (Year 11), Poetry New Zealand Yearbook Student Poetry Competition

Café Vienna

Statues press their mouths to the rims
of coffee cups
in the capital of Austria. Vines curl up
wooden beams in a nearby café.

Smokey scents of vanilla swirl
through the air. Sweetness caresses
the faces of the customers. Soft exhales drift
upwards and mix with the clouds.

I wonder what kind of drink it is?
'Let's order one,' she says.

Cream floats on coffee brown
as my lover's hair.

So she doesn't drown
her immune system, I take the cream
for her, scooping it onto a silver teaspoon.
Melting on my tongue: milk and cocoa.

She drinks the coffee, stirring
in a cosmos of sugar crystals.
We sit side by side, imaging the city
our drink knows.

Silver spoons clink against ceramic cups, just
as they do in the capital. Hands brush,
two tongues taste one drink.

What of Vienna?
Unfamiliar place, we imagine that
your mother is proud of you.

Viennese coffee, café Vienna, child of Austria:
Five dollars ninety-nine.

Learning how she likes her coffee:
foolishly, free of charge.

The Under-skins

Some rivers run deep — aquifers beneath earth's crust —
like-mindedness, like-heartedness, like survival.

Under pressure to assimilate, my children's father
made efforts to forget his native blood-song.
Now his tongue, atrophied, refuses to pass its music on.

The faces I love are brown, black, yellow, white,
birth-wrinkled, age-wrinkled, living and dying —
the living are dying, shedding their skins today,

or years away

and

across a quarantined ocean,
my parents' faces are so old,

I may never see them again.

Nicholas Wright

No Great Discovery

None please of the beetles and moths of Keats.
No ancient moor, nor eider shroud.
No single-minded weight in sod.
No round tales, no wake, no styx.

But here's an aboriginal stomach,
full legs twisted to cross, one alabaster
buttock cheek higher than the other,
two lips, wet with passing flesh.

The intolerable wrestle curved in the spine,
the pubic blaze, a cock turned left,
one hand nurtures a still, ripening breast
the other's in deposition — an index stiff in ruin.

Your head lost in an engendering field;
an ear engrained not deaf to seed.

David Wrigley

Post-human Desert Blues

i
The waistcoats of lovelorn bachelors, clouds
slung across three peaks

Ruapehu, bad-breathed ardent suitor —
his late summer mange a too-small suit.

The air carries a teenage funk
abandoned hostel stillness
atmospheres at the edge of a window pane

ii
It's cold here on The Desert Road
I should not have come.

iii
Army helicopters drift low across the skyline
Fat flies humming for murder and meat
They mortar horses here don't they?

Flies vibrate across my eyeline
slow and wounded
Battle-weary
Dragging their buzz behind them like a dead friend.

iv
The desert lends no trees behind which a man can piss
so stumble over mooning terraces
Slip into a gully like a spoon between unhungry lips
assume formal military aspect.
Brace oneself.
Unzip.

v
conduit between bone-black earth
and a stain of tired sky
The rain a worm unfaltering
carving lines of uncut gravity
on the mustness of passing through

vi
Disgust bends my neck
And there, beside me,
Two dead sheep
star-crossed
meant to be
entwined

a shared memory
in the dark-side craters of four eyes
adrift and pulsing
with my war-sick fellow travellers:
fat, black, beatnik flies.

Rheymin Yau

Holes

Like craters on the moon
they dot the landscape,
getting deeper with time.

Their weak edges crumble in
an attempt to fill themselves,
while the ground beneath
distances itself from the approaching voids —
like ghost worms tunnelling away from the light.

At times I see these holes and wonder
how they came to be,
and if they'll ever be filled.

Karen Zelas

Disinterring the past

after 'The Jewish Cemetery Near Leningrad' by Joseph Brodsky

1

I've seen my share of Jewish cemeteries,
though not the one near Leningrad, which Brodsky
chronicled. Like an orphan,

I seek my heritage in every one,
in a language I cannot understand.
In Prague, the foresaken graveyard holds

a still beauty. Leafy shade, stone tablets
unadorned: colour of earth and lichen,
the ancient script a mystery with meaning.

Headstones stagger, lean in, cling
like ancient friends, shiker on Seder wine,
shouting, *L'Shana Haba'ah B'Yerushalayim.*

2

In Berlin, we stroll summer trees searching
for Aunt Jda's grave. Sunlight plays a kaleidoscope
through leaves and coloured glass.

Interred, 1942. Who'd have thought? A simple
ivy-covered stone. Her husband, children: puffs of smoke.
Saltwater stings our eyes; we wash

the marble clean, as reverently, as gently
as any pair of feet. *Stolpersteine*, a brassy
shine embedded in their street.

3
In London, I walk the East End cobbles
in search of grandparents never met; find
a tree-dark cemetery near their bombed-out home,

one tiny city block in size, at shoulder height
to passers-by. I peer at chiselled Hebrew script; hope
blooms, if little else, in this dank

and rotting dark. County records eventually reveal
my mother's mother's resting place — not here,
but Northern London. A pilgrimage,

my dead mother immaterial at my side. For us,
I find her — my grandmother, my namesake — *Dora,
beloved wife of Simon*. The sexton finds

her husband in an unmarked grave, like a pauper.
My grandfather. What misfortune pursued him
after her demise is left to my invention.

4
For years, in Christchurch, my dear takes care
of Jewish graves, repairing the wrongs of vandals,
of — call it what it is — Antisemitism

broken graves that recall the broken lives
of history. He tries to heal the wounds — glue
and cement on the outside, knowing

the inside to be irreparable.

5
When her time came, my mother, forsook
a Jewish burial, followed my father into the flames.

We scattered their ashes under the same tree,
no distance but thirty-six years apart.

Shiker — tipsy

L'Shana Haba'ah B'Yerushalayim — next year in Jerusalem

Essays

A Clearer Dawning

This chapter ends with me standing at a podium in one yellow-lit, upper foyer of the Aotea Centre. It is the 2021 Auckland Writers Festival. I blink, my smile is wobbly. Almost to the day, I have been living in Aotearoa for 15 years and three months. I am 28 years old.

A Post-it Note-marked copy of *A Clear Dawn* is pushed into my hands moments before this moment. I've been told it is the first anthology of its kind. The subtitle on the front reads *New Asian Voices from Aotearoa New Zealand*. My words occupy one page out of 340. The contributors' copies are stuck in a dark container somewhere at the port, so I haven't experienced the book in three-dimensions until now. I don't even know where to find my place. The page isn't tagged because I am a happy last-minute stand-in.

This is my first time holding the book. I get distracted, running my fingers up and down its spine while I flip through, trying to find my name. The book is covered in a fabric I can't identify, the smooth-hard kind of cloth that zips when rubbed. It feels familiar . . .

My hands shrink. I can feel cold tile under my bare feet. The air is warm, heavy with soot, and after-monsoon condensation. Garlic sizzles in the small skillet on the stove.

I am running the fingers of one hand through the pile of fabric scraps stuffed into a plastic bag on the table. My other hand is buried in a tin full of buttons of every shape, size, colour and design. I'm looking for a blue one. It isn't easy because I'm too short to see into the tin. I have to pick up a handful of buttons at a time and hold them up to the light.

Lola taps some sardines into the skillet, straight from the can.

'Oh,' she says, drawing the vowel out, long and loud. 'I did not hear you. Repeat it again, oh.'

I drop the buttons back into the tin — one by one because I like the sound they make — climb onto a chair, and stare at the pieces of copy paper lined up on the frangipani tablecloth next to everything else. Lola has written letters on each neat square. I breathe in and read them aloud.

'A, e, i, o, u,' I chant. 'Ba, be, bi, bo, bu.'

As I continue through the alphabet, and then on to the diphthongs, there is movement across the table.

Lolo's face appears slowly from behind his newspaper. He puts The Philippine Star *down, pushes his chair back. It scrapes a low-pitched screech on the tiles. Lolo looks over his giant glasses at me.*

'Very good,' he says slowly, deliberately. Like he values every letter.

Then he nods for me to keep going, and stands up to check on the watermelon seeds he left drying on the windowsill.

I start again.

'A, e, i, o, u,' I chant. 'Ba, be, bi, bo, bu.'

I start imagining the shapes I want to make with my buttons. The fabric will need to be blue too, blue like the sky on Andy's wall in Toy Story. *The lesson continues. As I read, one hand stays inside the plastic bag. My fingers run through pieces of fabric, pulling on loose threads, rubbing the scraps together to make a soft zipping sound. The world hums in sync and I keep chanting above it.*

'Ka, ke, ki, ko, ku. La, le, li, lo, lu . . .'

I blink. My smile stretches until my cheeks hurt. I look up at the faces in front of the podium, encouraging under the yellow light. *A Clear Dawn* feels soft in my shaking hands, open now to the right page. I've found my place. It is March 15, 2021.

The air seems to ring at a frequency only I can hear.

I take a breath, and share the poem I wrote about Lolo.

'My granddad was a slow talker . . .'

In between, there was an email.

The subject line read: *Exciting Opportunity for Asian NZ Writers!* Gmail timestamped it: *Sep 5, 2019, 8:36 PM.* When it arrived in my corner of the cloud, I had been living in New Zealand for 13 years. To this day it takes up a few megabytes of space there, one of 107 in a folder of my inbox labelled *Poetry.*

It took a moment to understand who the sender was: a fabulous online magazine I had unsuccessfully submitted poetry to, once.

Apparently, Alison Wong and Paula Morris were compiling an anthology for Auckland University Press. The email called for submissions of poetry and prose from writers with Asian backgrounds. The deadline for sending in work was September 18, two weeks away. For 13 days I wondered if anything in my drive was 'Asian' enough.

In between, there was not much writing.

Lolo died peacefully and quietly in 2016. It didn't come as a shock. He hadn't been doing well. There were days when Lolo thought he was a priest, started reciting Mass prayers in Latin on loop until someone intoned 'Amen'. Other days he'd get bright and wide-eyed, talk like it was the 1930s and Japanese fighter planes hadn't yet blown up his violin. Some days he thought he was in Saudi Arabia, looked around the garden for bridges to build. Often he would speak languages from islands we'd never seen. Towards the end, he often called Lola by his sister's name. He left behind a windowsill covered in shrivelled watermelon seeds.

At least, these are stories I remember being told. I wasn't there for that part.

My last image of Lolo is made from sun on glasses, a toothy grin, a brown waving hand. It's hard to distinguish memory from amalgamation.

After the phone call, I got on my knees in the nearest chapel. I prayed I would next meet Lolo as himself, a spirit unweathered. I prayed I would one day know the stories behind all his cracks, hear his wrinkles redeemed by their meaning. My head was a list of questions I needed to ask him.

Why do you have a photo of yourself with a camel? Where were you going? Can you teach me mahjong? Did you let me win when we played chess? What were all the seeds for? Did you like living in the mountains? What did you build in Saudi Arabia? Have you ever smoked? How did you meet Lola? What were your parents like? What was your proudest achievement? Why didn't you go back?

Three years came and went before I could write about him. The poem, when I finally began it, was called 'Glass Questions'.

The refrain of my early drafts read: You. Children. Forget.

In between, there were poets, and missing things.

The first poems I took seriously were all about war. About young people who marched away with the conviction that they needed to be somewhere else to build something great. About fighting for place and people. About not recognising yourself. About coming back different. About changed dreams. The dissonance in Sassoon, Owen and Brooke — between here and there; between past, present and future selves — was flint and fuel for my imagination. It was some time before I perceived the resonance. Sometimes, I still don't see fairness in comparing migration and battle.

I'm alive. I live in a first-world country. There are so many things I never miss.

Like the machete wrapped in newspaper under the car seat. The heat. Going through bomb-checks every single time we go to the mall. So many malls. The heat. Cruise-ship rubbish washed up on the beach. Black, rancid water. Smog. Soot. Having asthma so badly we kept two nebulisers at home. Politician motorcades. Understocked libraries. The time-consuming chore of making water drinkable. Violent road rage. School starting at 7 a.m. The heat. These are all the things we said 'Goodbye' to. I never thought to farewell the good stuff.

Family. Fresh coconuts. The best mangoes in the world. Picnics in the American cemetery. Crazy market stalls full of real pearls on string. Bargaining. Bookstores with cafés inside them. Old stone churches. Saints' day parades. Easter flowers and Christmas lanterns. Sugar cane. Our back garden. Polished tiles. Lola's cloth cupboard. Mixing concrete with a stick, Lolo's hands on mine. Colours. Family.

I know when I go back, I will go back different. Some of the items on this list will lose meaning. Some will gain relevance. The ideas will churn and shift state. Simultaneously, I will try to keep, and to let go.

There aren't many poems about aftermath. About how to live with changed dreams. Even the soldiers didn't write about that.

In between, there was a choice. I decided to submit five poems. The selection process took two days. On the night of the deadline, I sat at my laptop with a draft email open in front of me. Alison's name blinked up at me from the address field. I had written my usual submission paragraphs, twisted them a little to suit the purpose of the opportunity. I was afraid to sound disingenuous. My poems were not about koi, rice or calligraphy. They were written entirely in English. They were Asian only because I was. Honestly, I didn't know if that was enough.

Four poems were already attached to the email. Three of them I would later re-label 'Unfinished'. I had room for one more.

I stared at my poetry folder, asked myself which poems I felt at home with. The answer was: none. Tabs closed. Tabs opened. I blinked again. Then I clicked on a folder I'd called, in a fit of creative frustration, *Detritus*.

'Glass Questions' was the only file in that folder. I attached it to the email without reading it through, thought of Lolo and untold stories.

It was late. My to-do list had a few more items on it. So I hit 'Send' and moved on.

A different chapter begins with me waking up on an aeroplane, pressing my nose to the window. I count the crystals forming between the panes of glass. Outside, the sky is blue like the walls of Andy's room in *Toy Story*. The sunlight is so strong it seems like a solid thing. I reach out, try to squeeze a beam between my fingers. The sea below looks like Pixar put it there. I imagine there could be choirs of rainbow fish beneath the surface, maybe even a mermaid.

It is 2006. I am about to step foot on New Zealand soil for the first time. All I know about the Land of the Long White Cloud is what I've seen in *The Lord of the Rings*, and the DVD the immigration people sent us in the mail. But Dad has been living there — without us — for 10 months. We almost believed him when he said he'd meet us blond, tall and bare-footed. There were no video calls. The map in my head was drawn email by email in binary, one eight-bit letter at a time. I itemise the puzzle pieces Dad has gifted us so far, try to build a picture from the edges.

You'll be able to see stars from the middle of the city. The air smells like living, growing things. School years have more holidays. We can go exploring. Everyone drinks straight from the tap. Drivers usually slow down for pedestrians. The Sky Tower is the only tall building in the country, but there are normal places like KFC and cinemas. Most waters are see-through. The sky has so many good days.

Dad is usually right.

Our plane banks. I'm blinded by the sudden glare. As we break through the clouds, I can see the ocean kissing the coast. The air seems to ring at a frequency only I can hear. My smile widens until my face hurts. Wheels meet tarmac. I blink, breathe in.

This feels like a clearer dawning.

Emily

> ... for me, poetry is the great unsettler. It questions the established order of the mind ... it works at the roots of thinking.
> — Alice Oswald

Poetry worth writing carries a two-pronged insistence; a mutinous one to *ruin* the epistemology of its day, then, riding along on the back of this, the drive to cut a track away from suppressing constraints, out into fresher air. A necessary precondition for this is an aversion to all the weary conceits of contemporary language, along with the nursed ambition to unhook it from its habituated forms. Revolution is what you are after; re-invigoration will never do. This intent unveils an obsession with unsettled and unsettling disquiet, married to the resolve then, to stabilise it into seditious form.

This is always the more confounding ambition.

In the most persuasive work, these impulses are very assertive and usually at loggerheads. So in an era teeming with skillfully managed verse — poetry that is finely toned and tuned, architecturally wrought and multifarious in its forms and ambitions — why does so much of it remain so comfortably wooed by containment? Here is deftly managed writing that never moves beyond closed doors, regulating a poetics of entrapment. Where is the acute awareness of the disparity between *lived* experience and the cultural intelligence of the day, which will always lack the capacity to describe or understand it, even as it imagines it is doing exactly that — imagines that simply by cavorting onward it will all come together?

This is why dissident voices set out on their own. The result is writing that issues from subjective experience in probing out beyond the common mantle, even where the sound is inevitably coloured by the cultural apparel of the time. For Keats, this lay in his infatuation with the classical, while Whitman's evangelical carnival was enamoured with the remaking of the American political idealism of the 1860s. Emily Dickinson played out the role of a Christian heretic.

Dickinson explored entrapment by probing away at it from all over the place in her emphatically choppy way, because, unlike most of our contemporary writers, she was living it, not simply trying to *think* it. You see this in lines like those in poem 599, 'There is a pain — so utter':

There is a pain — so utter —
It swallows substance up —
Then covers the Abyss with Trance —

which manages to be both harrowed *and* ecstatic. This identifies a crucial shift in where we have been moving in our efforts to explain our existential condition, because Western intellectual life has carried us to a point where we now think about the world as if we are living outside it. We have become separated, but don't carry an awareness of this. We cruise on as if we are still here, our understanding buried in the language, which as a result has become flattened and sterile even at its most freewheeling and subtle. It incubates the sound of what it feels like, to feel like, to feel, pretending this is a refined, conscious understanding.

About this Dickinson is sussy and sceptical as she claws her way toward a solitary independence, where, even at her most civil and cheery, you're never far from an anguish that can suddenly rear at you. Yet I always get a sense, skirting through even her most emphatic dispirit, that she knows there is a way through, she just hasn't *figured* it yet; and it is her robust scepticism that keeps sliding it from her grasp. She isn't looking for any easy answers, even as she trips right over them, only to decide, once again, to pull herself together.

In 274 she writes with jittery fright, and yet with great precision and delicacy, about an encounter with a ghost.

The only ghost I ever saw,
was dressed in Mechlin — so —
He wore no sandals on his foot —
And stepped like flakes of snow —

She was left greatly disturbed by the experience — she ends the poem in a flurry of foreboding — but it helped her open out the boundaries of her own conscious experience; in a later work, 670, she revisited it. There she compares the fears aroused by the spectre with encounters with a ghostly second *self*, roaming, loosed within her own consciousness. She identifies her careening fright as spawned by the understanding that she cannot command it.

Her door is jemmied open onto a view of consciousness and imagination that isn't confined within an individual self in the way we have come to presume. The jump she must make to embrace this, however, proves too chilling, and she immediately slams the door shut, while typically leaving her mind open and her speculation ajar.

> The Body — borrows a revolver —
> He bolts the door —
> O'erlooking a superior spectre —
> Or more —

In 646 she explores an alternative, less frightening, literary route through the impasse.

> The Vision — pondered long —
> So plausible becomes
> That I esteem the fiction — real —
> The Real — fictitious seems —

Here she gambols along upon imagination, while simultaneously laying her investigative lens over it. But this isn't a *directed* imagination — the imagination used, for example, as I scribble away at this, or again, to investigate the structures of the world — it is involuntary imagination, an imagination that takes us over, and over which we have little control and think of as carrying us away through dreaming, a very frightening experience when we are awake to it. This she must have experienced. We are locked back inside the world from which we are inseparable, and this threatens the cherished sense of personal control we have fabricated around the idea of an individual self, set apart. About this change she is absolutely explicit, characterising its governing persona in 593, as female.

> I think I was enchanted
> When first a sombre girl —
> I read that foreign lady —
> The Dark — felt beautiful —

How close is this to Homer's Circe? And with a comparable, though more covert eroticism woven into it. There is a characteristically clipped shift here from *reading* into *real*. It transmogrifies the world around her, bringing it to life, while at the same time — and this is what she is resisting — necessarily transforming her, tying her back inside it. This experience she identifies, following Keats, as beyond exegesis.

> I could not have defined the change —
> Conversion of the Mind
> Like Sanctifying in the Soul —
> Is witnessed not explained —

Here you can begin to see how this is visionary. She makes the link herself, tying it to a moral life, but she is a very secular mystic, riven with doubt and puzzlement, along with an exploratory erotic delight, as she makes her advance into transcendental experience from the secular side.

What defeats her, while also perhaps preserving her sanity — for this is a perilous business — is that she remains embroiled in weighing and censuring the conventional Christian strictures of her day. Would that she was born a century later. The 1960s would have set her free.

This Damned Helplessness

Time held me green and dying
though I sang in my chains like the sea.
— Dylan Thomas, 'Fern Hill'

Let me tell you a story. Once upon a time there was a girl who caught a glimpse of a mountain on the horizon, its brilliant peak a perfect cone in a clear blue sky. She longed to walk on those pristine snows, to breathe that rarified air, to stand on the summit and view the world spread for miles under her feet. And so she resolved to climb the mountain. But this was no climb for beginners, and to reach even the foothills she had to pass many tests, and she had to choose, the left-hand path or the right-hand path.

Both paths wound upwards and neither seemed easier or more direct, so she tossed her last gold coin. It came down heads, and she turned right. It was a long ascent. Every so often she looked up for a glimpse of the perfect mountain peak, but it was no longer visible. Eventually the woman (for she was no girl now, many years having passed) realised that the path, although still entrenched, had in fact levelled out some time ago. But where was the peak? Where was the wonderful view? Soon she was lost. She could hear voices somewhere ahead, and although she couldn't make out the sense she liked the tune and followed it. At last she popped out at the summit. The view was terrible. She saw another mountain.

On the other side of a deep ravine was a second peak, pristine and perfect against a clear blue sky. The voices were calling from over there. It seemed she would have to turn around, descend the first mountain, find the path to the second mountain and start climbing all over again. It seemed she couldn't be in both places at the same time.

∧ ∧

Let me tell it another way. I was a physiotherapist for 20 years, but grew dissatisfied, feeling somehow incomplete. So I quit. I turned around and retraced my trail to the mountain base, whereupon I chose the other path and began to toil up the second mountain. Strange magic! Suddenly the twin mountains were neither solid nor truly separate. What I had believed to be the first peak had, in fact, calved from the second. No, not that . . . it had been carved from the second. Some intentional act, long ago, had accomplished this. In nature these peaks belonged — belong — together. That, I realised, was the source of the incomplete feeling, the source of my yearning. I had become separated from an essential part of myself. What's more, I'd been labouring under the pervasive myth that the view from the 'first' peak was the primary view, and that the view from the 'second' was, well, secondary.

∧ ∧

There are lots of names for these imaginary mountains. Mount Rational and Mount Dream. Mount Day and Mount Night. Mount Fact and Mount Fiction. Mount Science and Mount Culture. Mount Body and Mount Soul. It doesn't matter what we call them, it's more important that we keep the path that connects them wide and open and well-used.

∧ ∧

> What are the roots that clutch, what branches grow
> Out of this stony rubbish?
> — T. S. Eliot, 'The Waste Land'

Rafael Campo, physician and poet, visualises Body and Soul (or Science and Culture) as unnaturally separated domains whose peoples have forgotten their original bond, and become antagonists. He calls the space that has opened up between them a 'wasted battlefield'. Note, not just a war zone, but a *wasted* place, with all the connotations of that word: exhaustion, atrophy and weakness, starvation, neglected opportunity and discarded trash.

For Campo, the key to transforming this bleak and blighted space into a 'living garden' is the imagination. 'How well I knew the data of his disease!' he exclaims in exasperation of a patient whose depression was non-responsive to standard medical interventions. It's only when his patient writes a poem which 'indelibly' describes his own experience that Campo can 'begin to intervene more effectively, to meet his revelations with some hard thinking of my own'.

Imagination, suggests Campo, gets you moving, can help you cross the wasted terrain. But, actually, 'cross' is not the verb that Campo uses, and of course not. The imagination is bored by straight lines. *Intervene. Meet.* No, it's necessary to get entangled with others out there. Expect delays. Expect complications. Expect looping back and reconsiderations and changes of direction. Expect to get involved, and to feel it.

Actually, expect to get intimately entangled — how else can the imagination be considered fertile, capable of producing life? For intervene, read *intercourse*. For meet, read *mate*. Little wonder, then, that keeping the imagination out of health care can seem a much safer option. Little wonder.

∧ ∧

The river's tent is broken: the last fingers of leaf
Clutch and sink into the wet bank. The wind
Crosses the brown land, unheard. The nymphs are departed.
— T. S. Eliot, 'The Waste Land'

∧ ∧

Psychiatrist and anthropologist Arthur Kleinman explains suffering as an existential experience, involving an unwelcome interference with 'the lived flow of experience' and having 'moral and somatic resonances' — that is, causing pain to body, mind and spirit. In this view, there is so much about suffering that falls outside the range of ailments that biomedicine can treat, or even what it can detect or discuss.

Biomedicine has evolved a powerful but narrowly focused gaze, and speaks in its own dialect. The novelist Andrew Solomon talks of the 'language gap' that opens up when a patient attempts to explain their symptoms to a doctor. On the one side is the reductive and classifying language of scientific medicine; on the other, natural human speech, digressive, emotional, uncertain and, perhaps, ambiguous.

The specialised vision and language of my physiotherapy training gave me certain powers. For instance, I could see by the way you walked into the room where you were sore, and, given the opportunity to examine you, my fingertips could locate the source of your pain. It wasn't magic, but sometimes it seemed so to those who hadn't been taught to read the body in this way. One of the things I'd learned through becoming 'body-literate', as it were, was that the site of the pain and the source of the pain need not be the same place. You'd come to the clinic rubbing your arm, for example, and I would treat you by rubbing your neck.

∧ ∧

A medical student, talking about the human body, once told Margaret Atwood: 'It's dark in there.' It's especially dark when (as Virginia Woolf put it) 'the lights of health go down'. This dark interior, the inner world of thoughts and feelings, is natural terrain for a writer. The literary gaze is a form of night vision, a torch. The writer explores, engaging the imagination, knowing nothing, feeling her way word by word.

∧ ∧

And so each venture
Is a new beginning, a raid on the inarticulate . . .
— T. S. Eliot, *Four Quartets*

∧ ∧

Reading, too, is an act of the imagination, is movement: toward another mind, toward connection, toward dialogue. Toward someone ahead who is carrying a torch in the dark. Toward the intercourse of story.

After his mother's death, Oliver Sacks turned to literature for help. 'Ibsen called to me,' he wrote, 'called to my condition, and his was the only voice I could bear.' Similarly, neurosurgeon Paul Kalanithi, who had majored in English literature before studying medicine, found himself returning to books when he was seriously ill with cancer. Reading restored his diminished sense of identity and treated his over-riding feelings of helplessness and paralysis. For him, too, imagination transformed a wasteland:

> Lost in a featureless wasteland of my own mortality, and finding no traction in the reams of scientific studies, intracellular molecular pathways, and endless curves of survival statistics, I began reading literature again . . . I was searching for a vocabulary with which to make sense of death, to find a way to begin defining myself and inching forward again . . . I needed words to go forward.

Sometimes — indeed, often, in extremity — the words one needs to go forward come in poetry. The torch in the dark for British novelist Samantha Harvey was a flower, Philip Larkin's 'million-petalled flower / of being here'. Desperately insomniac, this is the incandescent image that hauls her back to life at the death hour of 3 a.m. 'It feels,' writes Harvey, 'like a bell ringing distantly, like the heralding of company in what you thought was a desert or an abyss. Suddenly I don't feel lonely, I feel elated, and everything is soft and full of echoes and resonance.'

∧ ∧

It's only oblivion, true:
We had it before, but then it was going to end,
And was all the time merging with a unique endeavour
To bring to bloom the million-petalled flower

Of being here.
— Philip Larkin, 'The Old Fools'

∧ ∧

That's literature, though. Calls and searching, echoes and resonance. Pretty unreal. Pretty, unreal. Pretty: unreal. Doesn't all that belong on the second — the secondary — mountain? The convention about story in the clinic was this: you gave me your story, and I quickly cannibalised it for useful parts, selecting only the details that would augment my translation, and deleting what didn't fit. Then I'd give you back your story, corrected.

This would become, as between you, my patient, and me, as your health provider, the authorised version. This was because your story, being subjective, was simply not as reliable as my version. My story was objective, it dealt with facts, it proceeded proper noun by proper noun. Mine explained, delineated and categorised. Mine had a plot. It was nice and linear with a steady progression of cause and effect. Mine would tell you what had happened, what was happening now and what was going to happen next. Yours, frankly, was a mess. Mine would set the matter straight. My story would fix you.

And because of this, my story, on its own, was an immoblising device.

∧ ∧

Once upon a time, a patient came to see me complaining of leg pain. 'Complains of': that's the phrase I'd been taught to use as I began to record his side of the story, coded something like this: *c/o p (L) post. thigh.*

This man drove a bus for long distances every day. He told me that the edge of the seat cutting into his thigh had caused the muscle to get knots. It just needed a really deep massage, he said. The words 'knots' and 'massage' were irritating. I hadn't studied anatomy, pathology, biomechanics and a range of evidence-based manual therapy methods — all far more scientific, sophisticated and professional than *massage* — to be told by a bus driver what was wrong with his thigh, and how to fix it. After I'd examined him, I explained about referred pain and how mobilising his lumbar spine would help.

The bus driver attended for several weeks. He did not get better. At every session he told me again about the knotted muscle in his thigh that just needed a deep massage. I countered with the proper story, and treated the bus driver's back with my arsenal of rationally-selected mobilising techniques. He limped into the clinic, and he limped out.

The bus driver's final appointment was the one he kept only to tell me that he didn't need to attend the appointment. He'd found a 'proper masseuse' who had given his thigh a deep massage and unknotted the muscle. He was completely pain-free.

Sometimes the site of the pain *is* the source of the pain.

He'd told me that very clearly so many times. I had gone a fair way up the slopes of the first mountain at the time, and my imagination was well and truly cowed. Knots? Massage? I would not venture into the wasted territory between us to engage in any hard thinking of my own.

∧ ∧

Desire itself is movement.
— T. S. Eliot, *Four Quartets*

∧ ∧

There's no such thing as life without movement. Animated we are alive; inanimate, dead. The living body is always moving, even when asleep, even when profoundly physically disabled. 'The trilling wire in the blood,' wrote Eliot, and 'The dance along the artery / The circulation of the blood.' But so too my cat, snoozing on the couch. So too those sparrows out there at the foot of the garden stealing plums off the laden tree, and so too the tree, whose branches are being swept today by a gusty summer wind, and within whose xylem dances the sap.

The human condition — the how-we-know-ourselves-in-the-world — is more than the autonomic nervous system, smooth muscle or the stretch reflex. The human condition is to be conscious of death and conscious of not-knowing, and to desire to give life a shape in the face of this not-knowing. The human condition involves wanting to take action. A 'good life' is strongly aligned with volitional movement: the generating of the shape of one's own life by the exercise of choice. This is especially so in Western culture, where notions of independence and autonomy are threaded through the entire fabric of day-to-day life, personally, socially and politically. Freedom of movement, we call it, and freedom of speech, and free will.

∧ ∧

Annie Dillard's essay 'Waking Up Wild' asks what it feels like to be alive. Her prose reflects the sense of agency inherent in human consciousness. 'Who turned on the lights? You did, by waking up. You flipped the light switch, started up the wind machine, kicked on the flywheel that spins the years.' Her sentences rollick along, propelled by active verbs, full of weather and water and trees and rocks and sky, the page-scape peppered with sound. 'What a racket in your ears, what a scattershot pounding!'

And yet, writes Dillard, to know you are alive is also to be conscious of moving within bounds, to be aware of the existence of stronger forces wanting to push you in a different direction, perhaps crushing you into oblivion: 'feeling the planet buck under you — rear, kick, and try to throw you — while you hang on to the ring'. It's to sense the limits of mortality, to 'feel time as a stillness about you, and hear the silent air ask in so thin a voice, Have you noticed yet that you will die?'

And if you can't 'hang on'? What if the storyline of your life is suddenly cut through, leaving you dangling?

∧ ∧

'In every life,' writes Annie Proulx, in her epic novel *Barkskins*, 'there are events that reshape one's sense of existence. Afterward, all is different and the past is dimmed.' For her character René, the two life-altering events are a death and a marriage. After the death of his brother, René emigrates to 'escape the loss', ignorant of the fact that for the rest of his life 'he would carry sorrow enclosed within him'.

So there is that, too, the way we carry our stories through our lives, bearing the ever-increasing weight of them the best we can. Some events are so painful, so hot, that no matter how deeply we store them, no matter how many subsequent memories we layer over them, plumping ourselves up like matryoshka dolls, still at the barest breath of oxygen they flare up and burn.

∧ ∧

We tell ourselves stories in order to live.
— Joan Didion, *The White Album*

What I had been taught to believe: Stories have value as entertainment and escapism — hey, we all need a little fun now and then — but they cannot be relied upon as sources of truth. How can they be reliable, with their false premises, confusing timelines, expressions of wildly inappropriate secret desires, double (even triple) meanings, casts of crazy characters, metaphorical language and slippery conclusions? All that is bad enough in personal stories — daily gossip, anecdote, patient histories — but imaginative fiction takes it to a different level, deliberately and artfully employing these qualities to *make things up.*

It stood to reason, then, that stories, being immaterial — imaginative, non-physical — could play no part in treating pain and immobility.

∧ ∧

What did I think pain was? And immobility? I myself had shown a good deal of immobility with regard to the bus driver.

∧ ∧

Every so often my physiotherapy techniques effected something I
fondly thought of as a cure. Again and again, however — every single
time, in fact, and despite ongoing physical deficits and disabilities —
my patients healed themselves by recomposing the broken narrative
of their lives. *Once upon a time*, they would tell me, *I was* . . . a nurse, a
bus driver, a teacher, a builder, a tennis player. *But then this happened*:
the fall or the stroke or the occupational overuse syndrome, the head
injury, the sprain or the fracture. *And I am no longer who I was. Now
I am* . . . and as they talked they were weaving, talking the thread of
their story back and forth, back and forth, finding a way to bridge the
gap between who they once were and who they were now. I heard their
stories; they moved me and inspired me. Yet again and again I failed to
truly understand that *this* was why my patients could go on; *this* was
why they could bear it.

∧ ∧

Cures can be applied, but healing must be partaken of. Healing requires
patient involvement. Patient. Involvement.

∧ ∧

I thought, when I left the physiotherapy profession to spend my days
embroiled in literature, that I was going into a very different field of
work. The surprise has been to realise the deep connection between
physiotherapy and writing. Health practitioners and writers are both
profoundly engaged in the narrative arts, although only the writers are
allowed to claim this with full creative abandon, telling things slant and
reconfiguring timelines.

∧ ∧

No, I am not putting all of these things in their exact chronological order, I may as well confess it, but if I did I would violate my honor as a teller of stories.
— Tennessee Williams, 'The Resemblance Between a Violin Case and a Coffin'

∧ ∧

Story is something moving, something happening, something or somebody changing.
— Ursula K. Le Guin, *Steering the Craft*

Stories heal. I don't mean this in any abstract, airy-fairy or trivial way. I mean that illness paralyses and isolates, and story moves and connects. I mean that story is movement. I mean that being stuck hurts. I mean that stillness can feel like death. I mean that being able to move is a sign of personal agency and control. I mean that movement takes place in space and in time, externally and internally, visibly and invisibly, physically and metaphysically, emotionally and spiritually.

I mean that any movement at all — mental or physical — signals you're alive. I mean that language is central, and that body language and word language are intricately connected in the search for meaningful expression. I mean that humans crave meaning, thrive on a sense of personal agency and purpose, and that stories contain all the elements required for understanding how to weather the slings and arrows of outrageous fortune on this spinning pale blue dot.

I mean that stories are real, and the hunger for them is real, and the nourishment they provide is as real as vitamins from vegetables, as necessary as water.

∧ ∧

Listen: once upon a time there was a motherless and abandoned princess who ate a poisoned apple and fell into a swoon, who slept like death in a glass coffin until she was revived by the kiss of a prince. Once upon a time there was a boy who was made to sleep in a cupboard under the stairs but whose freedom and power was returned to him on his eleventh birthday when he found out who he really was.

And once upon a time (actually, about 1948, in the United States of America), there was a young man who was struck down by polio and placed in an iron lung. He could not be revived by kisses or spells, and he did not know, anymore, who he really was. He lay flat on his back, completely dependent, stripped of his autonomy, robbed of almost all bodily movement. He spent two years in hospitals 'helpless as a child', before going home paralysed and needing a respirator's help to breathe.

Some stories — a great many stories — are not about slaying dragons or saving maidens in distress. 'Conflict,' says Ursula K. Le Guin, 'is one kind of behavior. There are others, equally important in any human life, such as relating, finding, losing, bearing, discovering, parting, changing.'

∧ ∧

The young man's name was Larry Alexander. He was 27, fit and healthy, married to a wife he adored, and the father of a gorgeous baby girl when he fell ill. Really fell, although initially it didn't seem so much a fall as an inability to get up without throwing up. But the headache intensified, and soon his entire body was 'on fire' with fever. Alarmed, his wife summoned an ambulance. It was while he was being rushed to hospital that the next symptom began to appear. In the ambulance he tried, and failed, to grip the edges of the stretcher. 'To my terror,' he recalled later, 'my fingers wouldn't respond.'

Paralysis swiftly turned everything nightmarish. He was locked inside a metal cage, and the cage was careering around corners, someone else was driving and he didn't know who, and they were speeding somewhere (but where?) and he couldn't move and he couldn't call out (although he could hear the ambulance screaming) and he couldn't get a grip on anything (although something had a grip on him) and— It's about now that a nightmare bursts like an overinflated balloon, about now that Larry Alexander, 27, fit, strong and healthy, should sit bolt upright in bed, heart hammering, and say to his wife, 'Man, that was some nightmare!'

But the nightmare careered on. Nothing was as it ought to be, *he* was not who he ought to be, could not stop these slippages into horror — this plummeting fall, this 'sick feeling, like you get in a lift that suddenly dropped from under you', this sense of himself *disappearing*. This was not supposed to happen, it wasn't, as we say, 'in the script'.

Larry Alexander was wheeled into hospital on a gurney and placed in isolation. Masked figures in long white gowns appeared and disappeared like apparitions, and he caught a glimpse of two 'huge, monstrous' machines, for all the world like 'medieval instruments of torture'. These were iron lungs. A doctor came to the admission ward and offered him pain relief. Far worse than the pain, though, was the fear, and the fear was directly connected to the paralysis. 'It's this damned helplessness,' he told the doctor.

∧ ∧

The essence of terror is enforced immobility.

∧ ∧

The story is not in the plot but in the telling. It's the telling that moves.
— Ursula K. Le Guin, *Steering the Craft*

∧ ∧

No one could kiss Larry Alexander better, and he had not inherited magic powers. Except . . . yes he had. He had language, and he dictated his story to be published as a book. Published in 1955, it is called *The Iron Cradle: My Fight Against Polio*. The title and subtitle balance either side of the colon like weights on a scale. What's being weighed against what? The title's three words against the subtitle's four; noun phrase versus verb phrase — these are hints about the inherent weight of The Iron Cradle and the energy that will need to be mustered for a chance to weigh in against it. It's concrete object (well, an iron object) versus abstractions; the physical world versus the world of the self and the psyche; infancy against adulthood; dependency versus independence; circumstance versus the imagination. It's paralysis and recovery, the finding of a different way to move.

∧ ∧

Words move . . .
— T. S. Eliot, *Four Quartets*

∧ ∧

Can a story save a life? True, no one could kiss Larry Alexander out of a glass coffin — or an iron cradle — but he describes journeying farther and deeper into love than most princes and princesses (real or imagined) ever do. His storytelling magic couldn't release him from his personal cupboard-under-the-stairs either, but the telling created movement, and by moving he found out who he really was and gained his freedom — a most difficult freedom, scarred and limited, and so intensely felt that reading his book was like lifting the stopper from a dusty, cellared bottle to inhale a reviving dose of the very essence of life. Not a cure. Absolutely not a cure. A balm, perhaps, and perhaps also a kind of bridge.

A bridge between Larry before polio and Larry after polio; and a bridge between a young man who, more than 70 years ago, had to learn to live in a body that had been de-activated by one of the epidemics of his time, and us, his future readers, all of whom will one day need to tend terrifying immobility and dreadful pain with words, with breath, with imagination. A bridge, and someone on it, waving a many-petalled flower — a flower that sounds strangely and faintly like a bell — saying, *It has been done, it can be done,* saying *I see you there, human being, come on.*

∧ ∧

We tell stories to heal the pain of living.
— Niall Williams, *History of the Rain*

∧ ∧

Once upon a time, a time never so very far in the future, there is a person who strikes trouble. That person is you. You'll be stuck, in pain, and words will fail you. You'll feel a very long way away from everyone else. You will no longer be who you are as you read this, and you won't know what is going to happen next.

You will need to recompose yourself. You'll need words to go forward. You'll need to find a way to sing in your chains like the sea, a way to weave a bridge of sorts, even if precarious, and the chasm below so deep. You'll need to string the fragments of yourself together and re-attach your flimsy line — oh, but how? — to the million-petalled flower. You'll need to glimpse the incandescence in that flower. You'll need to catch a resonance, an echo.

Bring the mountains close again. Let those voices speak. It *is* all about the blood gases: without inspiration we die.

Works cited

Alexander, Lawrence. *The Iron Cradle: My Fight Against Polio*. London: Hodder and Stoughton, 1955.

Atwood, Margaret. *Negotiating with the Dead: A Writer on Writing*. London: Virago, 2005.

Campo, Rafael. *The Healing Art: A Doctor's Black Bag of Poetry*. New York: Norton, 2003.

Didion, Joan. *The White Album*. London: 4th Estate, 2017.

Dillard, Annie. 'Waking Up Wild.' In *The Abundance*. Edinburgh: Canongate Books, 2017.

Eliot, T. S. *Four Quartets*. London: Faber and Faber, 1944.

——'The Waste Land.' In *The Waste Land and Other Poems*. London: Faber and Faber, 1999.

Harvey, Samantha. 'It's As If I'm Falling From a 50-storey Building: A Year Without Sleep.' *The Guardian*, December 28, 2019. www.theguardian.com/books/2019/dec/28/its-as-if-im-falling-from-a-50-storey-building-a-novelists-year-without-sleep.

Kalanithi, Paul. *When Breath Becomes Air*. London: The Bodley Head, 2016.

Kleinman, Arthur. *The Illness Narratives: Suffering, Healing and the Human Condition*. New York: Basic Books, 1988.

Larkin, Philip. 'The Old Fools.' In *Collected Poems*, edited by Anthony Thwaite. London: The Marvell Press and Faber and Faber, 1988.

Le Guin, Ursula K. *Steering the Craft: A 21st Century Guide to Sailing the Sea of Story*. Boston: Houghton Mifflin Harcourt, 2015.

Proulx, Annie. *Barkskins*. London: 4th Estate, 2016.

Sacks, Oliver. *On the Move*. London: Picador, 2015.

Solomon, Andrew. 'Literature About Medicine May Be All That Can Save Us'. *The Guardian*, April 22, 2016. www.theguardian.com/books/2016/apr/22/literature-about-medicine-may-be-all-that-can-save-us.

Thomas, Dylan. 'Fern Hill'. In *The New Oxford Book of English Verse 1250–1950*, edited by Helen Gardner. London: Oxford University Press, 1972.

Williams, Niall. *The History of the Rain*. London: Bloomsbury, 2014.

Williams, Tennessee. 'The Resemblance Between a Violin Case and a Coffin.' In *The Best American Short Stories of the Century*, edited by John Updike. Boston: Houghton Mifflin Company, 2000.

Woolf, Virginia. 'On Being Ill.' In *Selected Essays*, edited by David Bradshaw. Oxford: Oxford University Press, 2008.

Michael Steven

Obituary: Schaeffer Lemalu (1983–2021)

On the weekend before the 2021 lockdown, the poet and painter Schaeffer Lemalu passed away suddenly in East Auckland. That weekend I lost a dear friend, as did many others. Aotearoa also lost one of its most sensitive, luminous and largely unpublished poets. In an era in which poems (and poets) have become marketable and thus commodifiable, Schaeffer held a rare and ascetic commitment to the study and composition of poetry.

I remember our first meeting, after we had corresponded for some years. The room he kept in a flat on Sandringham Road was like a monk's cell, or at least a minimalist painting of one. It was empty except for an unmade double bed, piles of well-read slim volumes by authors with names like Ashbery, Crane, Celan, Char and Duncan, and his notebooks. No furniture, no posters, prints or paintings adorning the walls. For a poet who lived always in the act of the poem, what else did he have need for?

To say he was unpublished, is to not say his work went unread. The composing and reading of a poem were for him occasions of intimate connection. Schaeffer was, by nature, reticent and shy. But he was always warmly attendant in conversation and correspondence, insightful and humorous. Like one of his heroes, the Greek-Egyptian lyric poet C. P. Cavafy, Schaeffer gathered his poems into small folios and distributed them (usually in PDF format) to his friends and peers. It was a subtle and brilliant way of circumventing the conventional (and public) channels of poetry publication. During his life Schaeffer published two chapbooks, *Sleeptalker* (2018) and *Sleeptalker 2* (2019). He leaves behind several book manuscripts and individual poems that are likely to be published in time.

What to say of the poems themselves when so much is to be said, in such little space? And how to say those things without recourse to dry analysis? Always, the poems were as jewelled and precise as the finest timepieces, holding their viewer/reader inside the perpetual enigma of what Schaeffer liked to call 'a fleeting present'. His work was open and inclusive, beguiling and etheric. It brought together high-minded philosophy, theology, music and pop culture in the same dance. Where else in our poetry do Freud and Young Thug hold it down with the movies of Michael Mann (yes, even the bad ones)? He could be difficult, but rarely was he obfuscating or obtuse. For Schaeffer, the poem was always prayer: his unique and private way of making supplication. For those of us who were blessed to know him and to read his work, he showed us God in the world.

Dropped Pin: Devonport, North Shore, Auckland

Summer was a new pair of Birkenstocks.
Freud's *Totem and Taboo*
in a laminated
Dover edition, from Book Depository.

Swimming stoned
each night before sundown,
you floated at the edge of the Hauraki Gulf's
basin of tepid green water

somewhere between Takapuna and Rangitoto,
while blonde promo girls
in string bikinis posed beside rockpools
and children screamed

down the faces of small waves
on boogey-boards,
and container ships reconfigured the horizon —
floating until you became the water,

floating until the water
became the memory of water
holding your body
again.

Reviews

David Eggleton

David Eggleton
The Wilder Years: Selected Poems
Otago University Press, 2021
RRP $40, 314pp

A selected works has arrived from the New Zealand
Poet Laureate: a solid, substantial hardback volume featuring a striking
cover painting by his collaborator Nigel Brown. Coming in at over 300
pages, this is a defining document of the multi-polar literary life of
the poet who came in from the cold (or perhaps the heat of his South
Auckland youth).

To appreciate this collection fully, an understanding of Eggleton's
personal history can give us some bearings. As the son of a working-
class English immigrant father and Rotuman Tongan mother, with a
Pasifika childhood transposed into the rugged environment of 1960s
and 1970s Auckland, Eggleton as a writer has a powerful outsider–
insider dynamic.

This is not to crudely reduce his writing to a mere by-product of
his background, but rather to contextualise a poet who has always
been deeply tangled up in the contradictory promises, realities and
mythologies of modern Aotearoa. His frustrations and swipes come
out of a deep sense of commitment, and a recognition of his nation's
uniqueness. Both of his world, and observing it from a distance,
Eggleton is a quantum anomaly broadcasting from multiple positions
simultaneously.

Leveraging radical spoken word styles as the Mad Kiwi Ranter of the
seventies and eighties — as a prescient and possibly one-man vanguard
of the live poetry eruption of recent years — Eggleton continued beyond
this self-carved territory, curving in a long arc over the literary firmament
to emerge late-career as laureate, critic, editor and public figure.

His first collection, *South Pacific Sunrise*, was published in 1986, in a New Zealand where Rob Muldoon had only recently been voted out of office. For a younger reader, this may as well be ancient history, given the technological and social acceleration and compression of the subsequent 35 years. Eggleton's formative era coincided with a melting of postwar consensus under the laser blasts of Rogernomics/Ruthanasia capitalist realism. New Zealand is now in many ways unrecognisable to those who can remember this past world, but no other New Zealand poet could make greater claim to tracking this turbulent age. Situated in time and space, this poetry balances on the fault lines of what social commentator Chris Trotter has described as the 'Old' New Zealand and the 'New' New Zealand.

It's political, but light-footed and often hilarious. Eggleton's profane, colloquial, wise-cracking and street-savvy lingo is utilised to undermine, satirise and reflect on what Les Murray described as 'narrowspeak', the conventional controlled narratives and dialects of the establishment. Yet Eggleton's poetry also functions at a higher formal level, informed by a quick intelligence and a sense of the infinite potential of language. Will Self once described the Scottish writer Alasdair Gray as 'a creative polymath with an integrated politico-philosophic vision', and this epithet could serve us equally well in a South Polynesian context for Eggleton.

The world is experience for Eggleton, as he examines the natural and social orders, collating, interrogating, declaiming in shifting, vibrant voices. Sometimes you get the anarcho-cyberpunk visionary, a William Gibson of comic affect ('Electric Puha Telemarketing Ode'), and oft times you get ghostly echoes of bush poetry, music-hall patter, long-dead Telethons and newspaper headlines ('Poem for Ben Brown').

Interestingly, we don't see a radical shift in style or focus over his career. Although there are occasional outliers, the dynamism of language is consistent, the themes panoramic but often returned to for further investigation. Despite the density of time-sensitive pop-culture references and news events, these poems rarely seem dated or obscure in their references.

There is a strong physicality to this poetry, which is defined by its visual and musical components, in the richness of image and metaphor, the rhythmic beat, the cadence. Those who have heard the poet read his work will appreciate this even more — an inimitable shamanic incantatory chant hybridised with the urgency of a TAB trackside announcer.

Eggleton's poetry uses engagement with place to instigate a chain reaction, a cascading series of responses and references that threaten to overflow all constraints. The poems in *The Wilder Years* range widely over the physical world, but have a dominant New Zealand focus. When I interviewed the author at the Dunedin Writers and Readers Festival in 2021, I noted that the two poles I found myself returning to in his poetry are Auckland and Dunedin: two cities that have profoundly influenced his writing.

Auckland is a space of sensory overload, chaos capitalism, a Polynesian cultural capital facing into the Pacific:

> I came out of the Manukau City shopping centre
> Doing the Manukau Mall Walk —
> the shoeshine shuffle, the hotfoot loogie, the baby elephant —
> ('Manukau Mall Walk')

Dunedin is a liminal zone, out of time, occupied by ghosts of its official and hidden histories, a remote outpost staring out into the vast Southern Ocean.

> ... in October, whaler pirates sail past Waikouaiti,
> In November, students blunder through the wee garden of Charles
> Brasch ...
> ('An Otago Gothic Calendar')

Always, there is the gimlet eye of a literary magpie darting for a shiny gewgaw, an arresting image or startling metaphor to transform the mundane into the visionary, or equally reduce the self-important with a surreal satiric barb.

As the poet himself has noted, he does not operate in the

confessional mode, which is a dominant key in much contemporary poetry, often subsumed in the internal life, the intimate relationship, a self-referential and self-deprecating personal world.

Eggleton's poetry says go big or go home, as it dislocates its jaws and swallows the world whole. From an outsider figure, both fascinated by and uncomfortably critical of a society in flux, he has become the pre-eminent poetic interpreter and chronicler of the New Zealand of his time, a status confirmed by his selected poems.

Rata Gordon

Rata Gordon
Second Person
Victoria University Press, 2020
RRP $25, 94pp

A stone. A mango. Six raw eggs. Tongues of small birds. A shoreline. In *Second Person*, Rata Gordon's first poetry collection, we wade through a flash of images to uncover slippery meanings. We float just out of frame, watching. Listening. From the first piece, 'The pregnant pioneer looks over her shoulder', shared here in full, there is an ordered instability, a breathless uncertainty finding its measure through unexpected imagery:

> I'm dressed in yellow leaking
> gorse seeds out my pockets like
> crumbs I am dressed in white skin
> drinking from the spout of a
> teapot the Waikato is
> clear and twisting onto my
> tongue rats are roaming under
> my skirt my son is sprouting
> legs like a tadpole a tree
> falls a tree falls a tree falls
> sparrows flap from my armpits
> spiders crawl on my sweaty
> nape the main issue we have
> is mud

There is a tender balance between quiet tragedy, awed beauty and sharp wit. We move in rising circular motion through the four sections, traipsing from the wonder of birth and childhood, 'pinching flakes for gold fish', and into the restlessness of young adulthood in a 'Small town' where:

> now the Barbies have plastic liver cancer
> and speak in hoarse whispers
> let's clothe the road-workers in clean sheets
> let's feed the grass
> some burnt toast

Following the weighted freedom of possibility in 'Where to go', we trek from India to the United States in the search 'to not be alone'. From the streets of Delhi, where 'the dust gets up your nose and into your veins', to the 'lesbian bar in San Francisco', we move back and forth between the sensual and the hopeless, between the experience of a quiet nakedness as 'a monsoon is arriving on heavy legs' and feeling like 'a maggot in a rotting sheep'. Still unsteady, we follow the discomforted return of a woman 'losing my way in a field of placentas and pesticides', and the increasingly aching search for a baby who may be 'sprouting legs inside a grapefruit in some far off universe'.

We are increasingly stalked by the ominous undertones of pollution, loss and the quiet horrors of being a woman, all of which are especially poignant in 'How I arrived' and 'Pacing'. This is an intimate search for balance between deep existential threats and the desperate hope for beauty, for connection, for identity, for little moments of meaning. Throughout this collection, we follow, suspended:

> In April you want to hurt
> yourself in the hotel room
> but you don't because a mango
> will make it better
>
> You walk through the streets
> in second person as if

watching yourself from behind
your backpack and your hands
are limp but your heart is
beating

This is all you have
to look forward to
your heartbeat and a
mango

This is a collection of self-discoveries, uncovered through delightfully unexpected pairings and an intense focus on flickering moments of being. We are reminded of the mythical in the mundane, where 'grey warblers sing like dust moving through the air', but even in its moments of warmth there is no solid ground here. Gordon keeps us off-balance through the pacing of these pieces, shifting unexpectedly between rapid barrages of images and sparse, languid lines. It is, perhaps, this — an appreciation of the unstable nature of being — which is best taken from this collection:

You can cause a wall to vibrate very gently by sitting
in front of it on a chair and playing the cello

and it is the unsteady trembling of a life which leaves the pages humming. In the end, words slip away into the inexpressible. We are bodies in movement, identities fluid and undefined. We slip away into the mangroves, 'in the water jungle where no words could find me'.

Jessie Burnette

Rhian Gallagher

Rhian Gallagher
Far-Flung
Auckland University Press, 2020
RRP $24.99, 96pp

I'm walking above myself in the blue light
indecently blue above the bay with its walk-on-water skin

It is with this sense of observation, somehow both omnisciently
detached and completely embodied, that Rhian Gallagher's fourth book
of poetry, *Far-Flung*, begins. At times playful and childlike, at others
cutting, but always infused with a sense of melancholy, this collection is
utterly devoted to the task of putting to the page 'what the body might
feel before thought'.

Moving through the two sections of *Far-Flung* — 'The Speed of God'
and 'Seacliff Epistles' — there is a growing sense that something dark is
being unearthed, something to which we must bear witness, something
which haunts us across the pages through time and space. It is, indeed,
a haunting; a scabbing trauma 'captured in carbon' and delicately
exposed through the testimony of the forest. From the beating wings of
contemporary grieved entrapment to the chorus of lost voices seeping
from 'the weeping wych-elm', the ambered moments captured in this
collection reverberate beyond the page.

As we move through 'The Speed of God', we pendulum from vivid
wonder at the landscape of present-day Otago to the hopes and fears
of childhood, before returning to a present now consumed by absence
and gentle memory shown through pieces like 'Short Takes on My

Father'. The momentum then carries us deeper into the past, down 'a line of descent' which brings us to 'Seacliff Epistles'. Here, we follow the clues of 'the long, tall voices of academics, utterly objective' and soft hints locked in the thistledown, the sea, the songbirds, to uncover the malignancy of Seacliff Asylum and the voices of its patients, strangled by history:

> the hearts
> I can't hear in the wind
> beating; the asylum
> locking me out — a ghost
> from the future
> come to haunt the past
>   — I listen.

Gallagher's attention to the rhythm and sonic flavour of each line carries us through the landscape, as we move from 'the cool, calm, cathedral-quiet of the beech forest; the milk-moss, fern-fanned floor' of the present day to the cold cruelty of nineteenth-century Seacliff Asylum, where:

> You move, you talk
> inside the room your sounds are human
>
> my name is so and so, you say, my name is
>   whatever
> the doctor, the guard, the attendant
> chooses to call me.

These lines have watched and listened; they hold in them the truths which can only be found through the body. Through them we hold the steady timing of the kōtukutuku, glide with the rising beat of the kāhu's 'riffling feathers', and spiral into the chaos of our uncontrollable destruction:

And as if God's rush were in us too we go about remodelling
faster and faster with our burning and breaking and the earth
reels with our speed and it looks and feels like a disaster.

Descending into the tragedy of Seacliff, we live in the skins of the
unseen many: 'the wild Irish workhouse girls', those who lost and 'felt
too much', those brought to the 'promised land' and told 'the Irish
need not apply'. The warming calm of the forest in 'The Speed of God'
slips away. We are 'estranged from the birds and the trees' and sucked
into the darkness of the sea, the 'great separator', and the wildness of
a landscape that seeks to kill even as it is itself being destroyed. We
are brought into a drowning land, where lines are only sunlit in tender
fragments such as 'Kevin's Treasure'.

In 'Night Descends' and 'Epilogue', we are finally returned to the
birds, the trees, the keepers of memory. Yet, there is still no safety. The
natural world appears more friendly when compared with a far greater
terror: a humanity that diagnoses, divides and silences, that 'puts on
its uniform' and demands order. There is a clear closing, yet there is no
closure — and rightfully so, because if there is anything to take from
Far-Flung it is that 'the past is never really passed' and we are all:

lying out there
between what's gone
and what's to come

Nina Mingya Powles

Nina Mingya Powles
Magnolia 木蘭
Seraph Press, 2020
RRP $30, 84pp

Reading *Magnolia* 木蘭 felt like seeing in colour for the first time, and then being dropped into a spring garden in full, technicolour bloom. It was an experience I did not want to end. Each poem demands, diamond-like, to be held in light for an entire day. Every position of the sun rewarded me with the discovery of a new spectrum of reality, and a rediscovery of self.

In this collection, Nina Mingya Powles has brought life to colours never seen. She has rooted herself in our literary geography as a voice of the freshest, most honest variety. Powles has made of herself a poet wielding beautiful, gentle swords. Journeying through her vibrant word worlds was in turns nostalgic, Miyazaki-magical, and future bright: a sometimes painful but always sweet awakening.

As I read 'Girl warrior' I caught myself reaching up to touch the obstinate, unwanted flick in my hair, the bit that no amount of brushing or layering could set straight. No matter how many times I had seen the film *Mulan*, I had never thought of the character as 'still a little messy', never felt a closeness with the pretty, perfect, animated hero. In three pages, Powles changed that. In three pages she had drawn in me an avalanche, lit a fire, changed a worldview.

I had never heard of Eileen Chang before I met 'Falling city', but in the landscape Powles paints I found echoes everywhere. The image she conjures of a woman in black-and-white has my great-grandmother's face. How many days did I stretch myself out on a tiled floor in an attempt to escape urban humidity? How many secret maps have Asian writers hidden away in the corners of our minds in favour of well-travelled studies of New York City? Poems like 'Colour fragments' fed the ignition points in my nerve endings. I could taste Powles's 'burnt up chemical sky', smell the saffron, feel the electricity.

In 'Field notes on a downpour', Powles washed away more of my preconceptions. Her close examination of the meaning behind different Mandarin numerical characters feels like a re-introduction to the universe, like I am meeting shopping malls, ghosts and pomelo at their cinematic debut.

The rest of the collection is a continuous blooming. With each piece, Powles stitches a volcano onto my horizon. 'Spring onion pancakes' made me wonder why I've never read a poem about spring onion pancakes before. Then I remember how I now only call ube 'purple yam', and I am confronted with the answer to my own question. The poem rings like sesame seeds spilling from a glass jar onto fabric. I lament as my bones 'turn soft in the heat. Collect up forgotten things . . .'

By the end of the closing poem, 'Magnolia, jade-orchid, she-wolf', I am full of cathartic satisfaction. If 'home is not a place but a string of colours threaded together and knotted at one end,' then *Magnolia* 木蘭 has brought me full-circle. But like the character Chihiro in Hayao Miyazaki's epic film *Spirited Away*, I have returned different, enchanted and aware.

When I next watch *Mulan*, there will be more dimensions to it. When I next flip through the photos of my grandmother's chilli plants and tamarind tree, I will see more than an over-exposed memory. When I next catch myself praising bubble tea out loud after my first sip, I will not apologise. A hunger has been awakened for poems about markets in downtown Manila, for Saturday mornings in Singapore, for meeting familiar faces in a Dubai airport. It's only recently, and mainly thanks to writers like Powles, Sherry Zhang and Modi Deng, that I have thought about penning such stories myself.

Magnolia 木蘭 has taught me to be proud of my own unique experiences, to celebrate them as more than exotic childhood fascinations. To praise them for the places they occupy in my life. I'm a better poet, a happier Asian, and a more complete human being for reading it. I am also very grateful to Powles for sharing these stories with us. But this is a book for living with, and living on. I hope that what Powles has begun with this book of gentle swords will be felt by many readers and writers to come. I hope this is only the beginning.

Murray Edmond

Murray Edmond
Time to Make a Song and Dance: Cultural Revolt in Auckland in the 1960s[1]
Atuanui Press, 2021
RRP $38, 360pp

'It was 20 years ago today . . .' opens the first track on *Sgt. Pepper's Lonely Hearts Club Band*. Well, that ground-breaking Beatles album is now over a half-century old and belongs to the decade of radical transformation in Auckland that Murray Edmond writes about in *Time to Make a Song and Dance*. In a sense, any take on history requires a looking over your own and other people's shoulders: the ways of looking are innumerable and often contentious. What intrigues me about Edmond's book is his weaving together of the personal and the institutional — *Song and Dance* AND *Cultural Revolt* — two facets that comprise an alluring but also surprisingly conflicted cultural history.

In 1960, 119 years after Auckland was declared New Zealand's first capital, Edmond turned 11. In the preface he avers 'my individual participation was never consequential', but his presence in the account of the decade is hardly incidental. This is indicated in 45 index references to him when he was a young student in the late 1960s, transitioning from Hamilton Boys' High to the University of Auckland, a budding drama devotee and political activist whose achievements over the ensuing 50 years would contribute to an exceptional career as an academic, dramaturge and poet.

Edmond clearly has skin in the game. The loosely-linked progression of 10 chapters, together with the preface and an appended 'finale' (a symbolic photograph of 'the statue of Sir George Grey in Albert Park,

---

1   I commend Diane Lowther for contributing a comprehensive index, a handy resource in the writing of this brief review.

beheaded, Waitangi Day 1987'), is purposefully dramatic. And the role that Edmond performs lies somewhere between a Greek chorus and *The Great Gatsby*'s Nick Carraway, part character, part confidant. Clearly, this is the story of what has affected him quite profoundly, and is part of a legacy he is at pains to see left in good care.

Needless to say, the points of intersection between the personal and institutional culture are complex and permeate the entire narrative. While carefully chosen individual 'protagonists' populate each chapter, grouped in three parts, the dramatic structure of the book falls more neatly into two halves. The first half is a kind of ramp-up, depicting unconventional personalities and events that have their origins elsewhere, predominantly the UK or in a discounted Māori culture, in the lead-up to 1960. The ramp-down picks up urgency in an increasingly homegrown manner and depicts younger, more activist approaches to achieving radical change. Here's the intermission point, circa 1965:

> In writing this book I have met with a tension between transformational moments, times that seem to create a pause in time, when the world 'turns' — Carmen walks out of court a free woman, Barbara Hepworth becomes the talk of the town, Samuel Beckett hits the headlines, The Young Aucklanders in the Arts Festival actually takes place — and that other thing, the flow of time, its gradual imperceptible waxing and waning. The moon, we are told, is only full for a few seconds in each monthly cycle . . . Music has this quality of temporal tension, between what we call the melodic and rhythmic, that flow in time versus the harmonic and simultaneous, those moments when everyone sings the same chord and steps off on the same foot — and the song and dance begins — or ends.

The push-and-pull is between a stopping dead and the oscillating, cumulative flow of time and the changes it occasions. The process can be quite brutal. Our characters, a couple of whom are mentioned above, constitute its heroes and villains. As Edmond aptly puts it, 'The motley crew who person the ship that sails through this book . . . don't make a coherent group, they are not bound by a single idea and they weren't working together.' The 'crew' is indeed 'motley', seeming almost ill-prepared for the part they must play under the spotlight, including several who have little more than walk-on cameos (Wystan Curnow, James K. Baxter, Bill Pearson, Karl Stead, Sylvia Ashton-Warner, Fleur Adcock, Mayor Robbie, Alan Brunton and Red Mole, Living Theatre Troupe, Keith Holyoake, Tim Shadbolt).

Those given prominence are as interesting in their own terms as they are in terms of their contribution to Edmond's argument (about which more shortly). An assortment mostly of oddballs, usually in combo, take the stage. There are no solo performances or soliloquies — chapters involve two, three or four key individuals, with the occasional crowd scene thrown in for good measure. This increases dramatic tension and the atmosphere of unpremeditatedness that Edmond evokes. He parades his characters, within and across chapters, sometimes highlighting similarities (Bob Lowry with Pita Awatere; Anna Hoffmann with Carmen; Molly Macalister with Barbara Hepworth and Jean Watson: 'quiet subversives'); sometimes comparing and contrasting (Ronnie Barker with Peter Tomory: 'overseas expert[s]'; Frank Sargeson, Janet Frame, Maurice Duggan, Jean Watson); sometimes emphasising implicit or explicit conflict or hostility (Hepworth and Tom Pearce: 'side-stepped the plodding Pearce to score under the posts'; Barry Crump and Jean Watson); with a final denouement given to the mob.

Actually, Edmond deftly weaves other layers of significance through the same narrative structure. Three of these layers stand out. One is the way recurrent motifs — Frame's 'lawnmower always wins' and 'terrible screaming called silence', Hone Tuwhare's prescient 'clear headed analysis of [his] society', and Allen Curnow's 'The Overseas Expert' — underscore the theme of near-futile opposition to an entrenched social conformism. Similarly, key figures — flawed heroes like Awatere ('the weight [he] carried was intolerable'), and Hoffman/Carmen — are approvingly and recurrently alluded to.

The third way in which approval and disapproval are meted out is stylistic. The career trajectory of the ill-fated Ron Barker, brought to New Zealand in 1958 to develop Community Arts Service (CAS) Theatre, is sympathetically contoured: a 'flamboyant, eccentric and demonstrative' UK-trained professional, who, in his experience of New Zealand society, 'sensed the horror beneath the surface', and was sacked by the University Council in 1962 because he 'had ended his usefulness'.

Not without some justification, valuative reassessments of creative artists are also in reasonably plain view. Barry Crump and James K. Baxter — who 'chose to don the martyr's sackcloth' — are disparaged because they 'performed acts of cultural contortionism . . . as professional rebels', whereas the dedication of Crump's lover and fellow writer, Jean Watson — whose 'short sweet simple love story' *Stand in the Rain* is admiringly and half-coyly awarded 'the Great New Zealand Novel' badge of honour. Her 'To chance and circumstance' dedication endears itself to Edmond. In contrast to the charlatans Baxter and Crump, Murray regards Watson, Frame and Tuwhare as the decade's genuine literary stars. Even Sargeson, whose *The Hangover* (1967) is rightfully celebrated as epochal, has the achievement downgraded because in real life 'his celebrity was based on a cloak of secrecy'.

At its heart *Song and Dance* is dedicated to the artistic dimension of social activism, and it fits this bill with aplomb. It is also assiduously researched. Pages of historical investigation background city council shenanigans around CAS, Auckland Festival organisation, Auckland Art Gallery governance; television; the founding of the Auckland International Film Festival (credited to Roger Horrocks and Wynne Colgan, also 'quiet subversives'); rapid demographic changes and the increased availability of education; and the advent of student and worker anti-war and anti-racism protests (Tim Shadbolt, Ngā Tamatoa, PYM, HALT and CARE).

Yet this is not primarily a book of historiography or scholarship. Research provides the choreographical ballast for a deeper purpose: the recovery and re-enactment of an originary impulse to act out of sustained creative revolt. The 'transformational moments' enacted by Edmond's cast outperform the extensions of time they necessarily occur within.

Beyond the obvious predicament of individual unbelonging, this raises the broader issue of historical revisionism. Such revisionism is pro-radical and pro-youth; pro-education and pro-artistic endeavour; pro-Māori and pro-feminist. It is anti-status quo and anti-establishment; anti-neoliberal and anti-capitalist; anti-apartheid and anti-war. In a curious way, it is also anti-cerebral, preferring plastic and embodied art forms (including those of Anna Hoffman and Carmen: 'flamboyance was a woman's right') to speculative thought. The *dramatis personae* are enterprising, iconoclastic, self-determining, unmistakably 'entangled with personal catastrophe'. 'The point was simply to rebel'.

More than a treatise that trusts in social transformation, or inclines towards a dint of transcendentalism (a reason perhaps why only minor appearances are granted people like Stead, Robin Dudding, Colin McCahon, Kendrick Smithyman, Baxter and Duggan, despite their own considerable self-transformations during the 1960s), the focus is on a present unfitting. It concerns disaffection and restlessness and the elusiveness of intended outcomes in an 'anarchic amoral world' (a phrase used in reference to Watson's novel). Perhaps this is the reason why Edmond's subtitle opts for 'revolt' in preference to 'revolution' (the name of a track on The Beatles' *White Album* of 1968).

Instead of the amelioration or reconciliation promised through 'progress', the prevailing atmosphere is of an abiding 'Theatre of Cruelty'. The phrase is Antonin Artaud's, that iconoclastic hedonist 'madman junkie' and 'tortured crazy man' originator of *The Theatre and Its Double* thrown in the mix: 'Artaud would be king'. Revolt without regard to outcomes — is that the ideal, the book's *leitmotif*?

While unquestionably presented as a celebration — witness *Song and Dance* and Pat Hanly's *Figures in Light No. 5* which graces the cover — the enterprise leaves me with feelings that are unexpectedly conflicted. This is not intended as a complaint — after all, the feeling of perplexity seems to be invited. Despite their undoubted verve, nobility and sheer ballsiness, many of Edmond's protagonists' endeavours and personal lives end in degrees of compromise, setback or tragedy.

Are we back in the days of Pearson's 'Fretful Sleepers' — with a sixties twist? Then, as nowadays, it seems that ill-gotten rewards invariably arrive at the doorstep of institutional conformists, while we other — ill-begotten, ostracised, creative souls — suffer underestimation, deprivation, exclusion. The takeaway impression is of a bifurcated world — moments of illuminating breakthrough bounded by preponderant disappointment, withdrawal, non-cohesion. Does revolt intimate a failed revolution, or does it simply indicate the way innovation and unusualness in New Zealand are constantly driven underground, or just away? Cultural innovation has thus far proved to be a rather painful journey, and promises to continue so.

Jordan Hamel

Victor Billot

Victor Billot
The Sets
Otago University Press, 2021
RRP $27.50, 118pp

> I wish these demands would forsake me,
> my heart and balls and guts tangled hopelessly
> in the murky business of the world.

The titular poem of Victor Billot's collection sets the table (pun intended) for the vast and winding journey to follow. It is a journey that shows the breadth of his poetic sensibilities, and presents him as someone who is not only comfortable but also truly excels in 'the murky business of the world'.

Billot's collection starts safely enough, at the sea, the speaker observing, reflecting, contemplating his own place 'on this fucking planet, this planet of death' beneath 'distant cores of stars' like any good southern man. But Billot isn't content with keeping his contemplation as grounded as previous poets of a similar ilk, instead choosing to use all 118 pages to roam between nature, history, family and the uncertain future, with a particularly strong middle section of biting and acerbic social satire, for which Billot has become known through his regular *Newsroom* contributions.

> Our isolated selves gathered by screens
> and we followed by tweet, post, insta
> the leisurely progress of an end.

Maybe it's because that's how I originally got into Victor's poetry or maybe it's because the section speaks so directly to my own interests, but I find his voice rings the loudest through the sardonic bile of the middle section. Billot has a rare ability to focus so intensely on a concept that you see it wriggle and turn inside out, revealing the real humour and ugliness inside. You see this in deadpan gems like '30 Arguments against the Climate Strike' and 'The Prince of Darkness attends a Work and Income Interview'.

> Sloth is no longer acceptable under new directives.
> It may be a revelation to you, Mr Lucifer,
>   but times have changed. I recommend retraining.
> There are always openings for those prepared to upskill.
> HR and marketing are growth areas which may appeal.

Perhaps this feel for the absurd and insane is most perfectly communicated in the epic diatribe written from the point of view of Aussie PM Scotty Morrison. 'How Good Is This?' is a true waltz of madness that will have you laughing and wincing before stopping you dead in your tracks.

> I turn around because it would have been good
> to talk to someone else or get a hug, or just even
> shake someone's hand, but there was no one there:
> just the darkness and the fire.

Billot could have filled the entire collection with this kind of satire and no one would have minded at all. But this collection is nothing if not ambitious, and, even if I found the sudden tonal and subject-matter gearshifts a bit jarring and disassociating at times, ultimately I think *The Sets* is better for it.

The collection, like all things in life, eventually returns to the sea with some quieter reflections and refractions. Although the collection feels a bit too bloated in places, this is the perfect destination. It highlights Billot's willingness to swerve deftly between the universal and the personal in the space of a line, and also his ability to be playful and use inventive language in ways that can be both hyper-visceral and pensive. No surprise, then, to see the likes of Michael Steven and David Eggleton referenced heavily in the acknowledgements.

> In time the strange becomes the expected,
> slumbering in wait to eat you from the inside out.

This ability to experiment helps carry the reader and hold focus, and will keep a wide range of poetry readers interested and engaged. I'm not sure what Billot will do next, but I hope we get more of him standing on the edge of this fucking planet, experimenting, making jokes, making sense, lamenting.

> There is survival, but no love where
> pressure bends life from its mould
> Night is absolute, eternal, cold.

Jordan Hamel

James Brown

James Brown
Selected Poems
Victoria University Press, 2020
RRP $40, 240pp

I've read some 'selected poems' collections of poets who I didn't think necessarily merited them. James Brown is not one of those. I hadn't been exposed to much of Brown's poetry before this book, outside of the odd poem online here and there, so having a pick of his greatest hits from the past 25 or so years is ideal. It provides a great stocktake of Brown's career so far, and it's clear to see why his writing has endured.

> There is too much
> poetry in the world
>
> and yet
> here you are.

The poems span a wide range of issues and ideas, and Brown's trademark dry wit and sharp observation shine through consistently. He seems to thrive when he gets to play — play with the reader, play with the idea of poetry, play with stark subject matter. In an RNZ interview about this collection, Harry Ricketts called Brown's style 'serious play', and I think that sums it up perfectly.

> Isn't it a shame how things don't seem to work out
> like that? Though maybe in some poems they do.
> Oh well, fuck. A bell is a cup, until it is struck.

Brown's fluid and often fractured relationship with his own medium particularly resonated with me. I get suspicious of poets who are too sincere or too enamoured with the form and all its subsequent baggage. The poem 'Good Books' comes to mind as the perfect example of Brown negotiating his praxis with himself, and his own place in it all, writing into the void: 'Poetry doesn't give enough / information. People don't like it / because they don't like absence.' Such reflections amidst the pithy phrases, inversions and diversions kept me interested; at 240 pages staying interested should not be taken for granted.

We spend too much time
doing things for people who don't
give a flying fuck about us.

What is a flying fuck anyway?
Is that line earning its place?
It could probably be cut.

The derision in his voice sets him apart from so many of his contemporaries, and as many older poets become lost to the sands of time I wonder if Brown's words, the 'blunt instruments' he conducts his music with, will keep him safely housed in the national memory. Because that's ultimately what a selected poems collection is; a memory. It's imperfect and subjective, and if someone else was tasked with recreating it, it would undoubtedly look different. But I like blemishes and missteps more than anything airbrushed, and even the quieter moments of this collection find a way to hiss and whine in distinctive fashion. If for some reason you're an ignorant luddite like me and have been avoiding immersing yourself in James Brown's extensive back catalogue, this is the perfect jumping-off point.

Not the best poem you've
ever read, but not the worst
I've ever written.

Emma Barnes

Emma Barnes
I Am in Bed with You
Auckland University Press, 2021
RRP $24.99, 88pp

> It is difficult to say meat over and over . . . we don't like to consider
> ourselves chewed up, swallowed and defecated by some higher-rung
> occupant
> — Emma Barnes, 'Meat'

I ask you, *What makes the xenomorph scary?* You say, *It kills people.* I
say, *Cigarettes kill people.* Perhaps the fault lies within my formulation
of the question. I consider my wording, then reassert — *What makes
the xenomorph horrifying?*

I've watched Ridley Scott's 1979 sci-fi horror opus *Alien* once a year
since age 15. I am, at time of writing, 24. It is often forgotten (and often
pointed out) that in *Alien* the xenomorph has a mere four minutes of
screentime. With this in mind, I have been in direct visual contact with
the xenomorph for a sum-total of 36 minutes. That has been enough to
permanently lodge its visage deep within my psyche and impregnate me
with a recurrent question: What makes this thing so . . . whatever it is?
In this moment I find myself wondering what Emma Barnes's answer to
this question might be.

Much of early psychoanalytical thought fixated on the advent of birth
as the first (and therefore) prototypical trauma. Freud argued that this
trauma came in the form of separation anxiety from the figure of the
mother. Barnes — or perhaps more diplomatically the figure of Barnes

within this collection — is equally fixated upon the trauma of birth, but, rather than feel anxiety towards separation from the mother, Barnes couldn't desire this separation with any greater intensity.

It isn't solely a separation from her own literal mother that Barnes desires, though this is present. Barnes's mother looms over the collection, an explicitly antagonistic force, 'from ten she was a skyscraper, her incredulity made her head wobble', 'my mother was at war with my body'. The desire for separation is also a desire to be separated from the symbolic role of motherhood that comes prescribed to the gender known as woman and from the bodily, physical ramifications of that prescription.

This is what makes the xenomorph horrifying. If we indulge this adjusted thesis that birth is the first trauma not because of separation anxiety but rather because of its radical and total experiential bodily-ness, then this horror becomes crystalline. Birth is a crucible that is non-voluntary and in-optionable, a nexus of trauma that once passed through (ideally) we cannot be made to reproduce. The xenomorph, without consent, takes us and re-inserts us into a reproductive cycle. A sort of chopped-and-screwed, hyper-violent exaggeration of our own. The xenomorph makes us into mothers.

This is a good juncture to explain why I've spent a considerable portion of this review discussing the Freudian particulars of the xenomorph. They are as follows: 1. I love *Alien* and will take every opportunity made available to discuss it, no matter how tenuous the link (027-███████, please call me so I can talk at you), and 2. a third of this collection, which clocks in at a lean 88 pages, chronicles dreams had with Sigourney Weaver. I choose this wording deliberately (in stark contrast to the remainder of this review); these are not dreams within which Sigourney Weaver features, nor are they dreams about Sigourney Weaver. These dreams are an activity undergone *with* Sigourney Weaver . . . and I like to imagine that somehow, however impossibly, that she dreams/dreamt/is dreaming them, too.

During this section I kept arriving at another question: Why Sigourney Weaver? Some answers to this question came quick.

Sigourney Weaver occupies a position within Gens X and Y queer culture as a lesbian matron figure — a mother of sorts. This is due to her resolute and historied support of the queer community, and a certain scene in *Alien* (you know the one) that serves as many queer women's *Oh fuck, I think I might be gay* moment. But this is surface. Why not Jodie Foster? Clarice Starling is as iconic as Ripley, plus Foster is herself a gay woman. Why not Tilda Swinton, who cemented her status as a cultural deity within gay canon for having played Orlando, a proto-transgender figure, in the film adaption of Woolf's novel? Sure, Barnes makes several allusions to Weaver's oeuvre, riffing on her greatest hits, but these could easily be supplanted by evocations of Hannibal Lector or *Panic Room*, I guess.

To dislodge Sigourney Weaver from this collection would dis-align a set of deliberately placed symbols. I think back to the first line of the collection: 'the woman impregnated the man and his body swelled full of tadpoles'. We arrive at 'the Sigourney Weaver scene' and we're discussing 'the delicate vulnerability of your [Weaver's] meat sack . . . they made you all nipples and a suggestion of labial folds'. It isn't erotic; it reads as body-horror.

In the poem that follows, 'Sigourney Weaver and the impregnation', Sigourney Weaver begins pushing Barnes into that motherhood role. Barnes manages to negotiate a de-literalisation of the birth: 'we spend the afternoon creating a blanket fort . . . with a vaginal canal'. This distancing metaphor isn't sufficient. Weaver 'is to laughter what the Wilhelm scream is to screaming'. She's too powerful to be diluted into symbol; Weaver is synonymous, Weaver is fucking monolithic and she wants your meat pregnant. Weaver is the mother 'at war with my body', and she's 'only one year, eleven months and three days younger than my mother', and holy shit this all so fucking brilliant! In retrospect, Weaver is described in ways not dissimilar to a hypothetical literary description of a xenomorph with long, slender limbs and sharp shoulders.

In the end, the dalliance with Weaver comes to a close, but there's no showdown, Weaver does not shed her skin, revealing herself to be the xenomorph Queen. There's no repurposed mechanical apparatus, no 'Get away from her, you bitch!' Just the shifting of an inarticulatable something and a post-relationship correspondence via email. It's beautiful and human and small.

There's much else I want to speak to, but I do not have the space. I wanted to talk categorical violation and misogyny in the genre of body-horror. I wanted to tie that back to the figure of the mother. Get more of Geiger's artwork in there. I wanted to reference Cronenberg's *The Brood*. I haven't touched the final third of the collection and its compelling depiction of the love of, and subsummation into, another's body as the transcendental sublime, an escape from gender and organ and the point at which that method of escape collapses. I was unable to return to birth trauma and discuss Wilfred Bion's theory of un-thought thoughts and sense impressions and how this speaks to the fragmented lexicon through which Barnes addresses her body.

I loved this collection and thought that penning an enthusiastic (if ill-conceived) half-essay proved that best. Go read it and think things for yourself!

A half-thought was called to mind as I read 'Good Girl, Good Girl', the collection's final moment. We've all looked at our bodies and been horrified, we've all looked in a bathroom mirror somewhere in space and time and thought: What is this thing? This thing is Alien.

Sam Duckor-Jones

Sam Duckor-Jones
Party Legend
Victoria University Press, 2021
RRP $25, 96pp

> Pay no attention to the man behind the curtain . . .
> Just kidding! please pay me lots of attention!
> — Sam Duckor-Jones, 'HI!'

It is an edict that has slithered its way into idiom that one should not, or rather cannot, judge a book by its cover. It has become equally common in our fuck-the-rules era of po-mo subversion to hyper-consciously pull a middle-finger and wave it in the face of this edict. I will here attempt a synthesis. I do not mean to subvert, conform or reduce, but I happen to think the cover of Sam Duckor-Jones' *Party Legend* is the first of many sublimely perfect moments in its salience.

Like much of *Party Legend*, the cover image is confidently Socratic, which I have determined to be the very soul of flirtation itself. It's a 'wouldn't you like to know?' And an 'I have the answer, but you'll have to find some way to slip it from under my tongue.' Who are these figures? They are Aryan, statuesque, possessing jawlines that I could only dream of. Are they friends? Are they lovers? Have they ever been?

They complete each other's features, lips, noses (genitals?). The face of one is partially obscured while we see the other only in profile. What are they hiding? Do they have scars? One chews a toothpick. Has he picked up this habit recently? We only see them throat-up; are they naked from there down? The eye of the left is the same tone as the skin of the right. Are they the same person? Some sort of super-ego and an id eyeing you up from across the dancefloor? Are they looking for a third?

Party Legend possesses a bold multiplicity of narrative threads, and, like the narrator, it defies categorisation along the lines of any axis. It does not want to be pinpointed along intersections of sexuality, politics, hobbies, philosophies, clothing, where it exists in time and space, what it's up to later, religion, etc. But it is also embarking on a wholly sincere (if slightly cheeky) quest to be understood. The opener (the titular 'Party Legend') is a sprawling eight-page thesis statement that takes the form of a campaign speech that builds on itself, slowly interspersing heritages, Judaism, historical narratives, allies, leanings and receipts. 'I may appear to you now as a velveteen seal pup w an enormous bank account / . . . Rebellion is in my blood!'

It has a joyously provocative sense of theatricality, absurdity and humour to it. 'Sweet constituents I love you like you were one of my own very numerous & successful racehorses.' I imagine it is a rally or a sermon that I'd adore seeing conducted in the flesh!

It's such an astoundingly entertaining and arresting opener that the formalistic decision to begin with the title drop almost slips you. It is a confident decision, a confidence reflected in the writing as well as the structure. *Party Legend* (the collection, not the poem) is separated into sounders that are delineated via an epigraph. These epigraphs range from deliberate misquotations of Charles Darwin to Dorian Corey from the Jennie Livingston documentary *Paris is Burning*.

I must confess that I didn't immediately recognise all of them prior to scanning the notes provided at the collection's conclusion (I am less familiar with the writings of Darwin than I am with *Priscilla, Queen of the Desert*), but every time I did recognise an epigraph, I felt as if I were being personally flirted with. It is a collection so brimming with electricity that the hum of its field calls upon influences from all avenues, so much so that the aforementioned notes section in its staccato eclecticism reads as a poem unto itself, wholly consistent with the Jewish esotericism and pop-culture celebratory queerness of the preceding collection.

Like all good art it is fundamentally loaded with, and acutely aware of, contradiction and the tension that arises from contradiction. But rather than concern itself primarily with the reconciliation or the making flat of these contradictions, the Sam Duckor-Jones of *Party Legend* is comfortably uncomfortable within the tension that arises from contradiction. It is embodied within the text as the sort of tension that might be embodied during the chatting-up of a stranger at a bar who you're looking to un-stranger (and in the process make yourselves both more strange!). It is the tension in the moment that you know sex is on the table, but you don't know the combination of words to get them into that room. You simply know that the combination of words is out there.

It is a possibility that you can de-mystify, an abstraction that you can make into a body, a tension and a contradiction that you can make into a mutual pleasure. Where another writer might obsess over the frustration, scrutinising academically the inconsistencies that occur within the holistic process of self-assemblage, Sam Duckor-Jones, with gay abandon, simply dances the fucking night away!

I do not want to be accused of, nor do I want Sam thinking that I am, diminishing this astounding collection to its most outwardly salacious and sexual elements. I want it to be understood that despite this review looking like a rather *jejeune* affair, I simply was not able to address everything. I have failed (a joyous act!), and rather than tying myself into knots (which may be fun under different circumstances) in an attempt to cover every literary and biblical allusion and pursue every reference, every evocation, I have instead elected to respond to the text in my best approximation of the spirit of the work. In summary, this is a lush, eccentric, playful and thoughtful collection, the very first line of which is a call for votes, so with that in mind . . . Vote for Sam!

Harry Ricketts

Selected Poems
Harry Ricketts

Harry Ricketts
Selected Poems
Victoria University Press, 2021
RRP $40, 224pp

As I began to read this collection I was worried that I didn't know enough about Harry Ricketts to be able to appreciate the poems fully, to understand some of the veiled references about events in his life. I need not have worried; the subtleties and the humour soon grew on me and I became comfortable. Keen to know more. Like making a new friend and gradually learning their stories over cups of coffee and drawn-out dinners.

Ricketts says his interest in poetry was fired by a poetry-writing weekend in the late-1970s run by Gavin Ewart (whom he terms a mostly forgotten English poet). One of Ewart's books was banned by the British booksellers W. H. Smith, the equivalent of being slapped on the wrist by Whitcoulls. On the first day Ewart had them write haiku, limericks and one-line poems. A man stormed out, saying that wasn't poetry, but it was a revelation for Ricketts, and the first poem in this collection is the one he submitted to the course for consideration. Of all those reproduced in this book it remains the most experimental in terms of white spacing and spread across the page.

Almost all the verse in *Selected Poems* has a tight fit to the left-hand margin. The form is conventional, but the words and sentiments are not. There is joy and humour suffused throughout — although not entirely, as eight lines titled 'Nice' show:

Why do you always have to be
so damn tolerant,

so bloody accepting?
It's not natural.

If you'd only shout, throw
a wobbly once in a while.
But, oh no, you're so fucking nice
it makes everyone sick.

As we age we turn more to our earlier stories, and with Ricketts these are memories of early university days in Oxford and teaching in Leicester. One of the things that I love most about this selection is his ability to take a common situation and turn it into a journey through history. Although all poets would probably call themselves lovers of words and books, I don't recall seeing many poems that look so deeply into the world of books themselves. 'Arty Bees: quality pre-loved books, bought, sold and exchanged' begins with a pre-loved book from the famous Wellington book emporium of the poem's title. The book plate tells us that it was third prize for attendance. Ricketts starts to speculate: what were the first and second prizes, why is a certain page missing, and what was the meaning of the scribbles across the illustrations?

A similar treatment happens in 'Wendy Cope in Newtown, Sydney', where the book in question is *Making Cocoa for Kingsley Amis* and contains a handwritten dedication from Hugh to Egg and a cryptic reference to page 42. On this page the poet vows to write poems that will win the heart. Ricketts's humour takes over, and he wonders if it was Egg who sold the book; whether Hugh failed to write the promised poems or whether they were simply not very good? Or did she find that Hugh was two-timing her with Audrey, that quiet girl from Summerhill? In true scholarly style Ricketts goes on to quote another line from Wendy Cope: 'There are so many kinds of awful men.'

Ricketts also indulges us in some ekphrastic writing, journeying through some works of art. His choice in 'The unmade bed' is obscure enough that many may not know the nineteenth-century painting of a young woman to which he is referring; we must rely on his words as the complete guide to what is on the canvas. I love the way he plays with old and modern, wondering if the thing in her hand is an iPod or iPhone, what she would be listening to as she emerged from beneath the blue floral bedspread. He picks up on items in the room, including the kissing couple in a painting on the wall, which he thinks may mirror her own situation. The notes at the back of the book give us the artist, and now I have seen the painting I can combine words and pictures. It is a wonderfully detailed painting, in which so many small objects are scattered through the room, that it is easy to spend time considering them all, why they were there, and what they symbolise.

In my journey through *Selected Poems* I became particularly caught up by a title that flows through the multiple volumes collected here. 'Your Secret Life' begins in 1989, and is addressed to Ricketts's daughter Jessie, coming home late from a party. In 2001, 'Your Secret Life 2' shifts to the telephone, and the opposite ends of the Earth. In 2015, 'Your Secret Life 4' is much more sombre in tone, calling on the lost years, overcome by tears. All the difficulties of childhood changing to adulthood, parenthood and fatherhood, especially from a distance, are chokingly caught in these brief lines. Number 3 did not make it to the collection, so I tracked down copies of the volumes from 2005 and 2012 to ensure that it existed and also find out what happened.

One of my absolute favourites in this collection rejoices in the splendid title 'Thirteen Ways of Starting a New Zealand Novel called Macrocarpa'. It is a joy of observation, humour and hidden scholarship. We see the keen eye of the scholar lurking beneath the mockery. I love the playfulness and spot-on observation. After a prose introduction from a genuine book about the trees of North America, we are equipped with numerous facts and figures about the Monterey Cypress (*Cupressus macrocarpa*); exact height from 20 to 78 feet, dark-brown to light grey bark and woody cones. Equipped with this raw material, Ricketts then lists 13 potential novels in various genres. I have cherry-picked six of my favourites:

3. That March when Wayne returned to the old homestead, he remarked for the first time the way the young macrocarpa cast its narrow, pyramidal shadow across the rotting pink hydrangeas.

4. Wally the Giant Weta was born in a pile of woody cones beside the 78-foot-tall macrocarpa.

6. Hidden in the stout branches of the macrocarpa, buffeted by high winds, sat Cheryl, the rabbiter's seventh daughter, biting her knuckles.

8. 'Macrocarpa, Monterey Cypress, *Cupressus Macrocarpa*,' mused Inspector Motz that afternoon, recalling Prof Brockman's lectures on arboreal forensics, 'but how to explain the glandular pits in the foliage and could these be connected in any way with the Vegemite stains on Cheryl Alabaster's prize-winning budgie?'

10. 'Women!' spat Bill, kicking vehemently at the pile of woody cones; 'at least you know where you are with a macrocarpa.'

12. 'O marcocarpa!' exclaimed Wayne, beating his forehead against the ridged bark, 'What am I going to do about Cheryl?'

Number 13 starts at the bottom of a page, lulling you into the expectation that it will be short like all the others, but when you turn the page you discover that it stretches out for a full half-page more of further madness.

Delve deeply, the gems are tight packed and well hidden. The poet is lurking among the pages. This is called 'Luggage':

Forty-something, you know
the goods are likely
to be damaged; that's just

how it is. So this battered
suitcase turning up in lost property
with its faded patchwork

of labels from around the world
should come as no surprise.
The lock's rusty; the key sticks.

How much you want to know what's
inside is entirely up to you.

Helen Jacobs / Peter Bland / Elizabeth Brooke-Carr

Helen Jacobs
A Habit of Writing
The Cuba Press, 2020
RRP $25, 58pp

Peter Bland
nowhere is too far off
The Cuba Press
RRP $25, 60pp

Elizabeth Brooke-Carr
Wanting to tell you everything
Caselberg Press
RRP $25, 66pp

I approached these three collections separately, but soon found them linked by a thread of age — age approached in different ways and taking varied tracks, reflections on life lived at different speeds, looking forwards as well as backwards.

Helen Jacobs is 91 and lives quietly, we gather from her poems, in a retirement village. *A Habit of Writing* is her eighth collection. Peter Bland is 87 and has published 22 previous collections of poems, four more for children, and a memoir before arriving at *nowhere is too far off*. Elizabeth Brooke-Carr was 79 when she died, and her friends and writing colleagues subsequently helped to complete her first collection, *Wanting to tell you everything*.

Worlds can be very small and also very broad. I am thinking in particular of Helen Jacobs' active life in a retirement village, where even a prescribed 45-minute walk can lead to a verse 'With the right shoes, flexible and cushioned'. There is plenty of humour in her lines, such as in the entirety of 'Jigsaw junkies':

Jigsaw junkies
eyesight intact
commune quietly
in the library.

The second half of her collection is called 'Pātea: the river series', eight short poems that beautifully recall a childhood there; the river and the railway that divide the town, the fishing trips and gathering driftwood. These are perfectly crafted memories.

Peter Bland's poems take us to London and Nevada and the Marilyn Monroe Deli outside Palm City, not to mention allowing us to travel through time to encounter him as a boy in wartime looking down at a dead airman on Scarborough beach. Peter may have been physically slowed by a stroke two years ago, but his mind continues to travel widely. The palpable sense of the loss of his wife, Beryl, is a constant emotional thread. Not only are there poems dedicated to her directly, but others also echo the empty space in his life. One fine example is the second verse from 'I dream of setting up my tent':

I dream of setting up my tent
close to the heart
of the Caliph's garden. It's
there I'll unroll
my lifelong carpet
among the nightingales and roses.

I'll arrive alone
in the cool of the evening
with the stars like split grain
in the desert sky,
and my love will be there
waiting to greet me,
with perfumed hair, wild honey and wine.

With Elizabeth Brooke-Carr you know you are dealing with someone
prepared to speak her mind. In 'Buzz Cut' we hear the horrors of having
your head shaved, and the platitudes that follow. She is having none of it:

Oh people say it suits me —
Some even dare to say it's stylish.
Bollocks!
I'm bald.
My head is full of sound and fury.

Elizabeth was preparing for a journey, and starts it with us, in a
poignant piece called 'On discovering your oncologist is a travel agent'.
Here are the first and last lines:

There is a choice, he says. The shorter route, without add-ons,
the 'no frills', no-treatment way would be faster, more direct.

One thing is certain. There's no going
back. That's not an option. Your name is on the passenger list.
You must pack your own bags and choose which way you will go.

Ruth France / Robert McLean

Ruth France
No Traveller Returns
Cold Hub Press, 2020
RRP $27.50, 102pp

Robert McLean
Enduring Love
Cold Hub Press, 2020
RRP $40, 221pp

By the time she died in 1968, Ruth France, who
published her poetry under the pseudonym of Paul Henderson, had
published two novels and two collections of poetry. She also left the
manuscript of a third collection, some of which makes it into print
here for the first time. *No Traveller Returns* gives us a fascinating and
tantalising look into a short life that seems shrouded in unknowns; not
so much mystery as privacy.

One of the few biographical details we have is that this Christchurch
poet lived on a boat in Lyttelton harbour, each day rowing her husband
ashore so he could get to work, and then again to take her son to
kindergarten. The sea and sailing are unsurprisingly prominent in some
of her verse, and she achieves a closeness which those firmly rooted
to the land would never achieve. A good example is 'The Ghost Ships',
which begins with these four lines:

Shatters the wind the cool glass of the ocean;
Smoothness ruffles, darkens, and the wind takes swiftly the water,

Tumbling the short seas into a soft sounding crashing:
Sheared, the wave turns back from the bow smooth-folded.

The fourth line brings to mind a farmer ploughing a field.

France also had a strong affinity for the land, the landscape of the South Island, the mountains and the high tussock, as well as the coasts and rivers. She is a poet grounded in her landscapes. In 'The Young Legend' the poet laments the difficulties of rural romance:

How do you make the untender passages
Of this island story coincide with the nightingale?

There was no smooth; there was shingle
On a clay road slicing the King Country;
Scrub; . . .
            And wherever I go
In this country the same deep hale

Hills elbowing in. It is crude
For love-making. Depends on petrol and
How many miles to the gallon and the mail

Left in a tin box two miles further on;

These two short quotes show that France was a lover of the semi-colon. Once noticed, I couldn't un-notice and started to count. There are nine in *Elegy* and 18 in the three pages of 'The Haunting Place', often in pairs, sharing the same sentence. One or two lines have three. In the final poem in the book I found the all-time record of five semi-colons in one sentence. It is worth a quote, to see it done:

A day of miracle? Scarcely; or even of more wonder
That would turn my eyes to the coolness of the garden
Where no strange bush, bell or bright blue gentian should surprise
On such a day; but does not; nothing new will appear there

> One may be certain; only the clear light of known leaves
> And awareness; of what?

Only that heavy lean on the semi-colon dates the poetry to a more distant time, the earliest being written over 65 years ago, but the poems nevertheless still feel fresh and relevant today.

In his fine introduction, editor Robert McLean calls France 'a thinker in verse, an animator of ideas'. He laments that of the five women poets published by the Caxton Press, her stock seems to have fallen the furthest. Three of her poems were in the *Penguin Book of New Zealand Verse* (1960; edited by Allen Curnow), and only four in the 1970 *Oxford Anthology of Twentieth Century New Zealand Poetry* (edited by Vincent O'Sullivan). She goes unrepresented elsewhere; I hope this slim volume will help to set the record straight. McLean thinks her obscurity may in part be due to her privacy, yet he also notes the vigour of her poetry and her habit of writing letters to the editor. A trip into the *Dictionary of New Zealand Biography* tells a little more, and reveals that she wrote many letters to *The Press* in Christchurch, and had poetry published in *Landfall* and the *New Zealand Poetry Yearbook*, as well as reviewing for the *Listener* and writing short stories.

The final poems, never before collected together, have a different feel, and seem more sombre, melancholy, from a darker time. This verse from the title piece of *No Traveller Returns* sets the tone:

> No traveller returns to find
> The scene of previous love is as tender
> Or as constant as he might have imagined.
> The leaves are faded now, and sunlight
> Enters the house with an effort.
> The sense of time beginning, of spring's clear air, is lost.

Robert McLean published his own collected poems with Cold Hub Press. You know that you are reading someone with a great deal more erudition than you have when the second line of the first poem sends you reaching for the dictionary: 'an orectic pause' forces me to stumble, and the dictionary gives me a one-word definition 'apperitive' ('having the quality of destiny'), so at last I'm on track again.

I feel the weight, the heft of scholarship behind the poems here, and sometimes I get what is going on, but sometimes it is far beyond me. One encounters Latin, French, Italian and German. McLean sums it up well himself in the poem 'The Second Life', when he says 'My mindfulness is wordy.'

In 2020, at the WORD Festival in Christchurch, both Bill Manhire and Vincent O'Sullivan made the same point, in separate talks: that audiences don't like it when poets use an 'I' that is someone other than themselves. I can't help but have this feeling here. For there are so many 'I's in this collection that we are never sure when and if the poet is speaking his own feelings. Both Boadicea and Napoleon are voiced as 'I'. In 'Alberti's Complaint' we are given the clue that this is Rimini in 1454, but even so are forced into Google to put some context around who is here and what is happening. Such forays distract from the verse.

The final section is composed of 32 previously unpublished pieces collected under the title 'Postcards from Atlantis', including some longer pieces. One of these, 'A Fantasia in the Voice of D'Arcy Cresswell', I enjoyed for its numerous levels. McLean uses numbered sonnets in the same way that Cresswell did in *The Poet's Progress* to outline snippets of his life in London. McLean's 15 sonnets cleverly reuse the last line of each in the first line of the next, and then end with a final verse made entirely of those repeated lines. Does that form have a name? I don't doubt that there are many hidden references within the verses, things beyond my limited knowledge of Cresswell.

I prefer McLean talking as himself — or at least I think he is. The poem 'Goldfinch and Hawk' stood out for me as a simpler, and more satisfying, monologue. Whether it is linked to anything from the Spanish baroque or from classical myth would be impossible to tell from these lines. On their own, I particularly admire their vivid imagery:

A long time before I am awake,
I begin to smell blood and rafters
burning, see the sky where the roof was,
bodies, and scattered parts of bodies.

Then comes the day. Goats at their tethers,
cool water in the well, swollen sun
heavy with heat, radios blaring,
children playing, garlic in the pan.

My wife — suave, dark-eyed, petulant —
loves me past conjecture. I flaunt her.
Lust makes us shiver. Life is a guest
Whom we entertain then bid farewell.

So there are signs — but warnings, never.
I know better than to expect them.
A hawk rises, crests, and dips its wing.
Black olives swell on silver branches.

Enjoyable, close, visceral, without the need for other players. Yet, does the
poet speak the 'I' as himself, or is there still another layer between us?

Bryan Walpert

Bryan Walpert
Brass Band to Follow
Otago University Press, 2021
RRP $27.50, 86pp

'Exhausted by all the rancor?' wrote a subeditor for the
online site *Arts and Letters Daily* in August 2021. 'Try poetry. It restores
the value of words in a culture intent on cheapening them . . .' That was
their clickbait to get readers to the beautiful reflection in *The New York
Times* by Tish Harrison Warren, 'Why Poetry is So Crucial Right Now'.

Although the poems in Bryan Walpert's new collection were drafted
before the onset of Covid anxiety in 2020, their tenor makes them very
well suited to the kind of calm, slow-mo reading and rereading that
lockdown affords. By the time you read this in print, early in 2022, I
hope we can all go to our local indie bookstores and buy poetry, literally,
by the hand. I'd suggest that Walpert's book would be an excellent
purchase. Buy it. Read it. Savour it.

In *Waiting for Godot*, 'crritic' [sic] is the worst epithet Vladimir and
Estragon can think of to hurl at each other when they argue, a joke
against critics that Beckett invented for his English version of the play.
Bryan Walpert is a good critic, and an award-winning tertiary teacher
to boot. He has published books of stories and a prize-winning novella,
as well as poetry. He is a multitasking writer, skilfully and humanely
engaging in a wide range of discourses. This brace of skills plays across
his new collection. That might be kind of deadly for readers if the
footnote approach lay too awkwardly on the page. Rest assured that
Walpert weaves his book together with panache.

There are three sections; the first, 'Prompted', and the third,
'Brass Band to Follow', have 11 poems each. These brace the longer
central section, 'Only Thine Eyes', with 18 poems. There may be some

numerological resonance to these numbers (11-18-11), or it may just be that the central section felt right at being nearly, but not quite twice, as long as each of the other two. Numerology might seem like a wacky thought, but this middle section is deeply soaked in the seventeenth-century rhetoric of science, from the writings of Robert Hooke, a crucial innovator in modern science based on observing the world intently (in his case through the double-lens microscope he invented); and also of seventeenth-century lyric poetry.

'Only Thine Eyes' draws also on one of the most beautiful of all Ben Jonson's poems, 'drink to me only with thine eyes'. This is a period where 'modern' ideas about science and being present in this real world of ours jostle with beliefs in astrology, the literal truth of the Bible, and the notion that numbers in sequence code our destinies.

The idea of channelling Robert Hooke's commitment to the real dominates this collection. Walpert is not directly conducting science experiments, but rather looking intently at the world with the precision of a scientist. He makes the dailiness of his life vivid to us. The collection ends with the title poem, 'Brass Band to Follow', where we find the poet at a Christmas parade, with very local stylings:

> . . . the Girl Guides,
> in their pink singlets, war veterans,
> the sun burnishing the fire engine
> as it rolls past . . .

The poet's son is on the last float, and then beyond, will come, by convention, the brass band of the title. We crane forward with the poet to see and hear the band, which the poem does not quite get to. The poem ends the collection with that in prospect: 'for what / has been written to come, to pass'. Echoing behind this we can hear Shakespeare's Antonio in *The Tempest* ('what's past is prologue, what to come / Is yours and my discharge'), and Yeats's golden bird, who sings to the court of Byzantium 'Of what is past, or passing, or to come.'

The longer poems here derive, I guess, from the mode of the

conversation poem invented by Wordsworth and Coleridge, where the poet does not commune with a spectral muse but rather talks directly to us. The cadence is then made from the light/heavy combination of stress patterns in iambic verse. Usually Walpert does not stretch to the full pentameter, often using eight syllables instead of 10. This is enough, though, to get the voice talking us through the experiences being evoked.

Walpert has an acute ear for when a shorter line or stanza will keep the energy going. For variation he will then break this up further, drawing on the haiku-like demeanour of hard-core imagism, such as the second part of 'Two Mornings':

> since you
>
> light's edges
> till the air
>
> your shadow
>
> flowers
> an exhale
>
> gathers rain
> the sunrise
>
> petals on the floor

A poet walks in the world, and brings that to us on the page. A poet then also walks daily through the world of words, constantly straddling the two realms for us. Walpert makes this look easy, but these beautiful poems have been 20 years in the making. His lines, as Hamlet requires, 'beget a smoothness' that invite repeated readings, grasping how much has been so adroitly, and so pleasingly, packed in.

Elizabeth Kirkby-McLeod

Kay McKenzie Cooke / Mary Cresswell / Jane Simpson

Kay McKenzie Cooke
Upturned
The Cuba Press, 2020
RRP $25, 98pp

Mary Cresswell
Body Politic
The Cuba Press, 2020
RRP $25, 68pp

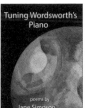

Jane Simpson
Tuning Wordsworth's Piano
Interactive Publications, 2019
RRP $29, 60pp

In *Upturned*, Kay McKenzie Cooke is always listening and watching. As she records what she hears and sees, we read juxtapositions of natural and human-made sounds and images.

McKenzie Cooke puts these natural and human-made images and sounds side-by-side, even as her subject and location changes. Some poems are firmly set in the New Zealand landscape, others in an alienating Berlin, others in memories and details of times and people she has lost. But throughout she is noticing how we rub up against creation; how we are ourselves created. It is signalled right there on the cover: a girl among the vines seems natural enough, yet she's painted yellow, pink and green — so clearly also created. It is there again most evocatively in 'Turn of events':

> We've passed so many frightened trees today providing shelter
> For woodpiles, standing in shock, up to their knees
> In chopped blocks of wood. Is that lest trees forget their eventual fate?

The standing trees are sheltering broken trees which have undergone a metamorphosis under human hands. Both the trees and the firewood are utilitarian in this image, one providing shelter, the other soon to provide warmth. Is that what they are to remember: their fate is to be useful to humanity? Is that all nature is to us?

Although not political poetry, by drawing our eye and ear again and again to the way we exist within the world, adding to and subtracting from its beauty, energy and noise, McKenzie Cooke's poetry connects us with the world we inhabit. There is a reason we want the sounds of rivers, waterfalls and bird song to ease us into our sleep, even as we are separated from nature and need the technology of sleep apps and earbuds to deliver it.

Mary Cresswell's *Body Politic* is in your face. She is angry and twinged with hopelessness, calling out the actions of the plutocracy, as in the poem 'Comfort Zone':

> We thought we could fix things — our plan was robust:
> progress comes first, cleanup comes after,
> we thought for sure we had it all sussed.
> But who believed that? Surely not us!

Technology — and today's plutocracy is found in the tech sector — such as drones and satellites, have an ominous presence. 'We move at speeds sharper than vision', a line from 'Holding patterns', seems to encompass her polemic: we can't see, or we refuse to see, what we are rushing ourselves and our planet towards. 'Contrary to opinion, we're none of us gods. / This is proved by what we intend for the world' ends the poem 'Remapping'.

Cresswell is able to get away with this polemic without it feeling didactic because her poetry skills are so strong. Shipwrecks are a reoccurring metaphor, an example for the Earth's fate. Humanity stands as both the wreakers and the stranded survivors. She takes children's fables like the Pied Piper and Little Red Riding Hood and subverts them, using satire to startle. She has a strong sense of rhythm and rhyme, of the sound of words playing on each other.

In the three distinct sections of Jane Simpson's new collection, *Tuning Wordsworth's Piano*, we see these ideas occurring again through three different interests of the poet. In the unnamed first section, Simpson's focus is on the natural world found in the context of a city, on the way humanity constrains nature for our own pleasure. We go to parks to admire 'unspoilt nature', but it is 'nature writ too small; / nature at our feet; / nodding daffodils saying "Yes"' ('Tuning Wordsworth's piano'); it is a lone rewarewa tree not in a forest but 'sold in a black planter bag' ('Rewarewa').

Where the true wilds might be takes our human effort to explore, and Simpson does this in part two, 'The patina of summers'. Recording a cycling journey through the Catlins, she develops a mental map we can use as an organising structure. She is searching for Hone Tuwhare's crib at Kaka Point, a place so isolated she gets lost on the way. When she finds it, she points out how only nature seems to have loved this unmarked crib, which has been left to the wind to 'blow kisses over weatherboards' and storms to 'leave love bites' ('Unmarked crib'). Yet, in 'The language of forests', we see that even here humans have reached in to change the landscape:

> the land is a woman
> > abused, stripped of her forests

all to make farms, perennial
>   ryegrass from valley to ridge.

In the unnamed third part Simpson returns to the city, where she engages with the cultural and spiritual, with other artworks and other poets, and with the great themes of life and death and love.

American environmental lawyer and advocate Gus Speth once said: 'I used to think the top environmental problems were biodiversity loss, ecosystem collapse and climate change . . . but I was wrong. The top environmental problems are selfishness, greed and apathy . . .' He goes on to say that to deal with these problems we need 'a spiritual and cultural transformation', and he calls on poets, among others, to bring this about. In different ways these three poets have responded to that call, asking us to re-examine our actions and identity beside, and within, the rest of creation.

Michele Amas

Michele Amas
Walking Home
Victoria University Press, 2020
RRP $25, 80pp

To begin at the end, in the titular poem that walks Amas toward her death: 'Let me borrow ideas from strangers / until I grow into my own'.

Michele Amas was an actor arguably long before she became a poet, but throughout this collection it's hard to find a clear division between the two, or between any of the roles she's taken on — and mastered — over a rich and many-faceted life. She *inhabits*. Her poetry, gathered here by her husband after her death, has a clarity and a documentary tone that cuts through artifice. She writes about motherhood, about travel and love and Brownies and conversations over the fence:

> I let her know we are
> hosting a teenage party
> there will be noise,
> she thinks I am inviting her
> hopes she can make it

Most of all, though, Amas writes for herself, leading her own way through the days and years. She vividly pictures the relationships that shape her life — beautifully, her daughter's: 'You hurt me / like a novice / I have thirty years on you.' She reaches out, embracing the messy connections that weave together to form the fabric of middle age. In the midst of the village of loved ones and passers-by, she also stands out as herself: 'Hold your own hand,' she says; 'Not the idea of it / or the theory of it', but the concrete identity that is revealed in ongoing struggle and strength.

She speaks boldly and directly, a woman who really doesn't have the time for things like Wellington's town planning ('still not finished . . . and the measurements / for the width of the streets / are a grievous error'), or being apart from loved ones ('The rooms become a burden so I live in one'), or the weather ('it's this wind making me crazy / I cannot think straight with tangled hair').

> A sparrow at the plastic station table
> possibly a relation
> misses a bit
> a huge crumb, dumb I think
> I want to point it out
> but who am I to judge
> I don't speak sparrow

Amas's words are powerfully sensuous, at times disconcerting, often funny. Then again, they often catch and pull at threads in ways that feel impossibly private — there are moments so precise it seems beyond intimate to witness them, like wandering into a room where pain or joy or worry is blossoming and bursting and burning up.

> The darkness she walks in
> is the darkness at your throat,
> your arm slides along the wall
> tipping paintings, sweeping, frantic
> to find the switch.

These poems circle around to a sense of utter completeness, not because they tackle anything more than usually profound — life and death have been done before — but because every word feels fully embodied, fully lived. A collection to be grown into and reread.

Elisabeth Kumar

Johanna Emeney

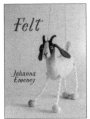

Johanna Emeney
Felt
Massey University Press, 2021
RRP $24.99, 80pp

For much of time, emotion and sensation have been
more or less the same thing. Passions and affections have worked
themselves out in bodies, bumped into each other and put small dings
in the world, poked holes through the walls that try to screen mind from
what's outside. In this collection, a satisfying fingerbreadth of poems,
Johanna Emeney explores the 'felt realm', bringing every sense she can
muster to the task of pointing at things that move worlds.

> Often when I tell strangers at parties/
> co-workers/contractors that I have pet goats
> they joke *Goats are delicious ha ha ha*
> *I once had this amazing curry*
> *in Hyderabad/from the Jamie Oliver Cookbook*
> and I try to emote amusement
> when what I'd like to do is dispatch them
>
> immediately to the paddock
> with armfuls of willow . . .

Jo Emeney is a chronicler of delight. She is also a teacher, practised at
persuading the ambivalent to fall in love with language and to look at
what's underneath. She is fearless and outspoken, without being quick
to conclusions: a born listener with a big mouth. She can make C. K.
Stead purr and Kim Hill sit quietly.

It's easy to tell — yes, to feel — that Emeney adores words, ordinary ones and decorative ones, adores young people and old people and, of course, especially goats. Her poetry feelers seek out moments from every day, the ones that you might blink and miss, and the ones that move a lever that will wrench somebody's history in an uncharted direction. These are the words of someone running her fingers over the fabric of lives, hers and others', finding the textures, pulling at threads. The world under her fingertips is solid, but still alive with uncertainty and possibility. The moments that aren't her own she witnesses tenderly, touches gently.

> Now, I've taken responsibility
> for many things in my life,
> but they were far smaller,
> like a forbidden water fight;
> a till, while the shopkeeper
> took a short break;
>
> a dog that skated on a frozen lake
> when I let him off-leash . . .
> but I have never held myself to blame
> for medicine's hit-and-miss treatments

It's that honesty that means this collection can hold an array of moments, some fizzy and delicious, others that stop and buckle where they stand. Each piece is courageous and watchful, grounded in the body and taking everything in. 'I would love a face that doesn't give itself away too easily,' says Emeney. Unfortunate, because these poems speak from a countenance that is generous and good.

Elizabeth Morton

Kate Camp

Kate Camp
How to Be Happy Though Human: New and Selected Poems
Victoria University Press, 2020
RRP $30, 176pp

'Man acts as though he were the shaper and master of language, while in fact language remains the master of man.' Such were the words of Heidegger, that talismanic but ideologically unsavoury phenomenologist. Kate Camp's *How to Be Happy Though Human* is a slave to the vocabularies and syntax of a world rich and writhing in its terrestrial meat. Camp is a phenomenologist of more wholesome ilk. This is her seventh collection, even though it is something more of an olio of heyday ballads and fresh tunes — the sort of mid-career rocker stage-show, where ciggy lighters and sing-alongs meet a Mexican-wave of hush.

Camp's new tracks are explorations of the body, as it exists in time. A prefatory quote by Polish poet and Nobel Prize winner Szymborska sets a theme of sorts: '. . . the body is and is / and has nowhere to go'. The slings and arrows of bodily afflictions, and the fragilies of the human mind, are a bathos in the face of survival's earnest trying. In 'Panic Button', Camp says: 'So many things can go wrong / inside a human life, it's almost comical'. Time's one-way trudge is spangled from the sidelines with 'glistening spheres of rain / on the renga renga, the pink twigs of the eucalypt', but the lament is clear — 'I can't do a damn thing about time'.

The world is not enough. 'There's only one of everything / one moon, one sun, one dad, one mum'. The manual of *How to Be Happy Though Human* is emptied of its confidence, and usurped by a question: Can we be happy, though human? Are the gulls, the fishing boats, the streetlights and the assembly halls enough to right a world of brute dissonance and existential doom? In the titular poem, 'How to be happy though human', Camp shows us the antinomy at the centre of things:

Before that we had been at the film
where three people taxidermied a baby zebra
caught in the moment of standing
for the first time

'Memory is a kind of mourning', the same poem reads. The conjuring of
nouns wet with scent and surface, which Camp does so well, is more an
ungraving of dead things, an anatomy museum of percepts already lost.
'Catalogue' holds those moments in formaldehyde:

The sour smell of towels, flannels
left hanging over shower glass.
Mattresses in too-small rooms.
Chicken blood rotting in the rubbish drawer.

The past is a reverb; it moves through us, abducts our body as a
medium. To be human is to be hostage — 'they might just be trapped /
inside the body of their lives'. How do we be happy, when gagged and
hogtied to our meats, saddled to the bollards of language's limits? The
answer is not obvious, but the Leibniz-type mantra is repeated:

We are fortunate to live in a world.
We are fortunate to live in a world . . .

The new poems stop. We are shunted back, to Camp's very first
collection, *Unfamiliar Legends of the Stars*, penned in the late nineties
— a world still ripe with Tupperware and cigarette machines, and told
by a young, laconic and attitude-heavy Camp. The philosophical edge is
there, 'the dead pay visits', but there is less ceremony in nostalgia, the
verse is deckle-edged.

There is a youthful angst, amongst the levity — premeditated ennui.
Camp opines the hazards of having a large heart, and, in some sort of
appeal to jump-start that dodgy pump, says 'it will take more than dawn /
to wake me up'. There is a sense of helplessness — 'I have nothing to

teach, just utensils' and, ultimately, 'no one is coming to rescue me'.

The sections that follow are a gift. Camp's vasculature of observation, language-play and thought experiment pushes sentiment from the centre, outwards. The gleanings are, at once, more temporal and terrene, but hold a more sophisticated metaphysics. 'I have always taken important things / extremely seriously' says one poem. In these sections, humour is not gratuitous, more an emulsifier of brute insights. In 'Admit one', from *Realia*, Camp moves from jocular simile to axiom:

> Cranes like cranes above the city.
> The city is a poem that says
>
> no matter what boat you take
> you cannot find
>
> the boat to take you from yourself
> to yourself.

In Camp's poetry, there is a place set for all the things, including those nihilist waifs and transients who inspire uncomfortable table-talk, who say 'nothing matters, man, nothing matters' over an after-dinner smoke. But Camp's grip on the beauty of existence is never derailed by her recognition that, as human animals, we're vigorously screwed.

> at the tops of mountains
> they could only feel the air
> and how little air was in it
>
> they were all so beautiful and
> exhausted.

And with this beauty, there is gratitude, a desperate gratitude:

> I don't want to leave this world

Elizabeth Morton

Fiona Farrell

Fiona Farrell
Nouns, verbs, etc. (selected poems)
Otago University Press, 2020
RRP $35, 212pp

Nouns, verbs, etc. (selected poems) is a showroom
where love, war, family and death are sold to unsuspecting customers
in the guise of mattresses, cabinets and toasters. Fiona Farrell ziplocks
the patriarchy, pops colonial militarism in shoeboxes, gift-wraps terror,
and serves it all with a congenial beam. You might walk out thinking
you've been played. And, yes, you have — but you'll go back and back,
fetching other packages of startling heft. This is an illusionist's sleight
of hand, the huckster's gentle scam. It is the gift of a confident and
consummate poet.

Farrell is that. She has notches to a literary belt by now so long it
would make a solid throwline. In her preface she recalls an early start in
crafting poems, stalled by the scoffing of some young *Landfall* alumnus,
in a 'world where men, past and present, stood about booming to one
another like so many kākāpō'. A return to verse, in her mid-thirties,
is the best kind of resistance movement. Poetry is perhaps the least
well-known of her forms, perhaps because poetry is a thing poets
read, and not all of them at that. These poems are selected from four
previous collections, in a chronology interrupted by thematically-cuffed
'uncollected' poems.

Farrell fashions myth from the most actual of things — punctuation
squirms and sets root, the harbour licks at your ear, men become
salmon, a hero with his cardboard suitcase sails away, fathers are bears
and mountains. There is a poem that preambles the story of the Three
Little Pigs from their mother's perspective. There is an all-grown-up
mention of the gingerbread man: 'I believe in / the gingerbread man. /

Who wouldn't run, / given the circumstances?' But these myths are rind, not pulp. Farrell's poetry is not the stubborn fairy-telling of someone intent on riddles and dreamworlds.

The cast of real, time-locked characters is circus enough. In her 'Passengers' series, from her 1987 collection *Cutting Out*, Farrell gives voice to nineteenth-century immigrant women, silenced by status and sex. These poems are simple, rhythmic 'songs', told by women whose servitude is defiant:

> But I'll never say 'sir'
> Or 'thank you ma'am'
> and I'll not curtsey more.

The poems in the sections that follow are more complex, more attentive to language's timbre. In the section taken from her 1999 collection, *The Inhabited Initial*, the alphabet is embodied and connotative. Haunting visions from the Iraq war of 1991 catch in the spindrift of ancient scripts — Semitic and Hittite cuneiform. There is horror here, a leaning-in to battlefield guns, birth defects and 'the weeping of children':

> This is the sound a child makes
> who is born with no head. This
> is the sound a woman makes who
> labours to bear a child without
> fingers, a child whose head
> swells like a pumpkin.

Mostly, though, Farrell's work is intimate, familial. Mothers and fathers, lovers and sisters, occupy the lounges of companiable homes. In 'The fathers', an 'uncollected' poem, we are gathered into the 'knotting of old jerseys / smelling of fish and vege / gardens and Best Bets . . .' In 'In a nutshell', sisters deal with the loss of their mother — 'huge with grief, two / fat babies struggling to get a grip'. Memory trespasses into the event of her dying. The tenderness is moving:

Each night she tucked us in
to bed, prayers said, so the
world rolled steady through
the dark. 'Roll over', she'd
say. 'Roll over. Face the wall
and you'll have good dreams.'

Farrell brings stories from her Irish whakapapa (from her paternal side) to a brutally colonised New Zealand. Ireland, and these islands, carry some shared burdens of history — a history that ultimately distils into 'the people the people the people'. In the section from her 2007 collection, *The Pop-Up Book of Invasions*, potato is set 'in black Kakanui loam', Cúchulainn, a Celtic Herakles-figure, occupies a poem with mingimingi, people traverse oceans — by sail boat or waka. Heroes are cut from ordinary folk, the journeys epic and harsh.

Poems about Christchurch's quake, from *The Broken Book* (2011), throb and buck and cry out for help:

The poem jolts at the caesura and all
the words slide sideways, slip from
the beam in dusty slabs. The children
who were learning how to say hello
tap goodbye goodbye in all their
voices, reaching in the dark for the
mother tongue . . . .

These are poems that let us hear love, when it is most desperate and raw. Farrell coaxes speech from the dead. She is a communication-board for people locked into fate.

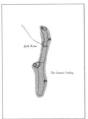

Jack Ross

Jack Ross
The Oceanic Feeling
Salt & Greyboy Press, 2021
RRP $38.99, 72pp

Jack Ross's collection ends where it starts, with '1913', not the year, but where 'you shout your fear into the storm'. *The Oceanic Feeling* offers us a bewilderment of death and grief and dying with all the rituals and pathos of PAK'nSAVE and Bible class on Tuesday. It's a collection where '[e]verything ages too fast'. The 'closed-in balconies' (to stop suicides) are ironic and earnest at the same time.

Ross fears not 'the primeval horror of the rat' (in 'Sylvie'), but the mundane horror of rest-home heaven — domesticity, dementia 'alone/ in the fog of [the] brain'. The pine tree is a recurring image, standing stripped-back, like his father 'at the end', like his bookcase, like 'my mother's failing memory'. Grief is reduced to a dead centipede caught on a web: 'his ship of eternity / lofty as the sky'; the names of dead relatives wait in the 'Family Plot', the plaque for his father still not made: bare like the pine tree, 'it makes you want to run out screaming / with an axe'. Maybe the cat needs to be euthanised 'with the sheer weight / of our love'.

The pity is tremendous, juxtaposed with the banalities of living. Ross is at times gratuitously *light*: 'less is more' in these mummified images, tokens of boredom (something even less than despair), ossified books, insects. Even great literature is reduced to chronology — time, and time descending — lower, lower — to zero: the fragments enact the emptying of a mind: dementia again, sepia-toned family portraits — the quiet mementos of loss. Even the memories are dying.

This collection of poetry is about death, and the lead-up to it (a 'dying alive'), and the fear that life is nothing more than a meaningless show of trade routes to the cat's food bowl, and campus redundancies. There is the crushing melancholia of being buried alive (like Antigone), or hanging yourself, self-analysis and family skeletons: the grandfather's suicide, the sister's suicide, and 'Mother's refusal / to hang onto *anything*'.

Ross does not want to be controlled by his antecedents, condemned to 'the same marionette dance'. Even the lighter moments feel 'futile / in the extreme' — the self-mocking academic who is crap at doing physical stuff (how ineffectual and useless compared to the 'sun-bronzed he-men'), the humiliation snapped by his new straw hat floating in the 'drink'. You've got to feel for him.

At times Ross *tries* to be dull, like a man who doesn't need to strive — 'those eager scrawls / sent off with such trepidation' for publication in *Poetry New Zealand*, as in the deliberations of the 'Communications committee', and the abstruse ruminations of the 'Oral exam'. The latter observes, however: ' "it's only dangerous / when the drums stop" ': 'Those are nice boots / Señor'. Beneath the surface, a rat is scratching its way out of the drear; 'Sometimes one fails to see / the glory'. But Ross wants us to fill the emotional gaps: what is the significance of the woman accosted by an Asian person from behind who says 'crude things'? Is this, to paraphrase the poem, one of the great mysteries of life? Ross is playing serious games, shooting in the dark.

'Checking into Facebook' feels to me like the physical and spiritual centre of *The Oceanic Feeling*. Here, all the themes and motifs of death, of memory, of profound boredom, accumulate. Is the body just a machine:

> without a ghost
> simply the illusion of
> Individuality [?]

> . . .

> in the eyes

of each murder victim
    a sense of relief
        what we *call*
        'Shakespeare'

isn't *Shakespeare*
the theatrical entrepreneur

Ross doesn't think so: 'the facts of the illusion / are so strong / they outweigh self-negation / confirm the heavy / burden / we lay down'. He seeks metaphysical consolation *in* tragedy, but fears, I think, the facts of the *illusion*, that life is meaningless; that beneath the skin, we're just 'a phrase-cranking / machine'. He strives to deny it, however. It can't be true. It mustn't. This is the nihilist threat that menaces the unbeliever, a bland terror (or the relief) that we become nothing, a spirit expelled 'when sneezing', ashes in a wooden urn. The oceanic feeling, I guess.

Mark Prisco

Marco Sonzogni / Timothy Smith

Marco Sonzogni and Timothy Smith (eds)
*More Favourable Waters: Aotearoa poets respond
to Dante's Purgatory*
The Cuba Press, 2020
RRP $25, 98pp

Only love purified takes us through the open door.
— Michael Fitzsimons

More Favourable Waters charts the course of Dante's journey through
Purgatory, reconfigured into the current vernacular of 33 New Zealand
poets — one for each canto. The setting for each is typically 'real-life-
modern', but tinged with a dash of magic that transforms, in Marisa
Cappetta's poem, for example, a recipe for pumpkin seeds into a
poignant tale of loss and regret.

Dante's original begins with the pilgrim arriving at the shores of
Purgatory, the place of atonement, where repentant sinners begin their
journey through suffering towards God, and where each one is made to
suffer the taste of their own sin, or a punishment that contrasts with it.
This is Dante's *contrapasso*: the aptness (and irony) of the Lustful made
to feel the flames of their passion, or the emaciated Gluttons, who see
but are denied the fruits that ripen on the trees.

And so it begins in the ante-chamber to Purgatory proper, which
is guarded by Cato or, in Steven Toussaint's poem, 'an agent with the
key'. In the latter, the 'newly-arrived' are merely moving house, but the
gloom and desolation is palpable, if obliquely 'understood'.

The theme of *Purgatory* is the purging of sins through suffering, and
so it is with this collection. The 'sins' however are less clearly defined,
more elusive and subtle therefore than Dante's rigid system of sin and

punishment, and the experiences and suffering invoked is of course earthly, more relatable therefore to our non-medieval sensibility. There's a certain amount of fortune involved: we are caught in our circumstances, victims of poor judgement, bad luck or the intervention of other people.

In Bryan Walpert's poem, a school bus is a modern-day Purgatory for the sensitive child. In Kay McKenzie Cooke's poem, the lament of Dante's avaricious (canto XX) is mirrored by the dismantled town of iron struts and dirty streams, by those who weep at their own song, at the memory of flush times. What's left is the 'steel vein' (the disused railway line) that runs through the town, the 'tangible' *contrapasso*.

Today, we slough our skins against the land that was stolen or befouled by Anahera Gildea's 'Mother-settler'. We lose our way and we suffer, through stubborn silences, poor communications, maybe even because of bad phone reception: in Sam Duckor-Jones' poem, 'the blaze of heaven's light' may yet penetrate the ordinary wickedness of a neglectful son, but bring only 'Howling and silhouettes that howl hello / / hello?' There is 'understanding' nevertheless, not in the grand Dantean manner of heaven's light, but an easy forgiveness, an acknowledgement of human weakness.

Dante's brutal scheme is based on the idea that joy or pain is linked to merit: 'just' reward or punishment. There is some truth to the idea that we get what we deserve: Andrew Johnston conceives The Fall as the despoliation of our planet — the garden of earthly delights, people! The 'big picture'. But the poets of this anthology have loosened the cords of Dante's morality and transformed it into something humane, and tenuous, like the joy or sorrow that attends falling in love.

Helen Rickerby reminds us that desire is the root not just of suffering, but of joy, too. It is 'something magical, or . . . deadly', and it can be made into 'something beautiful'. The poet's sins are those of regret for what she has *not* done, and her 'mountain' is the acceptance of joy and sorrow, of falling in love, and not, as it is for Dante, the overcoming of such human 'vices'.

Our experiences, and the consequences of our acts or omissions, are not contingent upon our virtues and transgressions; they are, unless 'governed' by Chance, determined by something more intricate and mysterious. This, as far as I can tell, is what all the poets in this collection want to tell us. Witness here from Anna Jackson the deprivation, and the memory of love in solemn tones reminiscent of Dante himself:

> but still from time
> To time we can hear a bird arrange
>
> Itself on a high branch and sing.
> All those songs lost in a cloud . . .
> What is a song, with no one to hear it?
>
> And now, this long silence . . .
> And now, this . . .
> And now, this . . .

Mary Maringikura Campbell

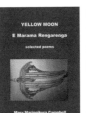

Mary Maringikura Campbell
Yellow Moon | E Marama Rengarenga
HeadworX Publishers, 2020
RRP $25, 84pp

Mary Maringikura Campbell's *Yellow Moon / E Marama Rengarenga* is a collection that combines the new and the old, a sampler of Campbell's work spanning 50 years of writing. The book is divided into two parts: the first, 'New and Uncollected Poems 1970s to 2019' and the second, the republication of *Maringi*, a collection originally released in 2015. The whole collection seems to exist as a kind of lifting up of Campbell's work into the light, a kind of *hey, this is what you have been missing out on.*

This book of short, direct lyric pieces starts with acknowledging her father, Alistair Te Ariki Campbell, and the tradition of poetry she continues in her own work. This opening poem also speaks to the insecurities around blood-quantum and skin colour that persist for pale-skinned people of the Moana: 'Do not judge me / because my skin burns in the sun / I know who I am'. She is moving towards Savaiki, the place her father has gone, where many of the Moana go when we leave this world. (We New Zealand Māori call this Hawaiki.)

The collection blurs together the Pākehā conception of past and future in this poem, featuring the man she comes from and the place that awaits us at the end of our lives. So much is caught up in these 50 or so words. These poems are consistently holding life and death together; for example, 'What the . . .' which takes us from doing the dishes to a character contemplating ending it all.

but if you jump off that bridge
make sure you have life insurance

because I have no time
to bury your arse

These are some of the no-nonsense, hard-hitting lines that animate this poem. This direct approach recurs across this section of the book. The poems 'Attitude' and 'Old man' both use this tone to speak to sexism:

Yes I am a woman
No I'm not your mother
Yes these tits are real
No you can't touch them

This snippet from 'Attitude' pulses between yes's and no's that reflect a woman's strained conversation with a man, digging into some of the tropes of sexist rhetoric that sadly come up in everyday conversation. 'Old man' references a checklist format to explore the idea that certain men only want women for sex. Campbell does a lot of good work recycling formats, especially in her poem 'The All Blacks Prayer', which takes the Lord's Prayer and turns it into an ironic critique of the way in which New Zealand deifies this sport.

The first section ends with 'In the Cooks', the poem that brings us back to that life and death connection: 'From the moment of conception / we slowly, we surely / begin to die.' I wonder what the book would have been like if this had been allowed to end the collection, but instead here we move from the collected works to *Maringi*. One of my favourite poems in the collection, 'Spiderwoman', is a really funny and sassy poem that just left me grinning. However, this section is where the collection starts to fall apart for me — not altogether, but some poems mortified me. 'Cutter', a poem about a girl who self-harms, moves between a strange binary of pretty girl to cutter which feels very dated.

. . . the cuts are so horrific
but she's so damn cute
with her yellow hair

She's as pretty as a button
WOW!

Maybe it's speaking to a specific kind of male gaze that tends to respond to women's pain in rather callous and objectifying ways, but for me the poem itself doesn't have enough in it to really underline this satirical perspective. 'Blind deaf and dumb' speaks to the ridiculousness of prejudice, again drawing attention to the ways in which patriarchy trains men to objectify women, but its ableist perspective doesn't sit well with me. These are the two big missteps for me, and I feel that the best parts of *Maringi* could have been lifted from that earlier publication to make a new expansive collection of selected works.

That said, a lot of the work towards the end really works, like the heart-breaking 'Who is to blame?', which speaks to the deaths of Indigenous people, in particular the murder and disappearances of Indigenous women.

'The Other Side' is a beautiful tribute to someone who has passed on, and ends with this incredible stanza that speaks to the start of the book and the travelling back to Savaiki:

How else would you have travelled
if it wasn't on the back
of a whale?

There is a lot of beauty and life and death here, and it doesn't all work, but I think that's the way with work, especially when you're sharing writing that spans decades. I for one am thankful this pukapuka is in the world. I keep being transported back to that image of the whale: wouldn't it be nice to be taken back home on a tohorā? Mauri ora.

Tayi Tibble

Tayi Tibble
Rangikura
Victoria University Press, 2021
RRP $25, 96pp

Eve is a Māori woman picking through the underbrush for the best weaving materials. And what she finds are all her ancestors stretching out before and behind her. She's gathering what we need, the tools we need. She's walking backwards into a haze. Not just the way time goes, but a haze that is man-made, or should I be specific and say coloniser-generated. And it's getting warmer. But we come from the Pacific, heat is what we're used to. When our ancestors got here they had to adjust. And now we're the generation made to watch as the sky reddens as it burns up. Ranginui impatient to close the gap between them and Papatūānuku. Story as old as time. Story way older than time.

I think — and I really don't know because I'm nowhere near old enough — every generation feels like they're marching towards some untimely end, right? The War to End All Wars (which unsurprisingly didn't), the rise of global fascism, the coming of the atomic era, and for at least 50 years we've been living and surviving under the cloud of global warming; for Indigenous people our worlds have ended and been ending so often outside of these global events. Look at our struggles. We know what the world ending is. *Rangikura* is the party at the end, knowing full well our ancestors have got this, either on this side of living or the next. You could catch hope like a viral disease off this book if you just let it. The ancestors are potent on the page, moving from dreams to reality, their dreams moving from idea and into action.

So I shrugged fuck it
and learnt to love the dark

where you can either
shine or disappear.

Tayi Tibble works in this darkness, taking all the evil out of it, taking all the sin out of it, all the colonial assumptions out of it. We live in darkness half our lives, why deny it?! She continues in the poem 'Mahuika':

The kind of girl who knows
that it's better to make
home in the black
and wait

for all the life that was stolen
from you to be recycled back.

She moves from embodying Mahuika, the atua of fire, to identifying with Hine-nui-te-pō. We are all of our ancestors, but this signifies a specific movement, gives a specific reason for the light. We dance for LAND BACK we dance for tino rangatiratanga we dance for Mana Wahine we dance for Mana Takatāpui.

Queen of the club scene grinding
with the gay devils and holding court
with the drag queens.

Hine-nui-te-pō as a modern Mary *come all you sick-as-frick queers and outcasts, here you have a poetry, here you have a chance.* Serve up some realness to topple governments to bring down the stagnant colonial empire of capital. We will have all we are owed in the end, this poem croaks into being. There is water full of pounamu and gold and bloodlines running through this pukapuka, places to stay and places to leave, people to fuck and people to love, and a people to fight for! Tibble asks the big questions in 'My Ancestors Send Me Screenshots', a poem that speaks to the specific kind of cross-examination that defines social media existence while drawing on the kind of ethnographic dissection that we as Māori have gone through since Pākehā got here. She spits questions mockingly back at these scientists of the colonial gaze:

> What the fuck is a whakapapa? Do I carry it in my pussy? In a tiny baggy? Like a real 1? Like a down-ass bitch? Do I have a heart? And does it bleed? Like a steak? If it's brutalised enough? If it's served? On a plate? With proper silverware?

Pākehā talk shit about how we are the cannibals when they've turned our whole existence into something to consume or throw away. We are uncontainable, this pukapuka says; we are smoke and make-up and swagger and hunger, we are fish and lizards and demigods, and we are the thighs that crush those demigods, we are M&Ms and orange dust, we are e hoas at a party, we are the rustling of bibles and tukutuku patterns, DBs and petri dishes, we are radical like the ancestors painting the skyful of whales. Read these toikupu out loud to the buzzing lights of run-down rental, to the thousands of satellites that Musk has pumped into Rehua's domain, read out loud to know that the ancestors fucking do ride with us and will forever as we ride with them.

We've got the tools to fix this mess, and this book points towards an Indigenous future with beauty and flare.

Ian Wedde

Ian Wedde
The Little Ache — a German notebook
Victoria University Press, 2021
RRP $30, 144pp

The thing to ask about a burlesqued wink or a mock sheep raid is not
what their ontological status is. It is the same as that of *rocks on the one
hand and dreams on the other — they are things of this world.*

The quote comes from anthropologist Clifford Geertz's famous essay
'Thick Description: Toward an Interpretive Theory of Culture'. Or
rather, it comes from the notes at the end of Ian Wedde's latest volume
of poems. In the poem itself, Wedde includes only the last 16 words,
which I've italicised here. Wedde explains the passage as follows:

> The term 'thick description' . . . became, Geertz wrote . . . 'a position
> and a slogan I have been living with since.' I have gone on reading and
> admiring these essays for many years and want to acknowledge that
> the concept of 'thick description' was my passport to the state of mind
> I hoped this book would occupy, where ghosts could be encountered in
> the everyday, material world, and in the phantom fragments of language
> which seemed to collate its meanings.

There are, of course, other names for this state of mind: in a fictional
context one might refer to it as 'Magic Realism'. But is that what Wedde
means by his own methods of 'thick description'? What exactly *is* it, for
a start? Another of Wedde's Geertz quotes may be helpful here:

Believing . . . that man is an animal suspended in webs of significance
he himself has spun, I take culture to be those webs, and the analysis
of it to be therefore not an experimental science in search of law but an
interpretive one in search of meaning.

So, for example, in poem 51, Wedde sees Turkish poet Nâzım Hikmet
Ran, who died in Moscow in 1963, sitting at a German café in 2014, and
carefully tabulating his reactions to:

> the perfect pitch of exile
> a tone found somewhere in the chord combining
> the demonstrators over at Wienerstraße
> the expostulations of his soccer companions
> and the voice of the German soccer commentator
> on the café's big screen
> during the quarter-final
> between Germany and France.

Shades of Geertz's famous example of the need to account for the
difference between a twitch and a wink ('as anyone unfortunate enough
to have had the first taken for the second knows')! Geertz's essay goes
on to add a third actor who chooses to *parody* the others' winks, and
whose behaviour is therefore even more culturally layered and needful
of interpretation than theirs.

Wedde, a New Zealander in temporary exile from his native land,
and eagerly trying to discover tendrils of ancestry in Germany, imagines
— or sees (need the apparition of a ghost *always* be taken as pure
imagination?) — the author of the epic *Human Landscapes from My
Country* carefully modulating his own way through all of these various
voices and layers of cultural entanglement.

Wedde's book — which might otherwise be taken as a simple
amalgam of travel notes and genealogical jottings — is actually
something far more ambitious: an attempt to decode the levels of
significance to be encountered by someone of his complex background

in an already immensely overwritten cultural matrix.

He has certain advantages, mind you. Some of his not-too-distant ancestors were themselves poets — one had a few poems set to music by Brahms, another was famed as 'the founder of Plattdüütsch dialect literature' — so their works can be interrogated with this concept of distant kinship in mind. With these advantages, however, come risks:

> it's the ghost of a smile I see
> when I read what Joseph Blos thought
> of Johannes Wedde's poems
> which though 'often very beautiful
> didn't sink in with the wider public
> on account of the scholarly ballast
> with which they were packed'.

There's a certain amount of 'scholarly ballast' in this Wedde book, too: 10 pages of notes and another three of acknowledgments. Personally, I'm inclined to think that there should be *more* notes, not fewer — not all of the German tags and quotations, most of them admittedly explained in the context of the poems they adorn, are actually translated, let alone referenced. That may not be every reader's view, however.

If there *is* a universal applicability to be sought in Ian Wedde's complex web of encounters and experiences during his Berlin residency, I suppose it comes by analogy rather than directly. And I find his struggles with communication in a strange land quite poignant, given my own halting German.

However, Wedde certainly gives as good as he gets to an arrogant librarian in poem 53:

> Failing to find it in the loan stacks
> I said to the narcissist of small differences
> as he glared at this Ausländer
> across his Ausgabeort barrier

Ich kann den Buch nicht finden
at which
having got it
he pushed the book against my chest
and jeered
Hier is der *Buch!*

Books are *das* not *der*

Given that this particular book — the second volume of Johannes Wedde's *Collected Works* — had not been taken out for 111 years, the current-day poet Wedde feels (not unreasonably) justified in unleashing the full force of his poetic fury against 'the thick-browed bureaucratic *Nationalismus*' of this 'bored pedant'.

Exile and displacement are subjects much on our minds at present. Now, 2013–14, when most of these poems were written, seems like a distant golden age, when free travel was still permitted (to holders of the right passports, that is), and the refugee crisis in Europe — though dire — was not yet catastrophic.

There are echoes of these things — the rise of extreme nationalism in Europe, for instance — in some of the poems, but to Wedde's credit he hasn't allowed second thoughts to distort the clear mirror of this particular experience.

This book appears 50 years after his first, *Homage to Matisse* (1971). What a career it's been! Wedde has always been one of the most internationally focused of New Zealand poets (witness his translations from Arabic poet Mahmoud Darwish, also published in the early 1970s).

There's a (much-quoted) phrase in Anna Akhmatova's *Poem without a Hero*: 'the bitter air of exile'. Wedde knows better than to borrow such an expression for his own voluntary sojourn abroad, his own constituting merely a 'little ache'. These letters from exile do, nevertheless, remind me of their distant prototypes, Ovid's *Sad Poems* and *Letters from Pontus*, written from his own place of official banishment on the shores of the Black Sea to the centre of culture in Rome.

Ash Davida Jane

Ash Davida Jane
How to Live with Mammals
Victoria University Press, 2021
RRP $25, 80pp

From the very opening, *How to Live with Mammals*
gives off heat and burning ozone. Cicadas scream while plants go to
seed, and we wonder how we will explain this world to our children —
'a piñata with apology / notes' is the poet's suggestion. Ash Davida Jane's
first poem 'hot bodies' reveals a tautness and urgency which stretches
across the collection. Climate apocalypse is an ever-present heat on
your neck, while you worry about Blu-Tack marks on rental walls. The
poet never lets us wallow, though, with touches of humour brushing by
in even the most serious pieces — 'we'll be starving / come winter / how
vintage' — and many of the poems are downright hilarious.

How to Live with Mammals is an image-soaked concoction of colour
and nature that draws you into a world whose beauty is evanescent and
painful. The struggle to be alive and belong somewhere comes across
keenly. Jane makes this experience personal and real, and certainly any
millennial will get a crick in their neck from profusely nodding along
to every stanza — particularly in 'we go to work' where 'capitalism is
a fuckboy'. We see 'a firefly or the moon' rise up and edge 'a blur of
gold light through the / shifting water'; we 'sleep naked even in the
middle of winter / and warm our hands on each other's stomachs'; all
while 'jogging into an apocalyptic future / in polyester shorts'. The
poignancy this collection invokes is deep, the narrator of 'marine snow'
encapsulating it with 'I'm not built / for this kind of grief / I start to
carry it / around and put a little / into everything I do / now'.

A blend of humour, sharpness, pessimism and an acute gentleness
makes each piece feel unique but wholly human. Particularly striking

is 'bird currency', which captures and examines self-consciousness and human-driven destruction. Near the opening, we are struck by the desolation of 'let's practise paying rent until we can do it / just right'. Before you can regain your breath, Jane follows this with lemmings tumbling off a cliff and the raw cruelty of splicing together the pain so everything looks good in 'the final cut'. The piece is imperative and harsh. The reader is told to 'take something you love / and empty it', to 'press it flat / like a flower / make it dead trying to make it / yours'.

And indeed, the lines make you feel flattened, witnessing the inevitable destruction done, and, without even malicious intent, a pressing kind of sadness. The piece ends with bodies being cut open, again and again, because 'you have to keep going / until you find something / otherwise none of the / dying means anything'. Each line of the close is a finely-tuned hit to the solar plexus. The piece is cemented as an unflinching analogy: humans are the lemmings and drivers, continuously pushing everyone off the cliff because they can't admit that they're in too deep, and that, perhaps, jumping off in the first place was a bad idea.

Some pieces also allow the reader to breathe. The well-considered placement of poems and lines form a balancing act between bursting hope and sinking nihilism. Straight after the visceral experience that is 'bird currency', 'self talk' comes along. The voice here is different, still very strong but imbued with whimsy and hope. It is the narrator's internal monologue, telling themselves what they will do, ranging from the sweet and relatable ('i will walk through the city and pet all of the cats') to the more touching and thoughtful ('i will wonder / how many small things I have to do to add up / to something impactful'). The piece does not drop the tension but rather softens it, showcasing the deft composition of this collection. Another poem which does this well is 'in the future'. Here the narrator imagines being a 'hermit crab real estate agent', showing 'prospective crabs through' and pointing out 'modern chic' features. A soft brightness suffuses this piece; it's a reimagining of our world in kinder hands: 'I could give back all the hermit crabs' money / with interest'.

How to Live with Mammals is deeply moving, and each poem could be read differently at least 50 times. Jane shows our lives in new and textured ways, with climate and moral degradation a stark and ever-present tragedy. But she also gives us her words and hope, and the courage to don our 'griefproof layer' and keep leaving the house.

Jess Fiebig

Jess Fiebig
My Honest Poem
Auckland University Press, 2020
RRP $24.99, 112pp

Even before you slip a single finger between the pages and open Jess Fiebig's *My Honest Poem*, the collection is transfixing. The pixelated woman on the cover stares. The effect of the hair and lips make it a striking cover, but it's the eyes that truly catch you. They are lapis, cornflowers and oceanic depths; vivid blue and carrying the magnetism of an old soul. Having read the back-cover blurb, I was prepared for difficult material and trauma, but not for just how beautiful this collection is.

Fiebig's writing style is an absolutely impeccable blend of narrative, image, voice and lyricism. Everything is honed, necessary and striking. I am reminded of the Gainsborough painting, *Louisa, Lady Clarges*. Just like the painting, *My Honest Poem* pays attention to colour and concrete detail, and at first glance the style looks to be intelligent and realist. However, the closer you get to Gainsborough's portrait, the more visible the subtle impressionism — the shaded fingers, the softened strings of the harp, the blurred edges of the purple dress — becomes. In this way, the work somehow becomes 'realist impressionism' and, just like this collection, tells a story which is intricate in detail and plot but oh-so rich in colour, texture and sensory stimulation. About four lines into the first piece, Fiebig pulls you that close, and you see and feel the unerring talent and impressive stylistic blend of her writing.

My Honest Poem is clever; the themes and narratives are so enmeshed that to draw one out requires all others to come, too. The word 'honest' keeps coming back to me. It's not only in the collection's title and its final poem, but also at the heart of every piece. It is not glossed-up clickbait proffered by the writer: 'oh yes, I'm just sooo open and honest'. The honesty is authentic, sweet, sour and blood-real; it's Sexton 'The Operation' real, it's 'here I am, look me in the eye' real.

This collection was certainly not light reading, but I could not stop. And I felt as if I owed it to her — if she is brave enough to lay all this out, then I had better bloody keep reading. That is not to say that the collection is sepia-sad; there is so much sensory detail that it is impossible not to see and breathe every scene in full technicolour. The air is thick with roses, jasmine, poppies, daphne, perfume from a 'baby blue' bottle and fragranced soap; the scents pull us into the lines and provide a comforting embrace when we need it.

Many traumatic events feature, and while at times fractures and gaps appear inside the narrator, most evident in 'Saturday Night in the Emergency Department', the beauty in every description displays a fiercely beating heart. 'This is Poetry' goes deep into the narrator's process, and its early appearance informs many of the later pieces. Emotions are felt like a 'hot iron', which burns the narrator until she describes:

> how scared I am to be alive, / how happy I am to be alive, / how confused I am / when words fly out / of my head like dried butterflies / but how good it feels / to tack their inky bodies on paper

Words and the beauty and sadness of language fully and bodily consume the writer. 'This is Poetry' explains the 'why' of writing, and the conclusion you are left with is: whyever wouldn't you?

So many pieces were standouts, for so many reasons. 'Sixteen' 'is sugar dissolving to salt / on your tongue' until it's 'like breath growing thick and sour / in the night'; loneliness is a 'neon vacancy sign' which lights up on Christmas. Interactions with men feature 'a wreckage of bedsheets'. In the poignant 'Loving a Depressive', 'he wants to wrap cotton around my thoughts, / but I like them jagged'.

One which really lodged itself under my sternum and still makes me cry is 'Nearly'. The opening lines say it all: 'it was winter / the six weeks I carried you'. Further on the narrator remembers how 'you unfurled / inside me'. Appearing at page 42, it is almost in the centre of the collection, and to me it felt as if the other poems were surrounding it and holding it in their warmth.

There isn't space to address the stirring titular poem which closes the collection, and space for only a passing mention of the numerous winged creatures — butterflies, starlings, cicadas, ducks, moths and ladybirds — those eternal signs of hope and freedom which flutter throughout the pages. This collection has it all, handing you butterflies pinned to paper, chewed fingernails, 'powdered sugar' and stomachs 'full of sand' — all honest and displayed 'caffeinated / in crisp sunlight'.

Siobhan Harvey

Siobhan Harvey
Ghosts
Otago University Press, 2021
RRP $27.50, 112pp

What is home and *where* is home are two huge
questions Siobhan Harvey's *Ghosts* has us asking. A multitude of first-
person narrators speak to displacement and belonging, corporeality and
translucence, and the ghosts are ever there, 'as we drift through / our
thin lives'. As you read, preconceived lines between the living and the
dead blur, and the ghosts rise within us, peering out from the skeletons
of our houses and reaching through strands of our inherited DNA.

Ghosts is structured into acts; feeling both classical Grecian
and indie-concept-album in its deliberate and effortlessly skilled
arrangement. The journey begins in the ghostly houses of Aotearoa,
state homes, new beginnings, enforced gentrification and people
othered from their homes. Sometimes a house will appear as the
prototypical mother, reaching out to encompass the cold and alienated
within her four walls and to keep the rain from their heads. In other
pieces, the mother figure is sorely lacking, as governments foreclose,
sell and demolish while protestors cry on. Pieces like 'Requiem for a
War, with Refrain' cry forth to be read aloud, while the first-person
plural narrator of 'The Evicted' conjures the thick emotion of works like
'Do You Hear the People Sing', with:

Remember our children grow
like sunflowers. Like solar panels,
they soak up the warmth

our love gives them, for tomorrow
they *will* take back our sky.

Berlin, Singapore and global expanses fill the later pages, bringing ghosts who refuse to be erased, who live in the static-flash of an electric charge but who are also unknown and elusive. Harvey's language is lyrical, and in pieces like 'The Ghosts of Wall Unbuilt' the lines flow softly into each other, releasing vibrant images which float in the air:

We hang in the heavens,
a kaleidoscope of monarchs, orange
as late autumn leaves, amber
lights or sparks.

The acts feel more intimate as they progress, with less separation between ghosts and narrators, and details becoming more personal. In 'My First Boyfriend is an Apparition of the Heart' we hear how 'something / inside me   inside him   broke / like a mirror, like the heart / snatched back'. 'If Befriending Ghosts' is a challenge for a reviewer; each line feels quotable, but doing so would end up just reproducing the whole poem. However, the last couplet is particularly moving: 'I will be their armour, their second skin / I will be their padded cell, their asylum.'

Ghosts includes a fair amount of experimentation, prompting the reader to consider Glyn Maxwell's discussion of the white space of the writer's page in *On Poetry*: 'if you don't know how to use it you are writing prose'. It feels as if Harvey is certainly considering all the spaces. The forms of her pieces are constantly moving; sometimes there are deliberate gaps and the stanzas become houses for the ghosts to fill. In other moments, the lines are close and flow through each other until it feels like the blackness itself is becoming ghostly and spreading unseen across the whole page.

It could be considered atypical to finish a poetry collection with an essay, but Harvey's experiment in adding one is certainly successful.

The 'Afterword' is a piece of creative non-fiction entitled 'Living in the Haunted House of the Past: or Renovation, Writing and How to Construct a Living Room While Searching for a Home'. It reads beautifully, shedding light on aspects covered or alluded to in the preceding poetry. But in its separation in genre and form, the afterword makes clear the distinction between author and narrator — although they are no doubt filled with personal ideas and images, these poems are not biography. Going suddenly from reading short to long form was not jarring, and in fact Harvey's skill as an essayist made me sorry when the final paragraph ended.

There is no small amount to take away from this collection, but, perhaps above all, there is an over-riding sense that homes are not simple things. They are mammoth intertexts of past and present, which vibrate with layers of memory, story and spirit until our bones ache. Occupants both visible and ghostly become intertwined in the search for somewhere to belong, and Harvey's poetry shows that we can so often find this sought-after refuge within each other.

Tusiata Avia / Courtney Sina Meredith

Tusiata Avia
The Savage Coloniser Book
Victoria University Press, 2020
RRP $25, 96pp

Courtney Sina Meredith
Burst Kisses on the Actual Wind
Beatnik, 2021
RRP $30, 72pp

I begin at the end. In the final poem of *The Savage Coloniser Book*, 'Some notes for critics', Tusiata Avia helpfully lists 31 notes to keep in mind when reading her work. Sarcastic and clever, it is a hilarious poem, with the humour being distinctly that of our Pasifika peoples. I once read it at a Wellington poetry event with a crowd of mostly Pākehā, and my cackle was louder than theirs. The lines are succinct and punchy, going for the hit each time:

12. Lay-ers
13. Samoan legends
14. It's not rocket science
15. Google it
16. Some writers don't include glossaries

This poem should be compulsory reading if you're white and about to critique anything Pasifika. While it is specific to Avia's literary experiences, it is also a poem for other Pasifika poets to carry around as a shield, to attach to our emails to editors and reviewers, to add as a footnote at the end of every poem we write.

Avia is blunt. She does not hide from the savage coloniser or try to turn every violent moment into a metaphor. When prominent politicians cannot see past their own white privilege and fabricate lies, like colonisation being beneficial 'on balance' to the colonised, this book answers. An answer that is covered in blood and gets heavier the longer you hold it. Avia gives space to those who are silenced by exposing some of the trauma minorities have suffered:

> Put all the refugees on Manus
> They will sew their mouths up red

The poem 'BLM' is perhaps the most confronting. It is short — only six stanzas, each being four lines. Each stanza is a lump in your throat that is so big it cuts into the skin. It hurts to swallow. I missed my step with the first two lines:

> I'm looking straight into the camera
> My ancestors standing behind me

I thought it was centring a Black person's experience. From those first two lines I was prepared for unwavering support for Black Lives Matter and their ancestors who were forced into slavery. But instead, it's six stanzas of white supremacy:

> Crushing the head of the black man
> This is my God-given white.

This book is heavy. I carry it around Wellington in my handbag and feel the extra weight.

Even though I read the last poem first, endings are not endings. As Pasifika peoples, our time is not linear, rather, as the common Polynesian saying goes, we look back to go forward. We walk in spirals, ever mindful of our ancestors and our future generations. Our connection to the past and the future means that the climate crisis always sits on our tongues. Climate change affects us first. Our islands are sinking, and the savage colonisers are to blame. This is summed up by Avia with the heart-breaking line:

> And the school kids have to sit cross-legged in their classrooms up to their waists in seawater

The most obvious thing this book does is invert the word *savage* and give it back to the coloniser who forced us to carry it first. We carry the history of this word in our scars.

I wish I could write about every poem of Avia's, but I would never have enough words. Avia's poetry is the jandal slap from the aunty who watches your every move, it is your ancestors' cackle when you correct an important Pākehā's pronunciation in a meeting, and it is an elder squeezing your hand as you shake and rage about the way your people suffer.

I am sure a white critic might describe this collection as angry and leave it at that. While there is anger, limiting an evaluation to just this word is lazy and ignorant, as it ignores all of the generational trauma Avia carefully unpacks, and, more importantly, it dismisses all the `ofa with which the poems have clearly been crafted . If I could give this book one word, I would name it as *tender*. Avia presents our stories and her stories so tenderly, despite the colonisation we have been forced to endure. She opens herself up and gifts us her words — and gives the savage coloniser a good smack in the face.

Courtney Sina Meredith's *Burst Kisses on the Actual Wind* is also tender, although in a different way. The tenderness in her poems come from sentences that feel like soft sun in the islands, from gentle words that float on waves, and from deep acknowledgements of racism and our hurting brown bodies. It also comes from Meredith's unexpected and playful use of language:

The silence wanted its throat slit
I sang to myself while I made dinner

The book opens with 'Could you connect me to a diverse community?', which is a great visual poem. It begins:

I am aware of my privilege. Could you connect me to a diverse community?

This sentence is then repeated 14 times, but each successive repetition redacts a new word, with it ending up as a fully redacted sentence. By doing this, Meredith takes the power back from such a belittling statement and question. Receiving tone-deaf communications like this from well-meaning Pākehā is a shared experience among Pasifika peoples. By redacting it, Meredith erases the performative behaviour of the person asking. This poem is deceptively complex and really, really funny.

Much of Meredith's work traces displacement and what happens to our connections to culture and people and place when we are somewhere new. It is that uncomfortable feeling of going home to the islands even though it is not your place of residence. You are both excited and nervous. Everything is how you remember, but nothing is in the same place:

You get back everybody says oh you're back!
You are back but everything has moved.

This book not only travels home, it also takes us all around the world — we are in Mexico City seeing piñatas suspended from buildings, we're in King's Cross, we take the shuttle in Honolulu, and accept advice from shop girls in New York. Despite travelling to all these places, this book has roots in Aotearoa. These roots cannot forget the Dawn Raids or colonisation or the history of Pasifika peoples in this place. We are now in Ponsonby, a suburb that built itself on our backs, yet only a few of us live there now:

We drive down Ponsonby Road and turn into a memory
I know this place
      my blood is in the soil

Meredith's work is heavy and hopeful. I walk through her experiences, looking left and right, amazed by the colours. I can feel my heart. It beats in time with her words. The final line of the final poem is beautiful and wraps up my journey tenderly. I am on a beach in Tonga, where the sun does not care about the time and my body slowly unlearns its colonised ways:

The horizon is vast.

David Wrigley

Ben Kemp / Vanessa Crofskey / Chris Stewart

Ben Kemp, Vanessa Crofskey, Chris Stewart
AUP New Poets 6
Auckland University Press, 2020
RRP $29.99, 114pp

The three poets in this book ask questions about states of belonging, about who is on the inside and who is stuck on the outside looking in. In this time of Covid and Fortress New Zealand, especially, these are questions worth asking.

Ben Kemp's poems come to us from Tokyo. He draws inspiration from his outsider position, indeed revels in it. In 'Four Tokyo Subcultures' he wanders out to the extremities, pulling us into worlds that are alien even to most Japanese people:

> Beings flaunt LCD eyes
> with hardwired electricity cables to their temples

There is a sense of another, post-human existence sprinting away from us, towards a future in which we will play no part. Kemp's still, snow-bound poems keep returning to the idea of people and persons in the wrong place. In 'Opoutere' we sit with the thoughts of a stranded whale looking for the first time at the world 'without the lens of seawater'. The poem is slow and undulating, eerily calm but suffused with the spectre of death. There is an alienness to the gentle rocking of the language, but one that suggests that connection is possible:

> We are one tree, one body . . .
> fed by the same root and connected by the same fisherman's knot

Vanessa Crofskey's poems are sarcastic, funny and righteously angry. Like the whales in 'Opoutere', she has been forced from the water to which she once felt she belonged ('we are born into buoyancy'). The male gaze and the approach of puberty drive her to the cold comfort of the land:

> Swimming pools only became terrifying once I noticed the public audience to my limbs

Her work is sculpted in the awkward spaces children and grandchildren of immigrants are forced to inhabit. She carves poems from immigration cards, asks us: Who gets to come in? What does a New Zealander look like? Readers must bear witness to the racist jokes of border security officers. Her work is often necessarily unadorned by poetic sentiment, a series of brutal combinations of conversational gut-punches:

> my best representation is in a section of Pornhub
> where all the skinny Asian girls and the mixed chicks don't speak
> have big tits, and white men cum all over their faces

Cracks of lyricism open up in 'The Capital of My Mother' as Crofskey contemplates her Malaysian whānau, and the rivers, harbours and oceans that unite and separate them:

> Kuala Lumpar means muddy confluence
> The city is born from the places two rivers
> merge then flow

> 'We don't speak the same language
> but we do share the same ocean [. . .]'

Her sense of herself as an outsider runs through these poems as a rich seam of rage, angst and comedy, whether considering her whakapapa, her place within New Zealand's often contrived multicultural melée, or wishing she was anywhere else than a moribund South Auckland theme park ('Postcard from Rainbow's End').

The careful craft of Chris Stewart's poetry feels like an attempt to make some sort of order from the chaos: the chaos of the universe, of the ocean, of the caprices of that most alien of invaders — a newborn baby.

His poems are spare, spacious, sometimes lonely things. Stewart finds himself in a domestic world in which he is unsure of his role, casting around for guidance from seahorses, penguins, pandas, mice, polar bears. There are no guides. Who can we ask for advice on how to be good fathers? Our fathers? Please.

> in another life I died of exhaustion
> a terrible swimmer caught
> in a storm-roiled sea with only
> small fins to steer myself

These currents that billow a new parent also cause him to reflect on the heavens:

> we glove the light in our skin
> find sleep in solar wind
> wrap ourselves in the gravity
> of your arrival

He shares with the other poets in this book a desire to use poetry as a vehicle to find a place in the world, to work out where they belong and where they do not. In the process they ask difficult questions of the reader, and even of the country and culture as a whole.

David Wrigley

Rhys Feeney / Ria Masae / Claudia Jardine

Rhys Feeney, Ria Masae, Claudia Jardine
AUP New Poets 7
Auckland University Press, 2020
RRP $29.99, 114pp

The three poets in this collection all excavate political, cultural and environmental problems, both ancient and modern, and dust them down with combinations of erudition, anger, humour and empathy.

Rhys Feeney's dense and information-rich poems immediately reminded me of Mark Fisher (like Feeney, a high-school teacher) and his description of British students suffering from what he called 'reflexive impotence'. The students knew what a terrible state the world was in but were paralysed by the certainty of their inability to change anything. They couldn't conceive of a world without capitalism, and so collapsed into an anxious apathy. Feeney, with wit and intelligence, manages to just stay ahead of the despair that bites at his heels.

His poem 'the world is at least fifty percent terrible' lies awake and gnaws on the threat of AI, the fate of battery chickens, the ecological disaster that is soy milk, New Zealand's own dairy-farmed demons:

after work get drunk go to maccas don't eat anything
    walk out into the cold look up at the sky
ask where are the stars where is the moon
    why don't they come out
did we do something wrong

In 'bioremediation' he treads a line between environmental despair and 'hope   in the form of spring daffodils'. He reminds us of Rachel Carson's *Silent Spring* and the near-eradication of DDT as a pesticide that followed its publication. In another poem '('t/w: dsh')', he writes of his own struggles with mental health and tells us 'My writing is connected to the chemicals in my body'. The soil and the psyche become soothed and saved by words.

Ria Masae's scathing poem 'SkyCity Scraps' also takes on the excesses of capitalism, tearing chunks from the gauche monstrosity that is Auckland's Sky Tower, a needle that:

> injects the wishful with debt and depression and false build-ups
> that plummet to real nothings

She follows 'a nomad, a no-man' through a night of state-sanctioned debauchery at the casino, an Id unconstrained by Ego, 'one rusted nail amongst thousands / on that discarded cross'.

SkyCity looms over Masae's Auckland, radiating alienation and despair. The poet follows the bad vibes into the hidden lives of the desperate: the school bully playing at tea-parties with his porcelain dolls (in 'Chipped China'), the shut-in peering through curtains at the action on the street outside ('Black Days'). The poetry is lean, muscular, unsentimental; it crackles with energy and hard-earned empathy.

Many of her poems play with the tension between traditional Samoan culture, life in Auckland, and the ways that tension plays out in English and Samoan language, and their awkward love-child Samoglish.

In 'There is No Translation for Post-Natal Depression in the Samoan Language', she tells us: 'Depression does not thrive in communities / where isolation and individualism are alien concepts'. She suggests here there are alternatives to capitalism's hegemony, but we've often left them behind us and are reluctant to return.

Masae's interest in the foibles and failings of language is shared by Claudia Jardine. In her retelling of the story of Orpheus and Eurydice she plays on the similarity between the Greek words for 'viper' and for 'no'. The timelessness of small phonetic misunderstandings and the infuriating durability of (half-) men's violence against women are displayed side by side — the political and the poetic, the tragic and the seemingly trivial.

Her interest in the classical world could easily be fusty or pretentious in lesser hands, but Jardine's work is scrupulously modern in tone. In 'Things that Spooked the Ancient Romans' she lists off a procession of oddball occurrences that could just as easily be news reports from modern Florida or environmental horror stories from anywhere:

> a pig is born with a human head   milk flows in the river
> two oxen climb onto the roof of a house in a fashionable neighbourhood

Jardine's poems are perfectly weighted, seemingly effortless, but with a seamlessness and grace that can only come with careful craft.

There is plenty to despair of in the here of New Zealand and now of today. The soil is filled with poison. Depression and anxiety are rampant. No one knows what to do about any of it. There is still hope, however, in carefully made poems that hold these problems up to the light, and ask us to consider them.

Contributors

Gary Allen has published 19 collections, most recently, *Bonfire Night* (Greenwich Exchange, 2021). His work is published widely in magazines including *Australian Book Review*, *Meanjin*, *Quadrant* and *Westerly*.

John Allison is an Ōtautahi Christchurch-based poet. His poem 'Father's Axe, Grandfather's Machete' was selected for *Best New Zealand Poems 2020*. A poem sequence 'The Poetics of Water' has been set to music by Pieta Hextall for a chamber ensemble. He is currently preparing his collected poems.

Aimee-Jane Anderson-O'Connor was the featured poet in *Poetry New Zealand Yearbook 2021*. She was awarded the 2018 Charles Brasch Young Writers' Essay Prize and was the co-winner of the 2017 Monash Undergraduate Prize for Creative Writing. Her work has appeared in a number of literary journals, including *Starling*, *Mayhem*, *Landfall*, *brief*, *Turbine | Kapohau*, *Verge* and *Minarets Journal*.

Philip Armstrong teaches English and writing at the University of Canterbury Te Whare Wānanga o Waitaha. His poems and short fiction have appeared in *PN Review*, *Landfall*, *Sport* and elsewhere, and his poetry collection *Sinking Lessons* (Otago University Press, 2020) won the Kathleen Grattan Poetry Award in 2019.

Ruth Arnison was born in Ōamaru and bred in the South Island. She travelled and worked in Europe for several years before settling in Windermere in the United Kingdom with her English husband, Barry. In 1986 they came to Dunedin 'for a year'; three children and 35 years later, they are still there.

Stu Bagby is a former winner of the New Zealand Poetry Society's International Competition. First published in *AUP New Poets 2*, he has written four books of poetry, a play and edited three anthologies. He lives in Paremoremo.

Rebecca Ball is a high school teacher based near Ōtautahi Christchurch. She has had poems published in *Landfall*, *London Grip* and *Poetry New Zealand Yearbook*, as well as a narrative study guide, *BA: An Insider's Guide* (Auckland University Press, 2012).

Holly H. Bercusson was born with a love of letters. Add to that a complicated childhood, a personality disorder and a dash of Jewish neuroticism, and you pretty much have a poet.

Tony Beyer lives in Taranaki. He spends as much time as he can reading and some of the time writing.

Claire Beynon is an Ōtepoti Dunedin-based artist and writer. In addition to her solo practice, she works on a diverse range of interdisciplinary projects in New Zealand and abroad. Recent collaborations include *Lifelines* (Antarctica-inspired theatre performance by Various People Inc., Adelaide) and a dance project with Dresden-based composer Sascha Mock. Her second collection of poems, *Balancing on air,* is nearing completion.

Tyla Harry Bidois is a Jewish poet, author, illustrator and musician from Mount Maunganui. Her work centres largely on poetic form, womanhood and the exploration of mixed-race cultural identity.

Victor Billot is an Ōtepoti Dunedin-based writer. His poetry collection *The Sets* was published by Otago University Press in 2021. His poems have featured in *Cordite Poetry Review, Landfall, Poetry New Zealand Yearbook* and *Best New Zealand Poems*.

Nikk-Lee Birdsey was born in Piha. Her first book, *Night as Day*, was published by Victoria University Press in 2019.

Cindy Botha lives in Tauranga. She began reading and writing poetry at the age of 59 while caring for her mother, who suffered from dementia. Her work has since been published in New Zealand and the United Kingdom and in *Poetics for the More-than-Human World* (Spuyten Duyvil Publishing, 2020).

Benjamin Brennan currently lives in Te Whanganui-a-Tara Wellington, where he is putting the finishing touches to a novel.

Erick Brenstrum is a meteorologist living in Te Whanganui-a-Tara Wellington. He has published *Thalassa*, a book of poems, and also *The New Zealand Weather Book*. His poems have appeared in a number of magazines including *Islands, JAAM, Landfall,* the *Listener, North & South, Poetry New Zealand Yearbook* and *takahē*.

Iain Britton is the author of several poetry collections. In the United Kingdom, his work has been nominated for a Forward Prize for Best Single Poem and Best First Collection. Work has been published in *takahē, Minarets Journal, Poetry New Zealand Yearbook, Landfall, brief, Harvard Review, Poetry Magazine, The New York Times, Stand, Agenda, New Statesman, Poetry Birmingham* and *Poetry Wales. The Intaglio Poems* was published by Hesterglock Press (UK) in 2017.

Owen Bullock's most recent books are *Uma rocha enorme que anda à roda* (A big rock that turns around), translations of tanka into Portuguese by Francisco Carvalho (Temas Originais, 2021); *Summer Haiku* (Recent Work Press, 2019) and *Work & Play* (Recent Work Press, 2017). He teaches Creative Writing at the University of Canberra.

Danny Bultitude has previously been published in *Landfall, The Spinoff*, Newsroom, and other national publications. He recently won the inaugural Bell Hill Apartments Poetry Competition but proclaims he is no poet.

Jessie Burnette is currently working to complete a Masters in English at the University of Waikato Te Whare Wānanga o Waikato. She is also passionate about creative writing and linguistics, and she is fascinated by the ability of poetry to capture slippery emotional truths.

Chris Cantillon lives in Whanganui and works in Marton. He is learning the piano.

Brent Cantwell is from Tīmaru and now lives with his family in the hinterland of Queensland, Australia. He teaches high-school English and has been writing for pleasure for 24 years. He has recently been published in *Fresh Ink, Milly Magazine, Poetry New Zealand Yearbook, Landfall* and *foam:e*.

Alastair Clarke, after years residing in the United Kingdom and in Australia, is re-seeing his country. His work has appeared previously in *Poetry New Zealand Yearbook*, *Antipodes Journal* and *Fresh Ink*.

Jenny Clay won the 2013 Kevin Ireland Poetry Competition, and the Graeme Lay Short Story Competition in 2016. Her poems have been published in print and online anthologies in New Zealand and overseas. She also researches, and sometimes writes, non-fiction.

Jennifer Compton was born in Te Whanganui-a Tara Wellington and now lives in Melbourne. Her eleventh book of poetry, *the moment, taken*, was published in 2021 by Recent Work Press, Canberra.

Imé Corkery is a poet by choice and chronic-illness warrior by design. She is currently completing her Masters in professional writing at the University of Waikato Te Whare Wānanga o Waikato.

J. Coté is a Raglan-born poet and Masters student at the University of Waikato Te Whare Wānanga o Waikato, and can usually be found neck deep in second-hand bookstores, trekking up mountains or brewing poetry.

Craig Cotter was born in New York and has lived in California since 1986. His poems have appeared in *California Quarterly, Chiron Review, Columbia Poetry Review, Court Green, The Gay & Lesbian Review, Great Lakes Review, Hawai`i Review* and *Tampa Review*. His fourth book of poems, *After Lunch with Frank O'Hara*, is currently available on Amazon.

Mary Cresswell is a science editor from Los Angeles who lives on the Kāpiti Coast. Her poems are regularly published in journals in New Zealand, Australia, the United States and the United Kingdom. Her recent books are *Body Politic: Nature poems for nature in crisis* (The Cuba Press, 2020) and *Fish Stories: Ghazals and glosas* (Canterbury University Press, 2015).

Majella Cullinane writes poetry, fiction and essays. Otago University Press and Salmon Poetry, Ireland, published her second poetry collection *Whisper of a Crow's Wing* in 2018. She was awarded a Copyright Licensing New Zealand grant (2019) and a Creative New Zealand Arts Grant (2021) to work on her third poetry collection, *Something to Say You Were Here*.

Vicky Curtain is a mother, teacher and artist. She lives in Kirikiriroa Hamilton.

Jeni Curtis is an Ōtautahi Christchurch writer who has had short stories and poetry published in various publications including *takahē*, NZPS anthologies, *JAAM, Landfall, Atlanta Review,* the *London Grip, Shot Glass Journal* and *Poetry New Zealand Yearbook*. She was the featured poet in the 2019 summer issue of *a fine line*. Her poem 'come autumn' was shortlisted for the 2020 Pushcart Prize. She is secretary of the Canterbury Poets Collective, and co-editor of poetry for *takahē*.

Semira Davis is a writer whose poems have appeared in *Landfall, takahē, Ika, Blackmail Press, Ramona Magazine, Catalyst, Poetry New Zealand Yearbook, Mayhem, The Friday Poem* and *Stasis*. They were a runner-up in the Kathleen Grattan Poetry Award 2019.

Brecon Dobbie lives in Tāmaki Makaurau Auckland and finds poetry to be her place of solace. Her work has appeared in *Starling, Minarets Journal, Love in the time of COVID* and *Poetry New Zealand Yearbook 2021*.

Doc Drumheller has worked in award-winning groups for theatre and music and has published 10 collections of poetry. His poems are translated into more than 20 languages, and he has performed widely overseas and throughout New Zealand. He lives in Oxford, North Canterbury, where he edits and publishes the literary journal *Catalyst*. His latest collection is *Election Day of the Dead* (Cold Hub Press, 2020).

Nicola Easthope (Pākehā, tangata tiriti) is a high-school English and psychology teacher who lives on the Kāpiti Coast. She has written two collections of poetry: *Leaving my Arms Free to Fly Around You* (Steele Roberts, 2011) and *Working the tang* (The Cuba Press, 2018).

David Eggleton is the Aotearoa New Zealand Poet Laureate 2019–2022. He edited *Landfall* and *Landfall Review Online* between 2009 and 2017. He is a recipient of a Janet Frame Literary Trust Award, an Ockham New Zealand Book Award for poetry and the Prime Minister's Award for Poetry. His *The Wilder Years: Selected Poems* was published by Otago University Press in 2021. His 'fridge magnet poem' is composed from a standard magnetic sheet of word tiles.

Amber Esau is a Sā-māo-rish writer (Ngāpuhi / Manase) born, bred and living in Tāmaki Makaurau Auckland. She is a poet, storyteller and amateur astrologer. Her work has been published in print and online.

Maryana Garcia is a journalist, poet, and picture-maker fascinated by everyday miracles. Her poetry has been published in *A Clear Dawn: New Asian Voices from Aotearoa New Zealand, Ko Aotearoa Tatou, takahē, Poetry New Zealand Yearbook 2018* and *2021*, and her photography in *Stasis*.

John Geraets is a Whangārei-based writer whose *Everything's Something in Place* was published by Titus Books in 2019.

Rata Gordon is a poet, embodiment teacher and arts therapist. Her first book of poetry, *Second Person*, was published by Victoria University Press in 2020.

Michael Hall lives in Ōtepoti Dunedin. Recent poems of his have appeared in *The Otago Daily Times, Queens Quarterly* (Canada) and Landing Press's anthology on housing.

Jordan Hamel is a Pōneke-based writer, poet and performer. He was the 2018 New Zealand Poetry Slam champion and represented New Zealand at the World Poetry Slam Champs in the United States in 2019. He is the co-editor of *Stasis* with Sinead Overbye and co-editor of a forthcoming New Zealand climate change poetry anthology from Auckland University Press. He is a 2021 Michael King Emerging Writer-in-

Residence and has recent words in *The Spinoff, Landfall, Newsroom, Re:, Poetry New Zealand Yearbook* and elsewhere. His debut poetry collection is forthcoming from Dead Bird Books in 2022.

Paula Harris lives in Palmerston North, where she writes and sleeps in a lot, because that's what depression makes you do. She won the 2018 Janet B. McCabe Poetry Prize and the 2017 Lilian Ida Smith Award. Her writing has been published in various journals, including *The Sun, Hobart, Passages North, New Ohio Review* and *Aotearotica*.

K-t Harrison: Ko Hapuakohe te maunga. Ko Mangawara te awa. Ko Tainui te waka. Ko Ngāti Paoa te Iwi. Ko Waiti te marae. No Te-Hoe-O-Tainui ahau. Ko tōku ingoa ko Gayle King-Tamihana. Ko tōku ingoa pene ko K-t Harrison.

Rebecca Hawkes is Methven born and Te Whanganui-a-Tara Wellington based. Her first book, *Meat Lovers*, will be published by Auckland University Press in 2022, and her chapbook *Softcore coldsores* was published in *AUP New Poets 5*. She co-edits the journal *Sweet Mammalian* with Nikki-Lee Birdsey, is a founding member of popstar poetry performance posse Show Ponies, and is co-editor of *No Other Place To Stand*, an anthology of poetry on climate change (forthcoming, Auckland University Press).

Jenna Heller is an American-Kiwi who lives and writes in Ōtautahi Christchurch. In 2021, she was the runner-up in the Caselberg Trust International Poetry Prize. More of her poetry can be found in places like *takahē, Landfall, Mayhem, Blackmail Press, Star 82 Review, Given Words* and previous editions of *Poetry New Zealand Yearbook*.

Liam Hinton is a Kirikiriroa Hamilton-based poet. He has had work published in *Mayhem, Poetry New Zealand Yearbook* and *Starling*. He co-runs One Question Theatre.

Marcus Hobson is a writer and reviewer from the hills near Katikati. He has been published in *Mayhem* and has just completed a novel for his Masters in professional writing at the University of Waikato Te Whare Wānanga o Waikato.

Dominic Hoey is a poet, novelist, playwright and small dog owner. When he's not writing about dogs and politics, he works with young people telling them they're awesome.

Lily Holloway (she/they) is a queer postgraduate English student and graduate teaching assistant at the University of Auckland Waipapa Taumata Rau. She has a Teletubby tattoo and a chapbook in *AUP New Poets 8*.

Alice Hooton lives in Mairangi Bay, Tāmaki Makaurau Auckland. She has been published in New Zealand and overseas.

Mark Houlahan teaches in the English programme in Te Kura Toi, University of Waikato Te Whare Wānanga o Waikato. He is very glad there are still new books of poems to hold and read in the hand.

Isabella Howarth sometimes writes poems after injuring her back. Her work has previously been published in *Milly Magazine*.

Jessica Howatson (she/her) is a queer, neurodivergent mother of two who thinks you don't have to be in love with someone to write them a love poem. Her words have previously appeared in *Mayhem* and *takahē*.

Amanda Hunt is a poet and environmental scientist from Rotorua. Her work has been published in *Landfall*, *takahē*, *Mimicry*, *Poetry New Zealand*, *Ngā Kupu Waikato*, *Sweet Mammalian* and more. She has been highly commended in several New Zealand Poetry Society competitions. In 2016, she was shortlisted for the Sarah Broom Poetry Prize.

Callum Ingram was born in Palmerston North in 1994 and grew up on a dairy farm just outside the city. He attended Freyberg High School and went on to study at Massey University Te Kunenga ki Pūrehuroa, achieving a Bachelor of Arts in English literature and a Masters in creative writing. He currently lives in South Korea and works as an ESL teacher.

Ross Jackson lives in Perth, Western Australia. He has had work published in many literary magazines and on poetry websites. *Time Alone on a Quiet Path* was published by University of Western Australia Press in 2020.

Ocean Jade was born in the United States and is a student at Otago Girls' High School. She is the winner of the Year 12 category in the 2021 *Poetry New Zealand Yearbook* Student Poetry Competition and has work published in the 2021 edition of the *NZPS Anthology*.

Adrienne Jansen writes fiction, non-fiction and poetry, most recently *All of Us* (with carina gallegos), longlisted in the 2019 Ockham New Zealand Book Awards. She is part of small Wellington publisher Landing Press, which publishes poetry for a wide audience. She lives in Tītahi Bay, Porirua.

Benjamin Jardine is a writer, poet and performer based in Te Whanganui-a-Tara Wellington. His fiction work has appeared in *Flash Frontier* and in the shortlist for the 2021 National Flash Fiction Day competition.

Eefa Jauhary spends most of her time writing and playing with her little dog, Daisy. Her published work can be found in *Mayhem*, *Sport* and *Stasis*.

Caitlin Jenkins is the winner of the Year 13 category of the 2021 *Poetry New Zealand Yearbook* Student Poetry Competition and the 2021 IIML National Schools Poetry Award. They are of Tongan (Village Fatai), Niuean (Village Toi) and European descent. In 2021 they attended Papatoetoe High School. Caitlin is a proud resident of South Auckland and lives in Papatoetoe.

Megan Jennings studied English literature at university in Aotearoa before spending a decade in London. She now lives in Tāmaki Makaurau Auckland, where she writes poetry and is working on her first novel.

Amanda Joshua has writing published in *Starling*, *Sweet Mammalian* and *Kate*, but her best work (unadulterated simp poetry about her partner) resides safely in her Notes app. In her spare time, she likes to read and contemplate dropping her law degree.

Hebe Kearney is a queer poet who lives in Tāmaki Makaurau Auckland. Their work has appeared in *The Three Lamps Journal, Starling, Oscen, Forest & Bird, a fine line* and *Poetry New Zealand Yearbook 2021*.

Brent Kininmont is working on his second collection of poems, the follow-up to *Thuds Underneath* (Victoria University Press, 2015). He lives in Tokyo, where he teaches intercultural communication.

Elizabeth (Libby) Kirkby-McLeod is a New Zealand author whose poetry and writing have appeared in a range of New Zealand journals, online publications, and in a public art installation. She has written several books, including her poetry collection *Family Instructions Upon Release* (Cuba Press), and is the editor of *Lit: stories from home* (OneTree House).

Megan Kitching lives in Ōtepoti Dunedin. Her poetry has appeared in *The Otago Daily Times, takahē, Landfall* and *Poetry New Zealand Yearbook*. In 2021, she was the inaugural recipient of the Caselberg Trust's Elizabeth Brooke-Carr Emerging Writers Residency.

Anthony Kohere (Ngāti Porou / Rongowhakaata / Muaūpoko / Waikato-Tainui / Ngāti Tūwharetoa) is currently in the midst of his Masters in professional writing at the University of Waikato Te Whare Wānanga o Waikato. He is writing two screenplays that recontextualise the genres of suspense thriller and espionage to a Māori setting.

Elisabeth Kumar is a lecturer in the Auckland School of Medicine's medical humanities programme, co-teaching (with Mike Hanne) a course called Unexamined Metaphors, Uncharted Stories. She is currently studying occupational therapy at Auckland University of Technology Te Wānanga Aronui o Tāmaki Makau Rau. She is particularly interested in literature around disability, madness, and dialogue.

Jane Landman has been writing on and off since she was a child. She writes poetry and short stories and is presently working on a creative non-fiction biography.

Jessica Le Bas has published two collections of poetry, *incognito* and *Walking to Africa* (Auckland University Press, 2007 and 2009). She was the winner of the 2019 Sarah Broom Prize for Poetry. Her 2010 novel for children, *Staying Home*, was published by Penguin Random House as *Locked Down* in 2021.

Wen-Juenn Lee is a Malaysian-Chinese poet from Te Whanganui-a-Tara Wellington currently living and writing on unceded Wurundjeri land. Her writing has been published, or is forthcoming, in *Landfall, Southerly, Going Down Swinging* and *Meanjin*, among others. She previously served as a poetry editor for *Voiceworks*.

Wes Lee lives in Te Whanganui-a-Tara Wellington. Her latest poetry collection, *By the Lapels*, was launched in 2019 (Steele Roberts Aotearoa). Her work has appeared in a wide array of literary journals and anthologies, including *Best New Zealand Poems, New Zealand Listener, Landfall, Poetry London, The London Magazine, The Stinging Fly, Westerly* and *Australian Poetry Journal*. Most recently she was selected as a finalist for the Sarah Broom Poetry Prize 2018, awarded the Poetry New Zealand Prize 2019, and shortlisted for The NZSA Laura Solomon Cuba Press Prize 2021.

Schaeffer Lemalu (1983–2021) was a Tāmaki Makaurau Auckland painter and poet. He was educated at Elam School of Fine Arts. He was the author of the chapbooks *Sleeptalker* and *Sleeptalker 2*, as well as numerous unpublished manuscripts.

Allison Li was born in China but is a Kiwi at heart and considers Aotearoa New Zealand to be her home. Her writing has been published in various journals, including *Landfall, takahē, Blackmail Press, The Cortland Review* and *Pif Magazine*.

Frances Libeau is a Pākehā writer and sound designer who lives in Tāmaki Makaurau Auckland. Their words appear in *Overland* (placing third in the 2021 Judith Wright Poetry Prize), *Poetry New Zealand Yearbook 2021, Oscen, Pantograph Punch* and more. A recent manuscript was long listed for the Nightboat Books 2020 Poetry Prize. Libeau's sonic compositions feature in interdisciplinary collaborations with artists worldwide.

Therese Lloyd has a PhD in creative writing from Victoria University of Wellington Te Herenga Waka, and in 2018 she was the Writer in Residence at the University of Waikato Te Whare Wānanga o Waikato. Her first full-length poetry collection, *Other Animals*, was published by Victoria University Press in 2013, and her second collection *The Facts* (Victoria University Press, 2018) was a finalist in the 2019 Ockham New Zealand Book Awards.

Olivia Macassey is a poet and editor whose work has previously appeared in *takahē, Poetry New Zealand Yearbook, Landfall, Otoliths, Rabbit* and other places. She has written two books of poetry.

Maitreyabandhu has written three books on Buddhism, two poetry pamphlets and three full-length collections with Bloodaxe Books: *The Crumb Road* (2013), *Yarn* (2015) and *After Cézanne* (2019), an illustrated meditation on the life and work of the painter. He was ordained into the Triratna Buddhist Order in 1990.

Vana Manasiadis is Greek-New Zealand writer born in Te Whanganui-a-Tara Wellington and now based in Tāmaki Makaurau Auckland after years living in Kirihi Ελλάδα. She is the 2021 Ursula Bethell Writer-in-Residence at Te Whare Wānanga o Waitaha Canterbury University. Her most recent book is *The Grief Almanac: A Sequel* (Seraph Press, 2019).

Jenni Mazaraki is a writer who lives on Wurundjeri land (Melbourne). Her short story collection *I'll Hold You* was highly commended in the Victorian Premier's Literary Awards for an Unpublished Manuscript 2020. Her work has been published in *Australian Poetry Journal, The Suburban Review* and *Headland*. She is currently undertaking a PhD in creative writing.

Liam McBreen graduated from the University of Waikato Te Whare Wānanga o Waikato with a Bachelor of Arts majoring in English literature. Raised in Taranaki, he moved to Wellington to study at Victoria University of Wellington Te Herenga Waka for two years before heading up to the mighty Waikato. He currently works as a school accountant and is studying towards his Masters in professional writing.

Jack McConnell lives in Te Whanganui-a-Tara Wellington, where he is studying at the International Institute of Modern Letters. His poetry has been published in *Mayhem*. He was highly commended in the 2020 NZPS International Poetry Competition and won the 2019 Charles Brasch Young Writers' Essay Competition.

Lucy Miles is a journalist, English teacher and writer who has lived throughout Europe. Currently she lives in Tāmaki Makaurau Auckland, where she is completing a Masters in English literature.

Sue Miles is a former journalist who has worked for many publications including the *Auckland Star, New Zealand Herald, The New Zealand Listener* and *Sunday Star-Times*. She is the author of several non-fiction books.

Anuja Mitra lives in Tāmaki Makaurau Auckland. Her writing has appeared in *Cordite, takahē, Mayhem, Starling, Sweet Mammalian, NZ Poetry Shelf* and *The Three Lamps*, as well as *A Clear Dawn: New Asian Voices from Aotearoa New Zealand* (Auckland University Press, 2021). She writes theatre and poetry reviews for Theatre Scenes and the New Zealand Poetry Society.

Layal Moore teaches art and BodyBalance and is the secretary for two local school boards. Her poetry, artwork and photography has been published in *Poetry New Zealand Yearbook* (2019 and 2021), *The Anthropozine, Mayhem, Hibiscus Coast Writers Inc Talents* (2018 and 2019) and *This Twilight Menagerie*. She is currently in her last months of study to become a secondary English and social studies teacher.

Margaret Moores has been a bookseller for many years and more recently a student of creative writing at Massey University Te Kunenga ki Pūrehuroa. Her PhD thesis investigates the aesthetic synergies between prose poetry and photography. Her poems and flash fiction have been published online and in journals in New Zealand and Australia.

Josiah Morgan is the author of two poetry collections and a forthcoming hybrid text. He is working on his first novel, *Road: A Postlapsarian Comedy*.

Elizabeth Morton is a teller of poems and tall tales. She has two collections of poetry — *Wolf* (Mākaro Press, 2017) and *This is your real name* (Otago University Press, 2020). She has an MLitt in creative writing from the University of Glasgow, and is completing an Masters in applied neuroscience.

Janet Newman's first poetry collection *Unseasoned Campaigner* was published by Otago University Press in 2021. She was second in the 2020 Poetry New Zealand Poetry Prize and a runner-up in the Kathleen Grattan Poetry Award 2019. In 2020, she completed a PhD in creative writing at Massey University Te Kunenga ki Pūrehuroa with her thesis, 'Imagining Ecologies: Traditions of ecopoetry in Aotearoa New Zealand.'

Piet Nieuwland lives on the Kaipara catchment edge. His book *As light into water* was published by Cyberwit in 2021, and his poems appear in numerous journals in Aotearoa and internationally. He is a visual artist and co-editor of *Fast Fibres Poetry*.

Jilly O'Brien is a poet and psychologist from Ōtepoti Dunedin. She has had poems published in *Landfall, Mayhem, takahē, Catalyst* and *The Spinoff*, as well as overseas in *Cordite, Rabbit, Stand, The Blue Nib* and *Not Very Quiet*. Her poetry has appeared in anthologies worldwide, as well as been displayed on the ice in Antarctica, on benches in Dunedin and on the back of parking tickets.

Alistair Paterson ONZM is a poet, editor of literary journals, essayist and anthologist, and former Fulbright Fellow. He has published a novel and a memoir and has won several awards, combining an extensive literary career with one in the Royal New Zealand Navy, from which he retired with the rank of lieutenant commander.

Kim Pears lives in Rotorua and is delighted to be published here for the first time. When she's not working on her novel or accompanying her elderly dog on slow walks, you'll find her dancing around her kitchen. Unsurprisingly, she's from Essex.

Karen Phelps is a full-time writer from Ōtautahi Christchurch. She has written about everything from colonic irrigation to interviewing Helen Clark. The poem in the 2022 *Poetry New Zealand Yearbook* is her first published poetry.

Mark Pirie is an internationally published poet, editor, publisher and archivist for PANZA (Poetry Archive of New Zealand Aotearoa). A long-term supporter of poets and poetry, he is a founder and former editor of *JAAM* , publisher for HeadworX and edits *broadsheet: new new zealand poetry*. Recent poetry collections include *Slips: Cricket Poems* (HeadworX, 2021) and *Bono Mato Poeia* (*Issue 42 of ESAW mini series*, 2021).

Mark Prisco is a PhD student at the University of Waikato Te Whare Wānanga o Aotearoa. He has had poems published in various literary journals.

Hayden Pyke lives in Kirikiriroa Hamilton. He a parent, partner and social worker who writes the occasional poem late at night when his 'real life' is asleep.

Mary Raleigh is a writer from Kirikiriroa Hamilton. She is currently studying towards a Masters in professional writing at the University of Waikato Te Whare Wānanga o Waikato. A secondary school English teacher for over 20 years, she loves both the process of writing and fostering her students' voices through writing.

Erin Ramsay is a nonbinary Pākehā poet. She uses she/her pronouns, mostly in the drag sense, and is currently working as a high school librarian. She lives in Tāmaki Makaurau Auckland but will be moving to Te Whanganui-a-Tara to pursue an Masters in history in 2022.

Kay Ramsbottom has a degree in graphic design from the University of Waikato Te Whare Wānanga o Waikato and is currently enrolled in a Masters in professional writing at the same institution, where she has begun work on her first novel — a creative non-fiction story set in the early European settlement in Wellington.

essa may ranapiri (tainui / waikato / maungatautari / waikawa / manakau / tararua | mātaatua / whakatāne / pūtauaki | cuan a tuath / guinnich / thames / highgate | takataapui | they / ia) is a kaituhi residing on ngāti wairere whenua. They will write until they're dead.

Vaughan Rapatahana (Te Ātiawa) commutes between homes in Hong Kong, Philippines and Aotearoa New Zealand, when Covid-19 permits. He is widely published across several genres in both his main languages, te reo Māori and English, and his work has been translated into Bahasa Malaysia, Italian, French, Mandarin, Romanian and Spanish.

Amanda Reilly's first love was English literature, which she studied at the University of Auckland in the late 1980s. Her second love was law, which proved to be more lucrative, and she is currently employed as a senior lecturer in commercial law at Victoria University of Wellington Te Herenga Waka. She never forgot her first love, though, and she lives in Wellington with her husband, Michael, and teenage daughter,Zelda.

Gillian Roach is an Auckland poet. She won the NEW VOICES — Emerging Poets Competition 2018 and was awarded runner-up in the Kathleen Grattan Prize for a sequence of poems in 2018 and 2019. She has been published in *Landfall, takahē* and *Poetry New Zealand Yearbook.*

Jeremy Roberts lives in Napier, where he works as an advocate, is MC at Napier Live Poets, interviews poets on Radio Kidnappers and posts poems on SoundCloud and YouTube. He has performed with musicians in New Zealand, Texas, Saigon and Jakarta. He won the Earl of Seacliff poetry prize in 2019.

Jack Ross's latest book is *The Oceanic Feeling* (Salt & Greyboy Press, 2021). He recently retired from Massey University Te Kunenga ki Pūrehuroa — where he's been teaching writing for the past 25 years — in the hopes of getting time to do a bit more of it himself.

Dadon Rowell is a Kirikiriroa Hamilton-based poet and short fiction writer. Her work has featured in *Mayhem, Foodcourt, Poetry New Zealand Yearbook, Sweet Mammalian's Exquisite Corpse, Aotearotica* and *Starling.* Most recently she co-won the NZYWF 24-hour Flash Fiction Competition.

Ruth Russ somehow finds time to write around four boys, a husband, a job and a DIY renovation. Her work has appeared in various literary magazines.

Amber Sadgrove is a Brighton-born queer poet currently living in Kirikiriroa Hamilton. In 2015, she graduated from the Guildford School of Acting in the United Kingdom and became part of the London poetry scene. After moving back to New Zealand, she completed a Bachelor of Arts majoring in writing studies at the University of Waikato Te Whare Wānanga o Waikato in 2020 and has become a regular in the creative scene in Hamilton.

Tim Saunders has had poetry and short stories published in *Turbine/ Kapohau, takahē, Landfall, Poetry New Zealand Yearbook, Headland, Flash Frontier,* and won the 2018 *MiNDFOOD* Short Story Competition. He was shortlisted for the 2021 Commonwealth Short Story Prize. His first book, *This Farming Life,* was published by Allen & Unwin in 2020.

Derek Schulz is a Kiwi poet, essayist and writer of fictions. His nine collections of poetry include *Orphic Light*; *The Last Great Mystery*; *Borderlands* and *DEREK SCHULZ — Selected Poems 1979–2019*. More recently he received the 2018 Caselberg International Poetry Prize, was runner up in 2019 and shortlisted again in 2021. His essays have appeared in *Strong Words* (Otago University Press 2019, 2021) and *The Spinoff*.

Ila Selwyn has a Masters in creative writing from the University of Auckland Waipapa Taumata Rau, two poetry collections and several chap books and is in three writing groups, an art class, a walking group and two dance classes. She is also attempting to learn te reo Māori.

Kerrin P. Sharpe has published four collections of poetry (all with Victoria University Press). She has also appeared in *Best New Zealand Poems*, *Oxford Poets 13* (Carcanet Press, 2013) and *POETRY 2018*. In 2020 she was placed second in the Acumen International Poetry Competition and was shortlisted for the Alpine Fellowship Writing Prize, and in 2021 she was awarded a Michael King Writers Centre summer residency.

Sarah-Kate Simons is the winner of the Year 12 category of the 2021 *Poetry New Zealand Yearbook* Student Poetry Competition. She is home-schooled.

Jane Simpson is a poet, liturgist and historian. Her poem 'Beneath them' won third prize in the New Zealand Poetry Society's 2020 International Poetry Competition. She has two collections, *A world without maps* (2016) and *Tuning Wordsworth's Piano* (2019), both published by Interactive Press.

Nigel Skjellerup works in the Ōtautahi Christchurch healthcare community. His work has been published in *The Press* and *takahē*, with more pieces to be published soon in the *New Zealand Poetry Society Anthology* and *Anesthesia & Analgesia*.

Courtney Speedy is a poet from Whangarei who has previously been published in *Write Off Line* (2014), *Re-Draft* (2014 and 2016) and *Poetry New Zealand Yearbook 2017* and 2022.

Michael Steven is the author of numerous poetry chapbooks as well as the acclaimed collections *Walking to Jutland Street* (Otago University Press, 2018) and *The Lifers* (Otago University Press, 2020). In 2018, he was awarded the Todd New Writer's Bursary. Recent poems appear in *Poetry New Zealand Yearbook 2021* and *Ōrongohau/Best New Zealand Poems*. He lives in Tāmaki Makaurau Auckland and is still pretty sore about the referendum result.

Melinda Szymanik is an award-winning writer of children's fiction, including poetry, short stories, picture books and novels. She also occasionally writes adult poetry. She was the 2014 University of Otago, College of Education / Creative New Zealand Children's Writer in Residence, and a judge for the New Zealand Book Awards for Children and Young Adults in 2016.

D. A. Taylor is a full-time writer and editor with Intelligent Ink, and managing editor for *Mayhem Literary Journal*. He lives between Tāmaki Makaurau Auckland and Waikato.

Richard Taylor is a Tāmaki Makaurau Auckland poet. His books include *RED* (Dead Poets Books, 1996) and *Conversation with a Stone* (Titus Books, 2007). He is retired but reads widely and continues to work on writing projects.

Feana Tu`akoi is a Kirikiriroa Hamilton-based writer who enjoys a lifelong love affair with words. Heard, spoken, read and written. In that order.

Rhegan Tu`akoi is a Tongan and Pākehā writer who lives in Te Whanganui-a-Tara Wellington. Her family hail from the grassy plains of South Canterbury, and the beautiful village of Holonga, Tongatapu. She has recently had words in *The Pantograph Punch*, *Sweet Mammalian* and *Mayhem*.

John Tuke lives in Ōtautahi Christchurch and has been writing poetry on and off for many years. John has worked in various work roles, including teacher, fire officer and probation officer. He now runs his own gardening and landscaping business, and still rides bikes.

Vincent Verhelst is a teacher and a writer who was born and raised in the French Flanders. He currently lives in Te Whanganui-a-Tara Wellington. He won the 2016 Une Autre Terre Award, for his debut novel, *Collision* (Valka Pahsser, 2015). His poetry has appeared in French journals like *L'Échappée Belle* and *Rétroviseur*.

Richard von Sturmer was born on the North Shore of Tāmaki Makaurau Auckland. His most recent book is *Postcard Stories* (Titus Books, 2019). He was the 2020 writer in residence at the University of Waikato Te Whare Wānanga o Waikato.

Janet Wainscott lives near Ōtautahi Christchurch and writes poetry and essays. Her poetry has appeared in publications including *takahē*, *Landfall*, *Poetry New Zealand Yearbook*, *Shot Glass Journal* and in recent NZPS anthologies.

Jade Wilson is the winner of the Year 11 category of the 2021 *Poetry New Zealand Yearbook* Student Poetry Competition. She is a student at Kaiapoi High School.

Sophia Wilson currently lives and works near Ōtepoti Dunedin. Her writing has appeared in various journals and anthologies in Australasia and abroad. Her poetry was recognised in the recent Kathleen Grattan Prize, Robert Burns Poetry Competition, Hippocrates Prize and Caselberg Trust International Poetry Prize.

Sue Wootton lives in Ōtepoti Dunedin and is the publisher at Otago University Press. Her most recent publications are her novel *Strip* and the poetry collection *The Yield*, longlisted and shortlisted respectively in the Ockham New Zealand Book Awards.

Nicholas Wright is a lecturer in the English department at the University of Canterbury Te Whare Wānanga o Waitaha. He is currently working on a book of essays on contemporary poetry in Aotearoa.

David Wrigley is a writer, musician, and former bartender. He lives in Cambridge with his partner and two children. He is currently between cats.

Rheymin Yau was born in Kuala Lumpur, Malaysia, and came to New Zealand in 2012. He has a Bachelor of Science from the University of Otago Te Whare Wānanga o Otāgo. He has published several poems, two of which appeared in *Poetry New Zealand 47*. He now lives with his family in Waihōpai Invercargill.

Karen Zelas is a Ōtautahi Christchurch writer of poetry, plays and novels. Her current project is producing a podcast of her latest play, *The Falling (concerning the final journey of Minnie Dean, 1895)*. Karen is also an editor and indie publisher at Pūkeko Publications.

Poetry New Zealand Yearbook, founded by Louis Johnson in 1951, is New Zealand's longest-running poetry magazine. It has been edited by some of New Zealand's most distinguished poets and academics, including Elizabeth Caffin, Grant Duncan, Riemke Ensing, Bernard Gadd, Leonard Lambert, Harry Ricketts, Elizabeth Smither, Brian Turner, Alistair Paterson, Jack Ross and Johanna Emeney. It is now edited by Dr Tracey Slaughter of The University of Waikato Te Whare Wānanga o Waikato. The university's financial support of the Yearbook is much appreciated.

Managing editor
Tracey Slaughter
editor@poetrynz.net
Website: www.poetrynz.net

Submissions: The submission dates for each issue are between 1 May and 31 July of each year. Email submissions are preferred. Email submissions and a covering letter should go to editor@poetrynz.net. Please paste your poems in the body of the message or include them as a MS Word file attachment.

Submissions by post and a covering letter should be sent to: Dr Tracey Slaughter, English Programme, School of Arts, University of Waikato, Private Bag 3105, Hamilton 3240. Posted submissions will not be returned.

Please include a short biography and your current postal address with your submission. Contributors whose poems are selected will receive a free copy of the issue in which their work is included.

First published in 2022 by Massey University Press
Private Bag 102904, North Shore Mail Centre
Auckland 0745, New Zealand
www.masseypress.ac.nz

Cover design by Jo Bailey
Typesetting by Megan van Staden

A catalogue record for this book is available from the
National Library of New Zealand

Printed and bound in China by Everbest Printing
Investment Limited

ISBN: 978-1-991151-11-7

The assistance of Creative New Zealand is gratefully
acknowledged by the publisher

THE UNIVERSITY OF
WAIKATO
Te Whare Wānanga o Waikato

Poetry New Zealand Yearbook 2022 is published in
association with the University of Waikato